Charles Kennedy is the Leader of the Liberal Democrats and the MP for Ross, Skye and Inverness West in the Scottish Highlands.

Born in Inverness in 1959, he was brought up and educated in Fort William, and attended Glasgow University. Following his graduation in 1982, he worked as a journalist and broadcaster with BBC Highland in Inverness.

He was then awarded a Fulbright Scholarship to attend Indiana University in the United States. In 1983 he was working towards a PhD at Indiana when the opportunity arose to seek the SDP nomination for Ross, Cromarty and Skye. He made a flying visit home, won the ballot and returned full time to the UK in April. The general election followed and less than six weeks later he was elected to the House of Commons, defeating the sitting government minister to become the youngest MP of the time.

During his term in parliament he has acted as a spokesperson on issues ranging from the welfare state to Europe, agriculture and rural affairs. He has served on the All-Party Select Committee that introduced the televising of the chamber. He was the first SDP MP to back the merger with the Liberals after the 1987 general election, and moved a successful motion to this effect at the party conference that year.

Charles Kennedy was elected UK Party President, the equivalent of party chairman, in 1990, and served in that post until 1994. In August 1999 he was elected as the Leader of the Liberal Democrats, and he was appointed to the Privy Council in October 1999.

THE FUTURE OF
POLITICS

Charles Kennedy

HarperCollins*Publishers*

HarperCollins*Publishers*
77–85 Fulham Palace Road,
Hammersmith, London W6 8JB

www.**fire**and**water**.com

This paperback edition 2001
1 3 5 7 9 8 6 4 2

First published in Great Britain by
HarperCollins*Publishers* 2000
Copyright © Charles Kennedy 2000 and 2001

The Author asserts the moral right to
be identified as the author of this work

ISBN 0 00 710132 5

Set in Minion

Printed and bound in Great Britain by
Omnia Books Limited, Glasgow

For my parents,
Ian and Mary Kennedy

ACKNOWLEDGEMENTS

In taking on a project such as this, many debts are incurred. While writing it on trains and planes, and occasionally automobiles, I have enjoyed conversations and brainstorming with too many people to give a conclusive list. However, I must first acknowledge the work of Matthew Baylis and Richard Grayson in pulling together the various drafts and for diverse thoughtful contributions. I would also like to thank Jamie Lundie for his assistance in the project. Rebecca McLindon, Claire Chandler, Daisy Sampson, Anna Werrin, Julian Brazil and Laura Brodie have all contributed enormously. In Parliament, Malcolm Bruce, Vince Cable, Matthew Taylor, Mark Oaten, Tim Razzall, Dick Newby, Steve Webb, Richard Allan, Robert Maclennan, Tom McNally, Bill Bradshaw and William Wallace have provided much wise advice. Vernon Bogdanor has been an invaluable stimulus for this and other work. I am particularly grateful to David Boyle for his advice on local currencies and community initiatives. For being marvellous ex-leaders, I am indebted to David Steel, Roy Jenkins, Robert Maclennan and Paddy Ashdown. For consistently good input and advice on a range of subjects I am also indebted to James Gurling, Clive Parry, Jane Bonham Carter, Mary Polak, Chris Rennard, David Walter, Gordon Lishman, Terry Maher, Bill le Breton, William Sieghart and Charles Marquand. For answering many queries on detail I would like to thank Duncan Brack, Paul Hodgson, Shaun Carr, Sally McLeod, Greg Simpson, Giles Desforges, Lee Wells, Judith Baines, Steve Bradford and Rob Blackie. Nothing of this nature can be completed without expertise from the publishing world and I have been ably assisted by my agent, Maggie Pearlstine, and by Michael Fishwick and Kate Morris at HarperCollins. Finally, nobody has displayed more patience and understanding while I have been working on all this than one Sarah Gurling. Thank you all so much.

CONTENTS

PREFACE TO THE PAPERBACK EDITION

This preface is being written at home in Scotland over the Christmas and New Year holiday period, 2000–2001. At the time of writing my thoughts and political preoccupations are very much focused upon what lies ahead during the next twelve months for British politics in general, and the Liberal Democrats in particular. By the time this paperback edition appears we will more than likely have been through a general election – or be in the middle of the campaign.

Politics and politicians have taken a further beating over the last year. In particular, as the hardback edition of this book went to press in the summer of 2000, something remarkable happened in British politics: direct action, in the form of the fuel blockades, came to the towns and villages of Britain. I refer, of course, to the fuel crisis.

It was remarkable for several reasons. First, such action, organized by individuals rather than trade unions, is rare in Britain. In some Western countries, particularly France, taking to the streets is a much-used part of the political process – and it has achieved its aims on many occasions. Indeed, only a fortnight earlier, the French authorities capitulated in the face of domestic protests over fuel – perhaps sending a message across the Channel. Usually, the British have done things more gradually, believing ultimately that all problems will, at least to some degree, be resolved by a general election.

The second remarkable feature of the fuel protests was the issue itself. There has been rumbling discontent over fuel prices for many years, but except in a small number of constituencies (my own included) it had never been a major election issue – and certainly was not one of the main reasons for the Conservatives' electoral eclipse in 1997, despite all that they had done to increase fuel taxes.

However, surely by far the most notable feature of the fuel protest was what it said about the state of politics itself. From all the diverse voices of the fuel protestors, one message came through loud and clear: the public want honesty on tax, and they are not getting it. If fuel taxes are necessary to protect the environment, people want politicians to say so – they do not want to be told, as they were by a government insulting their intelligence by seeking to shift the goalposts, that fuel taxes have now become necessary to pay for public services. Shifting the goalposts was exactly what Labour did. All parties had supported the principle that fuel taxes had an environmental objective when Norman Lamont introduced the fuel duty escalator (an automatic annual increase in fuel duty above the rate of inflation) in 1993. Indeed, Gordon Brown's 1998 Budget was big on the link between fuel duties and the environment. He said then that, 'only with the use of an escalator can emission levels be reduced by 2010 towards our environmental commitments'. He also spoke of the government's 'duty to take a long-term and consistent view of the environmental impact of emissions'.[1] But by September 2000, Gordon Brown was telling the nation that 'the existing fuel revenues are not being wasted but are paying for what the public wants and needs – now paying for rising investment in hospitals and schools'.[2] The subsequent opinion polls over that summer told their own story. The Conservatives' standing increased at the expense of Labour, as the Opposition inevitably does when the government faces a crisis. But the Liberal Democrats did better in the polls too – and our message was not a knee-jerk pledge to cut taxes, but a simple, restated pledge to be transparent as to the specific purposes of tax revenues.

Following on from the fuel crisis, came the floods – the other side of the story where climate change is concerned. During the flooding it became rapidly apparent that politicians are not talking nearly enough about the big issues, such as climate change, and that these will make a massive difference to the way that we all live our lives in the decades to come. Unless they start to do so, politics will never reconnect with the people it is losing – and politics will have no future.

This book is about the future, but it is also about me and it is about us – the British. It is one person's reflections on the United Kingdom, and that person's reflections upon himself. What makes this Kennedy fellow tick? What makes him angry, what makes him sad? What fires his passion? By the way, does he possess passion? Why is he a Liberal Democrat, and who are these Liberal Democrats anyway?

The story begins in the West Highlands of Scotland in November 1959 and I cannot tell you where it might yet end. My first visit to London was not until the age of seventeen; my third visit was as a newly elected Member of Parliament in 1983. A friend put me up, in those first few crazy weeks, in his spare bedroom in Hammersmith. I didn't know how you got to Hammersmith from Heathrow airport. I had no idea where Hammersmith stood geographically in relation to Westminster. It was a fast learning curve.

It was not until August 1999, when I was elected as Liberal Democrat leader by the party's members, that I experieced again anything remotely comparable. The party leadership transforms your life almost out of all recognition, but for the better. You learn every day of the week, and you are never really off duty, but you experience a profound sense of duty in the process.

This book is part of that process. It is about attitudes and aspirations, hopes and fears. It is also about ambition. I am extremely ambitious for the Liberal Democrats, for two solid reasons. First, I believe that we are more correct in our diagnosis as to the nature of the problems of the body politic – and how they can be cured – than are the other parties; second, I am convinced that we will secure the opportunity to put these beliefs into governmental action.

Back to the West Highlands. If you had told me, when I was growing up, that one day not only would there be a Scottish parliament, but that it would involve the Liberal tradition at ministerial level, then I think I would have been ever so slightly sceptical. It has happened. My friend, Jim Wallace, now presides over the system of justice in Scotland.

Due to the initial illness and then tragic, premature demise of Donald Dewar, Jim has also exercised full First Ministerial authority on two separate occasions.[3] Jim's staple diet these days is red boxes, decision making, trying to get public policy more right than wrong. He is a Liberal Democrat making a serious difference to people's lives; in December 2000 he became a Privy Councillor and was named 'Scottish Politician of the Year' by the *Herald*. In Opposition at Westminster you make sounds and faces; in the Scottish coalition, Liberal Democrats are taking decisions.

Leadership in contemporary politics has become too much about lecturing and not nearly enough about listening. Some politicians are prone to rant and rave, but Jim and myself have never been from that stable. We need more people of Jim's sort in public positions. And we need much more liberal democracy in public life. I am determined to help secure such an outcome.

Mine has been a distinctly curious political lineage, all things considered. I joined the Labour Party, at home in Fort William, aged fifteen. As I describe later, that entanglement didn't last very long. I soon found the dogmatic class war that many Labour activists were fighting thoroughly unpalatable. At the University of Glasgow I was sympathetic to the Liberals but joined the SDP, for which Roy Jenkins can be fairly and squarely blamed.

Out of the unhappy state of British politics in the late seventies, came Roy Jenkins' famous 1979 Dimbleby Lecture, 'Home Thoughts from Abroad'. Every so often in life, you hear someone articulate your own thoughts – and they do so with an elegance and eloquence which make you wish you had been able to say it yourself. Roy Jenkins' Dimbleby lecture had that effect on me. He brought sharply into focus the unease that I, as an open-minded, pro-European, moderate-thinking Scot, felt about the choices that Labour and the Conservatives were offering the British people.

Roy offered a vision of the type of political party I wanted to join. He spoke of the need for a party of the radical centre to bring about constitutional and electoral reform at the heart of our political life, to end the failures of the two-party system. The new political system that resulted would allow parties to co-operate where they shared ideas. The new party that Jenkins saw leading these changes would also devolve power, while advancing new policy agendas for women, the third world and the environment. He spoke too of the need to establish 'the innovating stimulus of the free market economy' without the 'brutality of its untrammelled distribution of rewards or its indifference to unemployment'.

The Dimbleby Lecture was a rallying cry for those who wished politics to move beyond the class war that it had become, and it struck many chords. It was a vision of a radical, decentralist and internationalist party, combining the best of the progressive Liberal and social democratic traditions. It was a vision of the party that the Liberal Democrats have become. From the first, I was clear that I wanted to be part of this new force in British politics. So when the SDP was launched in 1981, I was an early member. A blink or two later and I landed up as the youngest MP in the country, having defeated a Conservative minister in the process in Ross, Cromarty and Skye. There followed a lot of listening and, I hope, learning.

There is a popular, recurrent misunderstanding about the Liberal Democrat neck of the woods in politics. Many people – journalists and the wider public alike – seem to think that operating within the confines of the SDP, an SDP-Liberal Alliance, and the Liberal Democrats today, is somehow less demanding than being Labour or Conservative. Believe you me, it's not. It is every bit as demanding and, to a certain extent, even more so.

You have to fight for every column inch. You get two questions on a Wednesday afternoon at Prime Minister's Question Time – when the leader of the Opposition can rely on six. Contrary to popular opinion, the job of leader does not carry a salary. No complaint there. You occupy a certain space in the unwritten constitution of the land – from State occasions to the Privy Council – but somehow you are not quite part of the in-crowd. It is all very curious.

Since 1983 my world of politics has changed out of all recognition, and not just due to the party's achievement and progress over nearly two decades – the landscape of politics itself has altered. The key issues that set the tone for much of the twentieth century – socialism v. capitalism, public v. private ownership – are now no longer debated. Today the issues are quite different – professionalism v. the market, interdependence v. nationalism, community responsibility v. self-interest.

There is also the issue of women's rights and role in society, which is rightly coming far more to the fore of the political agenda. It should be a core issue for all in politics Despite the advances that women have made since receiving the vote, many still do not have equal life chances to men. A disproportionate number of women still suffers conditions of poverty in the UK. For women in work, the problems of part-time employment make a particular impact; and although women comprise 44 per cent of the workforce, the proportion of women in managerial and administrative roles is still only 32 per cent. Politicians are gradually recognizing these inequalities and deliverying policies which meet women's needs and support their aspirations.

We are also all coming to terms with post-devolution party politics. As a Scot I am acutely conscious of that fact; so is Prime Minister Blair, who has admitted his mistake in interfering in the politics of the Welsh Labour Party over the election between Rhodri Morgan and Alun Michael.[4] We even have the irony of the Conservative and Unionist Party leader seeming to welcome the fact that a combination of devolution and a degree of proportional representation has brought life back to the political corpse which his party had become in Scotland and Wales. Altered images indeed.

On the key issues of today, Liberal Democrats are in a better position than the other parties to set the agenda. We start off by trusting people. In 1865, Gladstone defined Liberalism as 'a principle of trust in the people only qualified by prudence', contrasting it with the Conservatives' 'mistrust of the people, only qualified by fear'. And I am always struck by Vernon Bogdanor's characterization of the nineteenth-century Conservative Party as pessimistic, fearful of democratic change, and inclined to rely on central rather than local government for political solutions. Little has changed in the modern Conservative Party. We are also different because we are strong defenders of the spirit of public service: we value the expertise of professionals, and want to fund them so that they can do their jobs effectively, particularly in health and education. We want to promote social justice through health and education. We alone, apart from the Green Party, stress the environment as a fundamental part of politics. We are an internationalist party, comfortable with playing a constructive role in Europe, but ready to reform it, and look beyond European frontiers. We recognize that women and ethnic minorities still face enormous barriers to involvement in public life. We are willing to champion the needs of sometimes unpopular minorities – essential at a time when the Conservative Party is willing to exploit the debate on asylum seekers for party ends. And above all, we tie these concerns together with a commitment to the liberty of the individual, a cause that the other parties cannot lead – Labour has a strong authoritarian streak, while the Conservatives tend to equate liberty with rampant market forces.

This is the territory upon which the Liberal Democrats now operate. Society seems to be defined by near-instantaneous flitting images; as a consequence we have to be fleet of foot politically. Our past weakness, support too evenly spread in every conceivable sense, is today a source of potential strength. We must be sharp, but, emphatically, we must not be concentrated only in some parts of the country.

Now exactly what, I hear you say, does he mean by that? Allow me to explain. There is no point in this or any other political party existing or campaigning without a common purpose and a collective attitude. The Liberal Democrats have that – and it is frequently infuriating. It questions, it ridicules, it gives the awkward squad an honorary degree for their troubles. The party dislikes top-down policies. And it puts people like me in their place. Frequently.

However, it is part of the spirit of the age. People do not trust their politicians much; there is a collective dubiousness out there which is a legitimate cause for concern. Certainty has given way to uncertainty, the council estate – where the residents tended to vote en bloc one way because they all worked at the same local factory – has changed out of recognition. That local factory, or coalmine, or steelworks, or shipyard, probably no longer exists. And the council estate these days is full of families who have bought their own homes and whose children send mail down the phone line.

But has the political establishment changed accordingly? Not really. We carry on, pretty much upon the same tram-lines, affecting modernization yet not, somehow, giving real vent to it. The nineteenth-century building that houses parliament all too often contains the remnants of nineteenth-century habits. We are failing citizens as much as we are failing ourselves. And yet, away from Westminster, 2000 showed that all is not lost.

Things have got better since May 1997. In particular, the government has spread more power throughout Britain through devolution than any Conservative government would have ever contemplated. And in that time we have had clear signs of how disastrous a William Hague-led Conservative government would be: slashing taxes for the sake of it, retreating from Europe, and still pretending that there can be improvements in health and education without paying for them.

The result of the Romsey by-election on 4 May 2000, coupled to our exceptional 28 per cent share of the vote at that day's local elections, demonstrates that the British people realize what is involved. In particular, it is clear that people are not taken in by Mr Hague's populist, saloon-bar rhetoric on asylum seekers. After the last election, people said the Conservative Party could sink no lower. But William Hague's behaviour did sink lower, and he got his just deserts from the people of Hampshire.

Nobody should underestimate the significance of that result. The Conservatives, while in opposition, have only twice before in the last hundred years lost an incumbent seat to the Liberal tradition at a parliamentary by-election. The first was in Londonderry in 1913, remarkably, given that the Liberals were in government. The second was the 1965 triumph in the Scottish Borders of a young man called David Steel.

There are, surely, two big implications which flow from the upheaval in Hampshire. First, there is no genuine, far less gut, enthusiasm out there for the William Hague Conservative Party. His narrow, jingoistic approach has next to no broad, public appeal. The Romsey result cannot be dismissed as the usual 'mid-term protest against a Conservative government'. There is no Tory government to protest against. On the evidence of Romsey, the Conservative Party is less popular than it was when it met its nemesis on 1 May 1997, and after the next general election there will still be no Conservative government to protest against. Since Romsey, moderate support for the Conservative Party has continued to fall away, and I was delighted to welcome Bill Newton-Dunn, the Conservative MEP, into the Liberal Democrat fold in November 2000.

Second, people have clearly learnt one of the major lessons of the 1997 general election: that it is vital to look at the local situation when casting your vote. People are no longer being guided simply by national trends or old loyalties when voting. They are looking at how they can best deploy their ballot with the maximum effect. In Romsey that meant that Labour voters made their vote really count – some for reasons of disillusion, others because they see an alternative Liberal Democrat opposition which they find more attractive to the administration of the day. It is now clear that the 1997 experience is being repeated, and voters are regularly prepared to use their votes with lethal intent where it can matter. I have this year chastised the BBC, for example, over their tendency to speak in terms of 'the two main political parties'. Apart from ignoring the disparate and distinct political systems at work within Scotland, Wales and Northern Ireland, it also overlooks electoral reality where the Liberal Democrats are concerned. In truth, as in Romsey, across large swathes of the country, we now have varied patterns of two-party contests – involving all three UK political parties.

I want things to get still better, and they can. In his Dimbleby Lecture, Roy Jenkins mapped out an approach to our political process which has been more than vindicated by events. Quite simply, he was correct. If, as a country, we had listened to and acted upon his prognosis, then a lot of subsequent history would have been different.

Which brings me to today. I believe that the individual is now king, the consumer is in charge. It is right to opt for interests of the individual and the community rather than those of the state. Ask Tony Benn or Tony Blair what they think instinctively about the structure of society, and their answers will tend to centre on the jobs people do and how much they earn. Ask most Conservative politicians and you will find that the Thatcherite mantra of 'no such thing as society' still dominates William Hague's party. Ask a Liberal Democrat and they will respond in terms that stress the relation of individuals to their communities.

It is an altogether different approach to life which needs to be understood clearly. We are in politics to promote the liberty of the individual – the best life chances for all, whoever or wherever they are. That is the core value at the heart of this book, at the heart of my politics and at the heart of the party I lead.

INTRODUCTION:
WHY AREN'T THE VOTERS VOTING?

'I'm not political' is a phrase I used to hear a great deal. Even in the ferment of Glasgow University in the seventies I was occasionally pulled up sharp when fellow students told me that their interests didn't extend to what I saw as the 'big issues' of the day: nationalization, inflation, trade union power, unemployment and Scottish devolution.

Of course, now that I am an MP, dwelling for the large part in a world populated by fellow Members, journalists, party stalwarts and others intimately involved with the theory and practice of politics, I don't hear it so often, but I'm fully aware that 'out there' in the real world, being 'political' does not always mean caring about how the country is run and trying to do something about it. It means something quite different, for instance, rigidly holding a set of outdated principles, having faith in and being involved in a process that for many people has no currency, and it means sleaze. To be 'political' is akin to admitting that you are a trainspotter or a collector of antique beermats – a crank, and not always a harmless one.

It's not just 'political people' who suffer as a result of this perception. For a large percentage of British people, the whole political process is deeply boring. It's obscure, it's impenetrable and, most importantly, it doesn't matter if you understand it or not, because – so the logic goes – it doesn't make any difference. Twenty years ago, it was still possible to find pubs where signs above the bar said 'No politics or religion', presumably because they were the two subjects most likely to cause a fight. Nowadays, you never see it, because either people don't discuss politics at all, or, if they do, it's conducted with such apathy that the chief danger is that the participants will fall asleep.

I was chatting with an acquaintance recently. I asked him if he'd seen the satirist and impersonator Rory Bremner on TV last night. He shook his head. 'He does too many politicians,' he complained, 'so I ended up watching the snooker.' I am not, I hope, out of touch. But it had never occurred to me that some people might find his show uninteresting precisely because a large part of its content is political satire. In essence my acquaintance was saying that politics is a turn-off, something that makes you want to change channels.

I don't blame people for having these opinions. There are many aspects of British politics I dislike. Westminster politics, structured around the two-party system for so long, often looks personal, petty and adversarial. Even with the advent of the so-called 'Blair Babes', Parliament often seems like an exclusive gentlemen's club. I do not believe in dismantling tradition indiscriminately, but much of the day-to-day ritual and protocol at the Palace of Westminster contributes to people's sense that what goes on there is distant from, if not irrelevant to, their lives.[1]

Members of Parliament often suffer similar feelings about their place of work. I remember vividly that when the Berlin Wall collapsed in November 1990, my colleague in the Commons Russell Johnston (formerly MP for Inverness, Nairn and Lochaber), suggested suspending the scheduled business, in order to hold an emergency debate on the titanic developments in Germany and their historic implications. This was ruled impossible, even though the bulk of MPs would have agreed and the Speaker was sympathetic. So the scheduled business went ahead, with run-of-the-mill turnout in the House. It was much the same following the release of Nelson Mandela. Both events filled me with optimism, but the sheer inertia and inflexibility of our own parliamentary system left me feeling gloomy afterwards. It seemed to me very poignant that, while Europeans were breaking down frontiers, the British Parliament was burying its head further in the mud of tradition.

I also view Prime Minister's Question Time with a measure of distaste. Before I became Liberal Democrat leader I rarely took part in it. I sat through many sessions during my time as a rank-and-file MP, but I never found it a particularly useful political device. Many aspiring party leaders seek to make their mark by launching jibes at the Prime Minister of the day, but tempting though it sometimes was, with characters like Margaret Thatcher and John Major at the dispatch box, that was never for me – it would be possible to count the number of questions I asked on the fingers of one hand. I usually find Prime Minister's Question Time an irrelevant piece of theatre – a tale of sound and fury, as the quotation goes, signifying nothing.

The problem is that, all too often, the weekly rant at the dispatch box is all the public sees of Westminster politics. William Hague is good at soundbites in the House of Commons: 'Frost on Sunday, panic on Monday, U-turn on Tuesday and waffle on Wednesday' was his summary of Tony Blair's baffling comments on NHS reform in January 2000. Later, outside the Chamber, our Prime Minister commented that William Hague might be good at one-liners, but lacked anything constructive to say. No surprise then, that after being exposed to such tit-for-tat exchanges, the voting public finds parliamentary politics a turn-off.

The televising of Parliament has, unfortunately, done little to reverse this problem, as surveys show.[2] There is even evidence to suggest that, far from making the process more open to public scrutiny, televising has led to changes in parliamentary behaviour which have, in turn, made the process seem even less relevant to the general public. In 1992, I drew attention to the fact that the number of bogus points of order seemed to have rocketed at exactly the point when TV coverage began. Some Honourable Members clearly found the temptations of appearing on the small screen more important than efficient scrutiny of the executive.

In terms of parliamentary coverage, the weekly session of Prime Minister's Questions is TV's finest hour, but, as I have mentioned, it is all too often little more than the swapping of insults. Predictably, the news networks tend to edit out the calmer moments and overlook the plentiful evidence of inter-party accord and co-operation, because it is not as exciting as a good row. The result is that the viewing public sees MPs as a highly undignified, hugely self-indulgent collective of ego trippers.

The structure of the House of Commons perpetuates this points-scoring ethos – the two facing sides of the Commons engender the sense that one half of the country is ranged against the other half. I would like to see the existing furniture scrapped and replaced with a horseshoe seating arrangement. Most European Parliaments have gone for this model, as have the Scottish Parliament, the Welsh and Northern Ireland Assemblies and the US Congress. People may say that cosmetic changes make no difference, but I disagree entirely. If the image you send out to voters through the media is of no relevance, why does Tony Blair spend so much money on his platoon of spin-doctors and image consultants? A rebuilt House of Commons would, in my view, achieve more than an army of Alastair Campbells. It would send out the message that politics is not a rugby game anymore, but a process of co-operation, hard work and winning arguments.

In spite of technological advances, the conduct of politics and its key events has changed little. Party conferences are still centred on an audience, a platform and a series of long speeches, culminating in forty minutes of rhetoric from the leader, but there is no law stating that every conference has to be like that. It is revealing to reflect that by far the largest proportion of party conference media coverage these days is generated on the fringe, in the studios and, doubtless, within the bars and the restaurants. The former Conservative MP Matthew Parris, now a respected political commentator, has said that the best way to keep a secret in Parliament is to make a speech about it in the House of Commons. That view finds a ready echo at the party conference: if you really want to know what is going on, then probably the last place to look is inside the conference hall itself. It could be different. The Internet offers great opportunities for people everywhere to ask questions, debate issues and even vote – but instead we only have a virtual tour of Downing Street. It is more common for TV soap stars to go on-line than politicians – in my view, it should be a regular segment of every politician's working life, as well as forming a key part of annual conferences.

Some key events in our recent history have served to harden public attitudes to Parliament and politics. The Maastricht Treaty was a classic example and typifies the problem – it proved a fascinating and instructive experience for my party and myself, but the public's view of the affair was radically different. In particular, it showed how damaging the adversarial system of politics that we have in Britain is. Too many people, both politicians and commentators, expect you to oppose whatever the merits of the case, and anything short of complete opposition from an opposition party is liable to be misunderstood. It is worth analysing the episode in some detail.

It is all too easy now to forget the depth of political depression which engulfed the centre-left following John Major's 1992 general election victory. Many of us had expected, prior to the election, that we would be taking our places in a balanced Parliament, in which no party had overall control. The prospect of working in a coalition, almost certainly Kinnock–Ashdown led, was an intriguing one. The prospect of real progress on fair votes for Westminster seemed near at last, but the Conservatives were returned in the face of an economic recession: if the non-Conservative forces failed to triumph against such a backdrop, then what chance was there of ever replacing the Conservatives in office?

John Major's personal position initially appeared unassailable. One photograph captured his and the media's assessment of the post-election Conservative invincibility. Attending a cricket match, he closed his eyes and turned his face skywards to bask in the sunlight. It was a telling image, which just added to my feelings of deep gloom.

Around this time, I had personal conversations with Robin Cook (at that point the Labour leadership campaign manager for John Smith) and later with Tony Blair and Peter Mandelson. The former occurred over a Chinese meal in a Pimlico restaurant – and since we found ourselves occupying a table immediately adjacent to the Conservative Education Secretary, Gillian Shephard, I cannot claim that the rendezvous was at all clandestine! It was clear that Smith's election was a foregone conclusion, and equally clear that he was emphatically in favour of devolution. I also knew that Robin had a sympathetic ear as regards proportional representation. For these reasons, we agreed to stay in touch, not least where a shared agenda on constitutional reform was concerned.

Tony Blair was anxious to be less public and eventually our trio broke bread at Derry Irvine's London residence. I knew Tony reasonably well, and we had recently appeared alongside each other in media debates during the campaign and afterwards on Channel Four News, which ran an inevitable 'Losers' Lament' segment on the Friday after the Tories' election victory. Although I have, throughout my career, had various Labour luminaries (including Mo Mowlam) urging me publicly to cross the floor and join their camp, this was not the purpose of the meeting with Tony and Peter. Their principal interest was in the potential for dialogue with Paddy Ashdown, but neither felt sufficiently familiar yet with his direction and policies. His post-election speech in Chard, in his constituency, tackling the future direction of the Liberal Democrats and our relationship with other parties, had caught their attention. I provided a positive thumbnail sketch and encouraged further contact.

So, purely informally, centre-left ruminations were taking place as some of us wondered aloud whether we had any prospect of a meaningful political career. I doubt many of us anticipated the scale of the political earthquake that was just around the corner. The source of the earthquake was equally surprising – a small nation famous for its bacon, but otherwise rarely in the British, far less the international, public eye.

On 2 June 1992, the state of Denmark suddenly became the focus of worldwide attention, when its citizens voted 'no' in their referendum to approve the Maastricht Treaty. The treaty essentially provided the framework for greater economic unity between all the European nations and changed the European Economic Community to the

European Union. Denmark's 'no' was, in a sense, a 'no' to the notion of Europe.

I was standing at the Members' Entrance of the Commons, awaiting a mid-evening taxi, when a journalist from the *Independent* broke the news that there was something rotten in the state of Denmark. The next morning, I awoke to an unusually uncertain Douglas Hurd on Radio Four's *Today* programme, insisting that the Second Reading of the Bill, giving effect to Maastricht ratification, would proceed as planned. Paddy Ashdown phoned me and said he agreed. Nevertheless, we were all overtaken by the rapidity of events – by mid-morning, government whips had decreed that the Bill would be pulled. It taught me the folly of parking one's political principles: while the government sat inert, Eurosceptics on both sides of the House were able to gather momentum.

Britain suffers the consequences to this day, in terms of its compromised position within Europe. While neighbouring states move towards closer union, and their citizens benefit from the greater stability and increased trade that this provides, Britain remains on the outside.

This profound tactical and strategic miscalculation propelled both John Major and John Smith into a parliamentary stand-off that was deeply injurious to themselves and their respective parties. If ever there was a case of the straitjacket of Westminster partisan politics triumphing over the greater good, then this was it.

It is worth standing back and reviewing the scenario at that point. A free vote over Maastricht ratification would, prior to the Danish 'no' vote, have commanded something like a four-fifths Commons majority in the division lobbies. Parliament was so essentially pro-European that there would have been practically no obstacle to us accepting the terms of Maastricht fully. Seasoned Tory Eurosceptics such as Teddy Taylor, Jonathan Aitken and Nicholas Budgen had become christened 'The Night Watchmen' for their readiness to keep the House sitting into the wee, small hours as they grilled ministers over the detail of harmonization measures. Long-standing Labour critics, including Peter Shore, Denzil Davies and Austin Mitchell, were characterized as 'the usual suspects'.

The essential guilt will always lie with John Major – it was his government's decision to postpone the Bill – but the late John Smith, much as I liked and admired him, has to shoulder his fair share of the blame as well. A combination of bad and short-term judgement on matters European would prove to be an exothermic elixir. As Roy Jenkins remarked to me at the time, Smith was 'doing a Harold Wilson' – ducking and weaving to appease both the modern elements of his party who were pro-Maastricht and the diehard Eurosceptics. He made certain that the debate centred disproportionately around the Social Chapter, the one element of Maastricht that every Labour Member agreed with, regardless of their feelings about the wider question of Europe. He was thus able to maintain an impression of party unity, without making any substantial steps towards ratification. His approach would, in fact, have prevented the treaty from being ratified, had my own party not voted with the Conservatives.

Postponing the Bill immediately elevated a decision made in Denmark into a meltdown in the so-called Mother of Parliaments. The (mainly) Tory Eurosceptics could hardly believe their unexpected good luck. They gained a foothold which they are still exploiting to this day.

John Major, meanwhile, fashioned a fumbling way forward and succeeded in throwing away what should have been an inbuilt parliamentary majority on this issue – a majority which was instinctively pro-Maastricht – and instead let loose Eurosceptical forces which were, ultimately, to destroy his premiership.

In the middle – literally and politically – were the Liberal Democrats. Rather than lament the past, I believe it is more helpful to analyse where we went wrong. We had said in our manifesto that we were pro-Maastricht and wanted to see its swift ratification. We did not back down from that position, even when things started to get worse, as they surely did. John Major, having blinked, then blinked twice. After postponing the Second Reading debate and vote, he then came up with a most curious constitutional device – a 'paving motion', so-called because it paved the way, by giving parliamentary legitimacy to further consideration of Maastricht. The Liberal Democrats had to vote for it on the basis of their conviction that Maastricht was right, along with the majority of Conservatives, but it was a marriage made in hell. And it was just a taste of things to come.

John Smith contrived successfully to portray this rather meaningless paving motion as somehow tantamount to a no confidence vote in the government – on the grounds that if Major was defeated, in part by a backbench revolt, it was a sure sign that no-one wanted him as leader. Labour's Machiavellian skill in this was more than matched by Tory ineptitude, as several Cabinet Ministers announced via the airwaves the need for a show of confidence in Major and his administration. Which was, predictably, not the best way to inspire confidence.

This placed the Liberal Democrats generally, and myself as European spokesman in particular, in a position of acute difficulty. I felt the paving motion was no more than a device to cloak the real issue, and described it as such in my weekly *Scotsman* newspaper column. This was seized upon by my Labour opposite number, George Robertson, and by the SNP Leader, Alex Salmond. However, we were determined to act out of principle and support the spirit of Maastricht.

The more the Tories worried over being able to carry the vote, the more they had to stress the 'confidence-in-John-Major' angle, as a means of reining in their Eurosceptic recalcitrants. But the more they stressed this, the more difficult it became for Liberal Democrats to vote for it. We wanted Maastricht but, needless to say, we didn't want a Tory government, so it stuck in the craw to be portrayed as saying, effectively, that we had confidence in it.

It was a tense and unhappy time, made worse by the fact that pro-Europeans in all three parties were finding themselves artificially divided as a result of Conservative maladroitness and Labour skullduggery. I defended our pitch along the media trail, but became increasingly unhappy that our consistent and principled approach was being sullied by association.

The *Mirror's* excited Political Editor, one Alastair Campbell, used a radio discussion with me to put forward the patently absurd notion that somehow a defeat on the paving motion could unleash forces that might precipitate a general election. This was sheer wishful thinking and I wasted no time in debunking the idea. The worst thing was that, while the other parties hijacked the issue for their own ends, the public completely lost sight of the issue that had sparked the whole affair. The principles of Maastricht – of greater European unity – became completely obscured. I was bombarded with letters begging me not to vote with the Tories.

With a bad taste in our mouths, our votes were cast with the government and secured them a tight majority on the night. There was great bitterness at the outcome, particularly from the Labour camp. Some Labour MPs behaved shamefully on the floor of the House, delivering highly personalized abuse in our direction, while one, a long-standing, normally friendly acquaintance, refused even to acknowledge me as we passed each other in the Central Lobby. This was jaundiced politics at its worst.

So it was, under these distinctly inauspicious circumstances, that the tortuous process of activating the Maastricht Treaty began. It was an experience that taught me some hard lessons about politics in general, and Westminster-style politics in particular. Because the government had a majority of only twenty, and could not rely on its backbench rebels – some of whom seemed to make a career out of dissenting – they depended on our support to secure majorities in key divisions. So we were key players, and at the time, particularly at 3 in the morning, that was far from easy. As with most hard times, the benefits have only become visible in retrospect. The Liberal Democrats entered, and ultimately emerged from, this sequence of events with their integrity intact and, I believe, their reputation enhanced. This was due, in no small way, to the political acumen of our leader, Paddy Ashdown.

Paddy got a central judgement absolutely correct from the outset: we would give our support on key votes based on the issue at stake – and not in return for favours in other areas. But we will never forget the widespread apprehension and distaste with which we found ourselves presented as propping up a deeply unpopular government on a near-nightly basis, for months on end. We gained from that experience, and the fact that the party remained unified was down to strong leadership from the top. As a result, the image of the party gained coherence and credibility. A useful by-product was that it put us in the news, and kept us there.

There were considerable behind-the-scenes dealings with the Tory government throughout this period. Archy Kirkwood, our Chief Whip, Russell Johnston and myself were in constant touch with Richard Ryder, then Conservative Chief Whip, about likely voting intentions. On particularly key issues, Paddy Ashdown and Douglas Hurd became involved, but procedural glitches meant that nonetheless the bulk of the Maastricht business ended up being debated on the floor of the House, rather than dealt with swiftly in the Committee Rooms, which meant very late nights and frayed tempers.

What disappointed me then, and continues to do so to this day, was the damage that the Maastricht affair did to the popular conception of European unity, and the wider public image of politics. At first, the risk was that the public would respond to the scaremongering, and view Maastricht as some scourge from abroad that threatened the Union Jack and could potentially topple the government. The letters in my postbag demonstrated the extent to which people understood the debate in precisely those terms.

Then, as the debate dragged on – and drag it did, from May 1992 to July 1993 – people stopped viewing Maastricht as a demon and simply lost interest in the many good things that it offered the nation. It was a classic example of the way adversarial politics and intra-party chicanery serve to increase public uninterest in the political process.

This increased – albeit limited – exposure to the workings of a government proved very instructive for me. It certainly confirmed in my opinion the importance of cross-party co-operation, even though, self-evidently, after such a prolonged period of untrammelled power, the Conservatives were unprepared for such a close relationship. I think they found having to deal with the Liberal Democrats a vaguely demeaning experience. We, on the other hand, learned to take an entirely pragmatic approach. If it was something we wanted, like Maastricht, then we could and would co-operate to get it. This was a vital lesson for us.

But while Liberal Democrats learnt lessons, democracy suffered. The Conservative attitude at that time was rather akin to the Labour attitude over the Welsh Assembly in the early months of 2000, when Labour in London was determined to keep Alun Michael in charge. Co-operation sometimes seems to be a dirty word in British politics, which often resembles a game of rugby: opposing teams fighting to be the single victor. This is apparent in the half-hearted response I have received each time I have called upon Tony Blair and William Hague to join me in establishing a tripartite approach to drugs and pensions. Until and unless the Conservative Party comes to terms with a more pluralistic conduct of politics, it will wait a long time before being readmitted to the mainstream. Until Labour does so less half-heartedly, it will miss opportunities. Unless British politics can accommodate itself to inter-party co-operation, the public will continue to view issues in the way they came to view Maastricht.

I have gained something of a reputation for myself over the years as a radio broadcaster, perhaps most noticeably in my *Today* programme broadcasts with Austin Mitchell, the Labour MP and the Conservative, Julian Critchley. The 'Mitch, Critch and Titch' trio may have been popular with the listeners, but I found that, even within my own party, it attracted some hostility, largely because people disapproved of the idea that MPs of different leanings could get on and have a laugh, even allowing their own parties to be mocked by the others. But have a laugh we do; whenever I am in Yorkshire or Shropshire, I visit Austin and Julian, and think nothing of it. Many people seem to feel that any suggestion of amity trivializes politics, but I feel quite the opposite, preferring to recount the words of Winston Churchill, who upon returning to office in 1951 said: 'Now perhaps there may be a lull in our party strife which will enable us to understand more what is good in our opponents.' All the while politics is conducted in hushed, reverential tones, all the while it takes itself so seriously, and perpetuates intense and entrenched rivalry, then the nation will find it trivial.

The tribal model of politics does not even reflect the way people vote. In the eighties, my party had an unchallenged record for coming second in elections across the board: local, national and European.

We did so because there was always a bloc of voters who would support the Labour or Conservative candidate regardless of the issues under discussion, but breakdowns of modern voting patterns show that people vote for a range of candidates and parties at different electoral levels. The old sectarian loyalties are breaking down and being replaced by a concern for issues. That is one reason why Ken Livingstone drew such wide and varied support when he stood independently of his party in the elections for London Mayor. A 1999 survey found that nearly two thirds of people polled had 'not very much' or 'no interest at all' in local politics and over one third felt the same about politics in general. Only 3 per cent of the country were members of a political party – lower than the figure for membership of the National Trust or the RSPB!

The voting public may be more discerning – and I welcome that – but it is becoming an increasingly rare breed. Disenchantment with politics is a national characteristic, but it affects certain groups more severely than others. It is particularly a problem among young people. A 1998 MORI survey of eighteen-year-olds revealed that four in ten young people are not registered to vote – five times as many as in the general population. The reported turnout of eighteen to twenty-four-year-olds in the 1997 general election was some 13 per cent lower than that for the electorate as a whole. It was also lower than in the 1972 election, so the trend is worsening. According to Vernon Bogdanor, Professor of Government at Oxford University, only 12 per cent of eighteen to twenty-four-year-olds say that they will consistently vote in local elections, and 52 per cent say they will never do so.[3]

The low level of enthusiasm for voting is a reflection of the critically low interest in political matters as a whole. Half of eighteen to twenty-four-year-olds surveyed by MORI in 1999 reported that they were not interested in politics. Over 80 per cent claimed to know little or nothing about Parliament, and 30 per cent said they had never heard of proportional representation! As someone who has visited many schools and colleges across the country, I can say without reservation that today's young people are just as energetic and curious as my own generation, if not more so, but the truth is that their interests are focused increasingly away from politics and onto other things. We politicians have clearly played a part in that process.

As someone who has attended nearly every Brit Award ceremony since entering Westminster, I find it telling that politicians are hardly ever invited any more to present one of the awards. It used to be a common occurrence, but they simply do not have that sort of status among the young nowadays. If MPs stand too close to a pop star, they are more likely to get a bucket of water thrown over them, as happened to John Prescott a couple of years back. I felt a great deal of sympathy for John on that occasion, but I thought the episode was a telling symbol of popular disenchantment.

Given that young people nowadays are less likely than before to be interested in politics, to be knowledgeable about the political system, or to have formed an attachment to a particular party, what does this say about their attitudes towards the whole democratic process? Surely their low levels of political interest and knowledge translate into mistrust, cynicism and apathy?

The figures support this contention. A MORI survey of sixteen to twenty-four-year-olds ranked politicians and journalists bottom on the list of people they could trust. The same survey asked youngsters whether they thought various schemes (such as polling booths in shopping centres and Internet voting) might encourage them to vote. The answer was an overwhelming no. Such is the level of disillusionment among the young – they are not abstaining because voting is inconvenient. They are abstaining because they quite plainly cannot see the point.

This attitude translates into a wider sense of alienation from nation and community as a whole. Over one third of those polled said they did not feel strongly attached to their community; a fifth said they felt the same about their country; and two thirds reported feeling little or no attachment to Europe. Over a third said they knew little or nothing about their responsibilities as a citizen. Politicians should be frightened by what these figures are saying: there is a whole stratum of young people who don't vote, know nothing about politics and don't feel that they belong anywhere.

Disillusionment is not solely a feature of adolescence, at least not in terms of politics. Youths who can't see the point in voting grow into non-voting adults. As a result, Britain's turnout record leaves a lot to be desired. The public seems to have least interest in European elections. For example, in 1979, 1984 and 1989, around one third of the electorate voted. In 1999 it was even worse – less than a quarter, making Britons the most reluctant voters in the EU.

Analysts have not undertaken any serious study of non-voting in European elections. It is generally assumed that the remoteness of the European Parliament and antipathy towards the EC/EU accounts for the low levels of participation. The unwieldy size of European constituencies also makes it very difficult for the parties – who are used to campaigning in Westminster constituencies – to work effectively on the ground in order to get voters out of their front doors and down to the polling booths.

Far more worrying is the body of statistics which shows that there is similar public apathy when it comes to electing our own governments. Turnout for the 1997 general election was 71.4 per cent, the lowest figure since 1945. Despite the unpopularity of John Major's government, over one quarter of voters stayed at home. We are not the most apathetic country in Europe, but our turnout figures compare unfavourably with those of Spain, Sweden, Greece and Italy. If we add New Zealand, Australia and the USA to the equation, then Britain has the fourteenth poorest voting figures out of twenty nations.

This is a nationwide problem. The electoral roll doesn't help, as there is a time lag in setting up the electoral register, which makes voting difficult for people who move around. The situation was also exacerbated by the hugely unpopular Poll Tax in the eighties, as large numbers of people took themselves off the electoral register in order to avoid paying the tax, but this predates the Poll Tax: the trend of turnouts in general elections has been downwards since a post-war high of 84 per cent in 1950.

Some elements of British society seem to be more disengaged than others. We have already seen that the young vote in disproportionately small numbers. There is also a huge variation in turnout figures when we compare different constituencies, which often ties in with levels of social deprivation, particularly with levels of unemployment. In 1997, turnout ranged from 81.1 per cent (Wirral South) to 51.6 per cent (Liverpool Riverside). In May 1997, the unemployment rate in Wirral South was 5.1 per cent, while Liverpool Riverside had a rate of 19 per cent unemployment, the third worst figure in England. In short, the poorest sections of society, those with, arguably, the most pressing reasons to make their voices heard and bring about change, are the most disillusioned with the political process and the least likely to vote.

Some of these concerns are far from new. I recently came across a fascinating book on the Chicago Mayoral election of 1923. Then, out of an electorate of 1.4 million, only 723,000 voted – a turnout of slightly under 52 per cent. *Non-Voting: Causes and Methods of Control,*[4] looks at some familiar problems, including the public views that 'voting changes little' and that 'politicians can't be trusted'. In the twenties, though, much of the blame for poor turnout seemed to be blamed on the cowardice, laziness, ignorance or stupidity of voters.

Today, we are far more likely to look at the failings of politicians rather than voters. This is, in my view, entirely correct. We created the disillusionment, and we have to find a way to solve it. I don't pretend it is an easy job. As the book on the Chicago 1923 election said, 'The disillusioned voter, who believes that one vote counts for nothing, presents a difficult problem of political control. The ignorant citizen can be informed, the indifferent citizen can be stirred out of his lethargy, but the sophisticated cynic of democracy cannot be moved so easily.'

So, where do we start? Is it enough to target the young and the poor, or do we need a broader, nationwide approach to restore people's faith in the political process? One thing is certain – until we have won people's trust back there is no way we can claim to live in a democracy. Democracy isn't just about everyone having the potential to change the way society works. Democracy is about a state where precisely that happens, because people are confident that their opinions matter and that they can make a difference. In a country where over a quarter of citizens don't exercise their right to choose the new government, and where the poorest have the least inclination to improve their lot, there can be little progress, only marginal improvement.

Politicians, for the most part, are not stupid. They have long been wise to the issue of public disaffection. What has baffled them is the solution. Previously, the tactic of all politicians across Parliament, has simply been to 'try harder'. Knock on every door, so the logic goes, appear in every newspaper and on every television programme, telling people how important it is for them to get out and vote, and you can make a change.

In this age of all-pervasive media, it is clear that this tactic is not working. It is not because people aren't aware of the key political issues of the day, or that they are ignorant about who the key politicians are, or what they stand for.

The problem is that we are working the wrong way round. This is the crisis facing politics: people aren't interested in voting, because they see it as a lip-service to true democracy. Individuals, families, communities, villages, towns and regions still have scant authority, and while so much power is disproportionately centred around a distant government and a single capital, it is no surprise if people are unconvinced that their vote matters. People won't turn out to vote for a new Prime Minister until they also have a chance to wield real power in their own backyards. Respect for government will only come about once people govern themselves.

And that's where the solution must lie. The challenge is to build a truly civic Britain, where power has been devolved to the local and regional level, and where we are playing a full role in Europe. Where people no longer expect change to come slowly and inefficiently from Westminster, but have power within their own communities and exercise it themselves. Where the can-do culture tears down the walls built by decades of disillusionment and cynicism. Until politicians stop governing on behalf of the nation and start to govern *with* it, politics in Britain will remain what it is today – a sheer irrelevance for larger and larger numbers of people – and the consequences for the nation will be disastrous. It will be, in a sense, a final victory for Thatcherism. We will be a nation that prefers to lock the doors, rather than see what's happening in the street outside.

It may seem inappropriate to speak of Thatcherism ten years after the end of the Iron Lady's reign, but eighteen years of Tory rule wrought lasting damage upon the fabric of our society, and rather than repair it, Labour has sometimes been too willing to appease the middle classes at the expense of the poor. This is not new in politics – for forty years, J. K. Galbraith has been warning of the political dangers of the affluent disregarding the poor. Without doubt, the current government is a vast improvement on the previous one, but it is dangerous that Labour has not done more to create an environment that is sympathetic to the poor. In political life it means that we face nothing short of an emergency, but to those who already feel disheartened enough to stop reading, I want to point out that crises merely provide us with an opportunity to take action. The remedy is in our hands.

We can only make the most of the future if we are clear about what we want to achieve. My aim in politics is to advance and protect the liberty of the individual, because I believe that this is the only way to achieve true democracy. That, in turn, means ensuring that all people have the maximum life chances and the maximum opportunities to make the most of their natural abilities, whatever their circumstances. How can we speak of 'democracy' otherwise? Rule by the people (which is the precise definition of the word) does not mean that small privileged elites exercise their power over the rest. It means that everyone has an equal capacity to exercise power, and equal liberty to govern themselves.

In this book, I shall be using the word 'liberty' a great deal, along with its more popular counterpart, 'freedom'. For me, politics is the machinery by which freedom is made possible. Freedom to breathe, in a safe and clean environment. Freedom from government, by devolving power to the communities, nations and regions of Britain. Freedom to innovate, and to trade with other nations. Freedom to develop one's talents to the full, and to raise a family in security. None of these freedoms have any validity if the people enjoying them are not also free from poverty. This, and government's responsibility to bring it about, is my starting point.

Chapter One

FREEDOM FROM POVERTY:
THE FORGOTTEN NATION

'True individual freedom cannot exist without economic security and independence. People who are hungry and out of a job are the stuff of which dictatorships are made.'
FRANKLIN D. ROOSEVELT, 1944

In my eighteen years as an MP, I have come to learn that the most effective politicians are those acting out of a very personal sense of injustice. I am often accused of being too rational, too reasonable, of rarely showing temper. This might be the case, but that does not mean I am not motivated by very clear and firmly held convictions, beliefs I have held since I entered the House at the age of twenty-three.

By then, I had witnessed the turmoil of the three-day week and the power cuts, and I was determined that people and government should never again be held to ransom in this way. I had also seen the disparity in incomes between some of the poorer families of my home town and the better-off workers who had migrated from the central belt of Scotland to work in the Corpach pulp and paper mill, which gave me a heightened awareness of inequality and its negative effects.

This crystallized when, as a teenager, I participated in the finals of the Scottish Schools Debating Tournament. For the first time, I came across people who were of my own age but from vastly different backgrounds. The disparity in outlook and aspiration between pupils from tough inner-city Glasgow comprehensives and those from fee-paying schools in Dundee and Edinburgh seemed remarkable to me. The wealthier participants were visibly more confident and outspoken, and carried themselves with self-assurance. I did not come from an impoverished background, but this was nevertheless the first time I had ever stayed in an hotel. I was awed by the experience, and this set me apart from other youngsters who treated the place as if it were an extension of their homes.

There was no difference in intelligence or eloquence – we were all gathered there because of our debating skills. But when you asked these teenagers what they wanted to do in later life, it became clear that those from poorer backgrounds expected less, and received it. They talked about 'a job', 'a house', whereas their more affluent counterparts had a very clear sense of what 'profession' they wanted and where they were going to live.

The experience was an eye-opener. It was, if you like, the beginnings of my sense of injustice. It gave me a determination to tackle the deep divisions within our society, which remains unabated to this day. Labour was once regarded as *the* party of social justice. The party believed in providing for the poorest, and that unarguable viewpoint was the party's keynote, for many decades. It is safe to say that prior to the 1997 general election, few voters or even card-carrying members could have told you much about Labour's foreign policy, or its attitude to European trade. They voted Labour and they contributed to its coffers because of its stand on social issues.

This does not mean that Britain should return to Old Labour policies. The dogma of class war, nationalization and tax-and-spend for the sake of it made a major contribution to many of the problems that Britain faces today. I want no part of any New Old Labour plan, yet in throwing out the worst of its past, New Labour has forgotten many of the people it should still be serving. As Mr Blair's close ally, John Monks put it recently, New Labour seems to be treating some of its most loyal voters like 'embarrassing elderly relatives' at a family party.[1] It was poignant that, on the night of the first vote to cut benefits in the new 1997 Parliament, Labour ministers supped champagne at Number 10 with a host of celebrities. Of course, had the politicians in question opted for tomato juice and an early night, the problems of Britain's poor and dispossessed would not have vanished, but as a symbol of New Labour's concerns, the juxtaposition was as symbolic as it was crass.

In an age where favourable media coverage and a carefully managed public image are lamentably as vital to a government as its policies, it was inevitable that we would see the Blairs hobnobbing with the Gallagher brothers and playing host to the stars of Cool Britannia. They can scarcely be reproached for that. Far more insidious is the growing body of evidence that suggests New Labour's chief concern lies in courting the approval, and the votes, of Middle England, and that, simultaneously, it has lost interest in the poorest sections of society.

Take the slogan 'education, education, education': Tony Blair claims that equal access to a free and high quality education is paramount in dismantling the boundaries between rich and poor. I do not disagree, but if we assume the role of auditor for a moment, and look at two very different regions of England, we immediately see significant disparities. In Cornwall, 14.9 per cent of pupils are eligible for school meals, yet since May 1997 its schools have received only £308 per pupil through the system of competitive bidding, under which Local Education Authorities and schools have to apply to central government for funds. Rutland, by contrast, is one of Britain's richest counties, with only 6.4 per cent of pupils eligible for school meals, yet it receives £1,006 per pupil. These figures suggest that the more disadvantaged areas of the UK are doing relatively badly when it comes to education funding, while the more comfortable, vocal and consequently more powerful regions grow even stronger. When the young people of Cornwall and Rutland compete in tomorrow's job market such disparities will inevitably have knock-on effects.

A similar trend seems to be at work when we look at unemployment figures. Since Labour came into power, the biggest drops in unemployment have been felt by the most affluent constituencies. Conversely, between the years 1996 and 1999, the constituencies where unemployment fell the least were among the poorest. Constituency unemployment figures are not the most representative way of examining poverty as a whole, but these figures suggest that affluent communities have benefited more than poorer ones under New Labour. The two constituencies with the biggest improvement were in the most affluent region of the UK, the south-east, and the two seeing the least improvement were in Lancashire, in the second poorest region.[2]

The government has over-trumpeted its successes in reducing unemployment. The National Institute of Social and Economic Research has concluded that of the 191,000 young people who have passed into jobs under the auspices of the New Deal since its launch in April 1998, 115,000 would probably have found work anyway, due to the strength and growth of the economy. The New Deal was Labour's attack on unemployment, giving eighteen to twenty-four-year-olds who had been jobless for more than six months the opportunity to receive 'in-job' training, and offering employers incentives to give such people temporary work and training. After a four-month gateway period in which work is sought, there are various further options, including subsidized employment on short-time education and training. It marked a bold attempt to undermine the benefits culture and replace it with a work culture, but there is no point doing that when there is not enough work to go around.

In practice, the New Deal has turned out to be nothing more than a repackaging of the old Youth Training Scheme. Employers have benefited from a cheap source of temporary labour and cash sweeteners for using it, but in more than a fifth of cases, there were no real jobs for trainees to go to after the period had ended. Sixty per cent of the starters to the full-time education and training option had left by September 1999. Of the 191,000 'placed' in work, at least 50,000 were back on benefits within three months of completing the scheme. The National Centre for Social Research has shown that only a quarter of New Deal leavers were continuously in employment for six months after completion of the scheme. Such figures indicate that little is being done to erode the benefits culture.

As with the boom in the eighties, there are plenty of social groups who have not benefited at all from the recent economic upturn. An estimated 1 million children live with parents who are both out of work. Labour's policy has been to provide incentives for parents to take work, even if it is low-paid, but it is facing an uphill struggle. The British Household Panel Survey showed that between 1991 and 1997 only a quarter of couples with children who were out of work in any given year were able to find work a year later. The figure for lone parents was even more depressing – one in ten.

But there are large numbers of parents who do mini-jobs – that is, they work fewer than sixteen hours a week, which is the limit beyond which people cannot claim Income Support. The Institute for Social and Economic Research found that the more hours people put into these jobs, the more likely they were to secure a job offering more than sixteen hours work a week in the following year. It follows that government ought to be encouraging these small part-time jobs as a route into more full-time employment and out of poverty, but we still have a punitive benefits system, the principles of which have not altered for decades. People have to declare every change in their part-time earnings – even though many such jobs are ad hoc. People can also only earn between £5 and £15, depending on their circumstances, before money is deducted from their benefit. All this discourages people from taking any job that is less than full time, regardless of the opportunities it may lead to later.

In its failure to think flexibly it is no worse than previous governments, but no better either. Labour appears prepared to understand work only in terms of the traditional model of nine to five, five days a week, and benefits in terms of a weekly sum of money. And because it has stuck by this rigid perspective, people are losing out. For example, under the present system, unemployed people receive a weekly sum of money and, on top of that, a few entitlements, such as free eye check-ups and prescriptions. As soon as they stop receiving weekly benefit, the other benefits cease as well, meaning that even though they are working, they may be worse off than when they were entirely dependent upon benefits. Instead, people working a few hours a week, and all people on low incomes, should retain a range of entitlements, such as subsidized transport, free prescriptions and milk, so that they have incentives to enter and then remain within the world of work.

In 1996, Tony Blair said, 'If the Labour government has not raised the standards of the poorest by the end of its time in office, it will have failed.' Mr Blair made the pursuit of equality a key feature of his agenda – I do not argue with the depth and sincerity of his conviction – but the fact remains that, back in 1996, this was a subject of immediate contemporary concern. New Labour were characteristically astute in capturing the mood of the nation. It is still an important issue in the nation's eyes, but it would be even more so if the government made a crusade of the issue.

It is easy to see why it was such a public preoccupation. In 1992, an estimated 13.7 million people were living on breadline benefit or on half the average wage. This amounted to one quarter of the population of Britain. UNICEF warned that Britain's children were the worst off in Europe. By 1994, 4.2 million – roughly one third – of the children in Britain belonged to families living below the poverty line. Meanwhile, the gap between rich and poor had widened. By 1994, the wealthiest 5.5 million people in GB (i.e. the richest 10 per cent) were an average £650 better off for every thousand pounds they had earned in 1979. But the poorest ten per cent were worse off. For every £1,000 they had had in 1979, they now had £860.[3]

Unfortunately, it takes more than three budgets and a New Deal to reverse major trends like these, and undo the damage already caused – benefit cuts were almost the hunting cry of the Tory party in the 1980s. The most vulnerable sections of the nation are still suffering them under Labour. Anyone who receives invalidity benefit and has a modest private pension (£85 a week or more) will lose benefit at a rate of 50p in the pound. Severe disablement allowance has also been abolished, placing many severely handicapped people below the poverty line. The state pension was 20 per cent of the average income in the early eighties. It has now fallen to 15 per cent and is still falling. The government's answer was to make a derisory change which amounts to 75p a week for the average single pensioner. Meanwhile, a study by the University of Kent has shown that half those over eighty are surviving on less than £80 a week. Pensioners, distressed at their treatment under the present government, are among the most regular and vocal contributors to my daily postbag.

We can also see how little things have improved for the poor when we examine public health. Areas such as Glasgow, Newcastle-upon-Tyne and Liverpool have premature death rates more than twice those in affluent southern counties like Buckinghamshire and Berkshire. Within London, poor boroughs such as Woolwich have premature death rates twice as high as wealthy boroughs like Kensington and Chelsea, as well as disproportionately high rates of asthma, eczema, heart disease and depression.

The urban poor face unique sets of problems which Labour is doing little to address or even understand. A 1999 University of Glasgow study pointed out that Britain's twenty major cities have been hardest hit by unemployment. The decline of manufacturing industries has led to huge numbers of male manual workers being put out of their traditional employment. The report indicated that the cities had lost nearly a quarter of their 1981 stock of full-time male jobs by 1996 – equivalent to over 500,000 jobs – and these people are not going on to find work elsewhere. The service industry, it is often said, is expanding, but it is, according to the study, doing so least in our cities. The decline in skilled manual jobs has, on the whole, resulted in downward movement for most urban men into unskilled, lower-paid jobs, or into unemployment, casual work and the black economy.[4] The upshot is that there is a massive jobs gap in our cities – that is, large numbers of men able to work, and no jobs for them to go to.

Labour's current policies are directed towards equipping the urban unemployed with more skills and motivating them to find work. All this is totally missing the point. In the words of the study's authors: 'national economic and social policies need to give greater emphasis to *expanding labour demand* in the cities'. Of course, training and motivation are vital – but they are pointless when there are no jobs for people to go into.

We must also not overlook the very real problem of rural poverty.

It's not just farmers who are angry about the present government. The Rowntree Foundation interviewed sixty young people from rural backgrounds, and found that only two of them had secure accommodation and financial independence, and all felt that the only long-term solution to their housing and employment difficulties was to leave the countryside. Poor transport, lack of affordable housing and decline in the traditional sources of rural income are creating poverty blackspots in areas many urbanites still think of as idyllic. The problems of the countryside are likely to be exacerbated by the government's decision to make benefits payable by Automatic Cash Transfer rather than over the counter at Post Offices. This means that many rural sub-post offices will become economically unviable and be forced to close, and since these are usually twinned with village shops, rural Britain risks losing a vital hub of community life.

On a recent visit to the West Country, a farmer asked me why Labour had seemingly abandoned them, even though it held more rural seats than ever before. I knew the answer, and it becomes clearer every day. The present government has more rural constituencies, certainly, but among them plenty that it neither needs nor wants. The bulk of its ministers are from an urban background, and its outlook is consequently not particularly sensitive to the needs of the rural population. Many of Labour's rural seats are expendable – it doesn't need them to stay in power – that's why they can happily tell farmers to stop whingeing and diversify.[5]

Wherever it occurs, poverty breeds poverty and further exclusion. In our nation, significant numbers of people are growing up with limited access to the sort of services that are normally considered essential for full participation in society. A recent study by the University of Newcastle looked at people's access to energy, food, telephones, banking and food retailing in two poor neighbourhoods. It was clear that service providers, like phone and other utility companies, as well as the discount supermarkets, were physically withdrawing from low-income areas. The more limited the access to a service became, the more it cost the people who could least afford it: for example, pre-payment electricity meters, small food shops, public telephones and loan sharks all cost the user significantly more. This is the Tory legacy of 'market forces' and 'no such thing as society'. It is the ultimate proof that the market is not the guarantor of freedom. To escape the cycle, people need to find jobs, but when they have to spend their benefits travelling into town to charge up the electricity meter, there is understandably less spare cash for making phone calls. So the cycle repeats itself – across Britain, in our cities and villages, there is an underclass, with significantly lower life expectancy, lower levels of health and fitness, and with compromised access to good education, to transport, to society itself. How can we talk about democracy when large numbers of our people are disenfranchised in this way?

The real question is whether New Labour has either the attitude or the ability to reverse these worrying trends. I started to worry when I heard Tony Blair calling the public sector 'inflexible'. Certainly, there are areas that need reforming, and there is still too much Old Labour sentiment in some small yet influential areas of the union movement. But is it really inflexibility that leaves patients on trolleys in hospital corridors and forces pensioners awaiting cataract operations to fly to India to bypass eighteen-month waiting lists? That compels the NHS, in the grip of a flu crisis (the idea of which was in any case exaggerated to cover up Labour's health failures), to send patients to France because our hospitals have reached critical mass? Or that leaves children in schools with woefully inadequate books and equipment?

Arguably, in some areas of the public sector, there is a little too much flexibility. In Britain's universities, there is a profound sense of unease over the working conditions of academics. Increasingly, universities are being forced to hire people on short-term contracts, often for a term or a year, and often on a part-time basis. Academics, particularly young academics seeking to make a mark, are forced to publish at such a rate of knots that their work does not meet the quality that would have been expected only a few years ago. In the university environment, where we need people to think in a considered and long-term manner, that is far from ideal. Yet that is what flexibility breeds, and in the university context, it is self-defeating.

The real problem is not inflexibility. It is a deliberate reluctance on the part of New Labour radically to address poverty and the countless other injustices blighting our society. A reluctance born of the fact that New Labour dare not be honest about the money it needs to spend to put these things right, for fear of losing the support of the wealthiest sections of society, who have benefited from New Labour's concessionary attitude to tax.

I am not delivering a blanket criticism of the Labour government. A recent University of Cambridge study suggested that the incomes of the poorest tenth of the population have risen over the last three budgets, while the richest tenth have, on average, not become any richer. The study said that the poorest families with children have seen their income rise by 16 per cent. At the same time, Labour's welfare programme was met with howls of discontent from the start. Witness the furore when Harriet Harman announced in autumn 1997 that she was going ahead with the Conservative plans to phase out additional benefits for single mothers, and the similar uproar when the government cut disability benefits, and introduced tuition fees for students in 1999.

In contrast to the Cambridge study we also have to consider the figures released by the Office of National Statistics in April 2000, which indicated that the gap between the earnings of the richest and the earnings of the poorest has widened to its highest level since Margaret Thatcher was Prime Minister. The government was visibly embarrassed by these findings, which overshadowed John Prescott's plans for a ten-year drive against poverty in the inner cities, launched only days before. They argued, in response, that the figures were unrepresentative, because measures such as the New Deal and the Working Families Tax Credit had simply not had time to take effect.

We cannot deny that Labour *is* spending money – but its record of benefit cuts indicate that it is doing so very selectively. There have been no universal increases in cash benefits – though academics have argued that this was what was desperately needed for a country where nearly 14 million received below half the average income.[6] They have also *not* funded these increases from income tax.

In fact, they are still adamant about cutting income tax, because

Labour believes this is the right way to win middle-income voters back from the Tories. This in turn means that, whatever Labour does for the most disadvantaged, it cannot do nearly enough to address the problems facing them. In 1997, journalist Nick Davies wrote:

> Labour thinking seems to take no account of the damage which has been inflicted on the poor in the past twenty years ... that by flicking the switches of the benefits machine ... people can be manipulated into families or into work or out of crime, as though they were carefully calculating their rational self-interest, as though their lives and sometimes their personalities had not been scrambled by the experience of the last twenty years.[7]

His words are just as true now. And the solution is not simply to raise taxes and throw more money at the poorest sections of society. The solution requires as much of a revolution in thought as in deeds.

The Alternative

I have repeatedly stated that Liberal Democrats do not and will not inherit the vacant lot to the left of New Labour. Such a strategy would be tantamount to our party embarking on the search for a political cul-de-sac, but, at the same time, I believe that our party is the only party truly concerned with social justice, and we will fight the next election on that basis.

This is not a new stance for the party. Nor is it something I have chosen because it is fashionable – or unfashionable, for that matter. Far from it: Liberals and Social Democrats have a long tradition of fighting the war against social inequality. Some of the key thinkers of twentieth-century politics, who had a decisive impact on the shape of millions of people's lives, were Liberals. William Beveridge produced the proposals for social security that became the bedrock of the post-war welfare state, and John Maynard Keynes was the economic guru of much of the post-war economic settlement. Before them, turn-of-the-century New Liberals such as L. T. Hobhouse and J. A. Hobson were among the first people in Britain to make a persuasive case for a government role in fighting poverty. We are and must always be the definitive political movement of conscience and reform.

Hobhouse's view that 'the struggle for liberty is ... a struggle for equality', is the basis of liberal attitudes to social justice. For all to be free, argued Hobhouse, there had to be equal access to opportunities for education and employment, and only individuals together, acting through government, could ensure that happened. Progressive social reform has deep philosophical roots within the Liberal Democrats.

It also has deep roots in Labour history, but the current leadership seems to have forgotten this. As a result, active public enthusiasm for New Labour (as opposed to national opinion polls) is at an all-time low. The desultory turnout for the 1999 European elections clearly indicated the nation's deep cynicism towards the political process. At a time when war in Kosovo had been raging for seventy days, less than a quarter of the population found European politics sufficiently relevant to leave their houses and vote.

People only pay attention to politicians when they are dealing with issues that immediately concern them. From my travels across the country, I know that inequality is an issue of great contemporary concern, but the present government has all but stopped trying to redress it. It feels it is doing enough, because it can always churn out figures that prove it is. When one of its own ministers, Peter Kilfoyle, resigned from office because he felt that Labour was not doing enough for the poor in his own Liverpool constituency, the response from the leadership was an embarrassed silence. There was much talk about regretting his departure, not so much about regretting what he said – or whether it was true.[8]

One practical measure in particular would make a radical and immediate improvement, and put issues of inequality at the centre of political debate. Just as the Budget dominates the national news once a year, so we need an annual Social Justice Audit of similar importance, which would examine the impact of all government policies that have any link with social inequalities. It would be published in full in the newspapers and be publicized to the hilt, and every year the government would be expected to show whether they had met the targets of the previous year. This would, combined with an audit of their environmental performance, and the traditional Budget, establish a 'triple bottom line'. The government is already encouraging ethical companies to report upon these aspects of their yearly performance; maybe it should learn the lesson itself.

Such an audit would have to be genuinely independent of government, and carry significant weight behind its conclusions. A variety of bodies would be consulted in its creation, and a panel of respected independent figures would be established. It would include representatives of, for example, the Economic and Social Research Council, the Bank of England, the CBI, the BMA, the National Audit Office and the Audit Commission. Not all of these bodies are primarily associated with the cause of social justice, and so they would not be seen as having axes to grind, but they could all provide significant expertise at evaluating evidence produced by government departments. In addition, they would be supported by a permanent team of researchers, independent of any government department, whose job would be to examine the figures produced by government. With such support, finding any inaccuracies in government figures would not be difficult – as Liberal Democrat researchers regularly prove even without such support. This would be an enormous improvement upon the government's present self-congratulatory Annual Report, an exercise which ranges from the anodyne to a brazen attempt at political propaganda at the taxpayers' expense. Mercifully, nobody appears to pay much attention to it.

What would this audit look like in practice? It would begin with the announcement of Bills in Parliament. Take some of those put forward by the government in the final Queen's Speech of the last century, November 1999. The audit would apply two key questions to them. First, how would different parts of the country, and the inequalities between them, be affected? Second, how would the inequalities between social groups be affected?

Measures such as the Care Standards Bill, intended to promote better care for the elderly, would have to include information on how those measures would affect people with different incomes and savings. If the Bill increased the access of people on low incomes to high quality care, then it would pass the Social Justice Audit. As the Bill presently stands, it would not pass, and nor would the Electronic Communications Bill, which does not consider how disadvantaged groups can take advantage of new technologies, nor how government can encourage them to participate.

The Social Justice Audit would be similarly scathing of government transport policy, which has not met its targets for traffic reduction, and has decreased spending on public transport. This is a social justice issue just as much as it is one of the environment, for car ownership is only possible for people above a certain level of income, and those below it have to rely on public transport. We need to subject every government policy to intense scrutiny if we are to have a more informed debate on the inequalities in Britain, which goes beyond mere questions of tax and benefits.

I do not pretend for one moment that a Social Justice Audit would solve all of Britain's social problems, but, given sufficient priority by government, it could change the nature of our political discourse, so that politicians would be forced to be clear about how they will tackle definite inequalities, and be held accountable when they don't deliver. If a Bill is judged to have failed, it might be automatically rescheduled for reworking in Parliament. The Audit would also highlight the extent to which social justice is affected by a wide range of policies – a fact often overlooked. For example, in terms of the environment, poorer areas suffer most from pollution.

Refocusing politics and reshaping our political language, so that politicians reconnect with the real concerns of millions of ordinary people, will have a tremendously positive impact on the quality of our democracy. It will give genuine meaning to politics, for people who at present feel that it has little to offer them. Otherwise we face a future in which 25 per cent election turnouts are seen as the norm, rather than a cause for concern. And we will continue to live in a Britain in which privilege, rather than ability, determines the achievements and the resultant quality of life.

Tax for Freedom

New Labour is reluctant to mention the word taxation, except, of course, to *claim* that it is coming down, but if we accept that every citizen of our nation has a right to first-class education, to comprehensive health care and a welfare safety net, then we also have to accept that we all have a responsibility to make those priorities possible. They cannot be achieved without radical changes in the way our taxes are applied and collected. To pretend otherwise is simply to con the voters.

I am not arguing for a simplistic 'high taxes, high public spending' model. I believe that the main increase should be in terms of efficiency. Increased efficiency in the way taxes are imposed, gathered and, most importantly, spent. Four guiding principles should govern all socially responsible policies on taxation.

The first is *adequacy*: taking exactly and only what is needed, from precisely those who can give. Penalizing the successful only deprives the nation of entrepreneurial talent. Bleeding the rich dry as a policy has more to do with old-fashioned antipathy – what Winston Churchill called 'cool-blooded class hatred' – than the search for social equality. At the same time, government cannot be starved of the money it needs to pay for good schools and teachers, quality health care, adequate pensions and people in need. That is why I urged the present government to spend its 1999–2000 budget surplus on the public sector, instead of sweetening the least needy sections of society with tax cuts and patching up the shortfall with the surplus cash.

That is also why I greeted Gordon Brown's 2000 Budget with scepticism: £1 billion goes into education, but £2.6 billion is devoted to a further cut in the basic rate of income tax – a clear indication of Labour's priorities. The Budget will do nothing to provide nursery education for all three year olds, and little to reduce class sizes in our secondary schools, or to address the backlog of repairs. Nor will it do anything towards abolishing or reducing tuition fees for higher education, or addressing the massive gap between the needs of business and the training on offer.

Physics tells us that matter can never be destroyed – it simply converts into other forms. Similarly, in politics you can never cut taxes unless somebody else pays. In the case of New Labour policy, much of the tax burden has shifted away from income tax and on to council tax, which has risen by a third in four years. Much of the pain will also be felt by the young and the old, as education loses out, and as do the pensioners, who received the staggeringly generous sum of an extra 75p a week. The only provision of extra money for pensioners was in a small increase (£50 – less than £1 per week) on the one-off winter fuel payment, when it is clear that what is required is an increase on weekly income across the board. That would be far more empowering than handouts on fuel. Perhaps the only consolation we could take from the Budget was that things would have been far worse under the Tories, but still, current Labour taxation policy does not satisfy the criteria for adequacy.

The second principle for responsible taxation is *honesty*. Politicians need to be straight with people about the choices involved. It is simply not acceptable to say, as William Hague's Conservative Party has done, that you can have tax cuts and more spending on schools and hospitals. That is an implausible position to take, and one clear indication of why the Conservative Party has become so irrelevant. In the run-up to elections, politicians must tell the public precisely how much their programme of public sector spending will cost, and how it will be paid for. Wherever they wish to introduce new taxes or set different levels they must explain exactly why the changes are occurring, and where the new money is going.

Liberal Democrats have produced a fully costed manifesto at both of the last two general elections. We have shown how much our plans would cost, and how we would pay for them. Some people have responded to this by saying, 'You can afford to be honest about it because you're the third party.' But being the third party does not mean we can get away with being out of touch with the mood of the nation! Our decision to be honest about taxes is based on an awareness that this is what the nation wants.

When we first proposed that we would, if necessary, raise taxation by 1p in the pound to pay for investment in education, commentators believed it would be unpopular. It was the subject of much passionate debate within the party before the 1992 General Election. People like Robert Maclennan, Simon Hughes, Matthew Taylor and myself were strongly in favour. I supported it because it was such a clear-cut, honest platform upon which to fight an election, and it was a definite departure from 1983 and 1987, when no-one, least of all ourselves, really understood what issues we were fighting on. Most importantly, it sent out the message that we were a party prepared to be honest about the money we needed in order to change things. Now, polls regularly indicate that as many as seven out of every ten voters are in favour of paying an extra penny on the pound for education or health.

Hypothecation is a term redolent of something technical and extremely complex. In reality it is just the opposite. It is the principle that people are able to see exactly where their money is going. If more money is needed for schools and hospitals, then hypothecation means that government will explain the costs to people, and where the money will be raised. People do not resent giving money in such a situation. I want every citizen to receive a statement with their tax return, which sets out in simple terms where their money has gone. It should also say what the main targets were for the public services, and how far they are being achieved.

The third principle is *fairness*. Taxes must be applied and collected in a fair way. It is grossly unfair that, at the moment, someone who earns £8,000 pays the same rate of income tax as someone earning £25,000. We should demand the greatest contribution from those with the greatest ability to pay. I strongly favour asking those who earn over £100,000 a year to pay more, through the introduction of a 50 per cent rate for anything earned over that figure. That would enable us to help the worst off in Britain, by taking around half a million people out of paying income tax altogether.

The fourth is *sustainability*. Taxes must favour job creation and the environment. Rather than being seen as the government's penalty upon the wage earner, taxes must be presented as the means by which we achieve a fairer and healthier society. Cutting tax for the low paid would be a major step in helping to create jobs and encourage people into work. Tax should also be used to discourage pollution by taxing the use of fossil fuel energy sources and the use of harmful chemicals in industry. The money raised can be used to reduce tax in other areas, so that people are not hit twice. I want to see logic prevail in the way taxes are used. For instance, putting money from petrol taxes straight into asthma research or money from tobacco straight into cancer research. At present, some industries are able to undermine people's health – whether by the sale of cigarettes, alcohol, junk food, or by pollution. Taxing them is one way of redressing the balance, so that they start to pay some of the costs they are presently imposing upon us.

There has to be a shift in the way the money gathered from taxation is spent. We would set our long-term policies with the aim of building a fairer society: reforming and investing in education; giving more of the nation's wealth to the NHS; increasing job opportunities for the long-term unemployed and others disadvantaged in the workforce; making more affordable housing available; and working for a healthy environment. With a Social Justice Audit in place, the government would have to state its aims for social spending and report each year on how well these were being met. That way, we could see whether policies were in fact expanding opportunities and promoting a more equal Britain. There was a time when manifestos were a new concept: that government should say *in advance* to the electorate what it intended to do was a strange idea. In the modern world, surely it should not be too much to require the government to explain whether it is achieving its promises. It is the logical progression of the manifesto.

We could also achieve better results through different types of spending. In education, we have to focus new spending on early years education to give children the best possible tuition in core skills of reading and writing. In the area of health, much greater attention needs to be paid to preventive medicine, and it needs to be realized that environmental factors make an enormous impact on health. That could mean GPs being able to prescribe home insulation as a pre-emptive treatment, instead of waiting until somebody is ill with pneumonia before treating them.

Britain clearly needs a more efficient and accountable tax system to fund a programme of social repair, but more money is seldom the only answer, and sometimes pouring resources into a bottomless pit can exacerbate the problems it was supposed to solve. The state has a duty to act as a safety net, but it has an equally pressing duty not to become a permanent crutch, lest people lose the will to walk themselves. We need to be agile in our thinking when it comes to bridging the deep social divides at the heart of Britain and, rather than simply providing funds on tap, we have to encourage individuals and communities to help themselves.

Help Yourself Politics

The responsibility for social disparities and their swift repair lies *with* the state, but many of the means to effect long-lasting change lie *beyond* it. The state should encourage and support the groups with the know-how and utilize their expertise.

This has not been happening because too often governments have taken a dim view of the voluntary sector as a whole. Perhaps because those in power draw a salary for running the country, there is a dangerous view that only the salaried are competent. Volunteers – even though they often use the same skills by which they can also earn a living – are seen by some as well-intentioned sources of interference. Others feel that a thriving voluntary sector symbolizes the gradual withdrawal of the state from every responsibility apart from the protection of property. It is – so the thinking goes – dangerous to over-encourage charities or voluntary work, lest the government give up altogether.

A vigorous voluntary sector is not a sign that the state is abdicating; instead, it is the sign of a healthy nation. A strong interest and involvement in voluntary groups shows that civic Britain is strong. That there is a lively public spirit, and that citizens are willing to work together for the benefit of others, can only be good news, but this community spirit has been in crisis for the last two decades. While the machinery is still in place, and our nation is enriched by the activities of a diverse and vibrant voluntary sector (Age Concern alone reports 250,000 volunteers nationwide, and receives a third of its annual £27 million income just from donations), the notion of community was dealt serious damage by the egocentric culture of the eighties. How could it be otherwise when the leader of the country said that the pursuit of equality was a mirage and that there was no such thing as society? Meanwhile, as the Pet Shop Boys sang 'Let's Make Lots of Money', city bonuses soared. Benefits for the poor were systematically undermined, while TV advertising extolled the virtues of ambition, self-reliance and basic greed. Small wonder concern for community hit an all-time low.

At the same time, I believe we can only pick through the rubble left by the eighties for a given time, and that time is past. After a decade, and a change of government, the time has come to start rebuilding a civic Britain, in which individuals and communities look out for each other.

A thriving voluntary sector signifies a healthy society because it shows people do not expect government to be Sole Solver of All Problems. As a postgraduate student in the early eighties, I spent time in the USA, at Indiana University. This experience proved to be a powerful influence on my view of the world: what impressed me above all about the States was the tremendous can-do energy.

It is interesting to compare the way that people complain about things here and in the States. Here they tend to say, 'What is the government going to do about it?'; over there, they are as likely to say, 'Get the government off my back so I can do something about it.' Americans are also more likely to see government as responsible to the people, rather than accept the state as master. That is more than a turn of phrase – it illustrates a state of mind.

There is a belief, rooted in the American culture, that every individual has huge opportunities as well as a responsibility for their own destiny, which results in a real drive among individuals to carve out their own future. It is a spirit reinforced by the decentralization of power and authority in the USA.

This can take a variety of forms. Jonathan Freedland's provocative book *Bring Home the Revolution: How Britain can live the American Dream*[9] has some interesting tales to tell. In Hanover, New Hampshire, the local people bypass government altogether once a year with direct democracy. They meet every May in a school gym and then vote on their own proposals about how the community should be governed. For the rest of the year, citizens can call an emergency meeting through a petition. Their achievements are considerable and even include keeping the ubiquitous McDonald's out of their town. In Ithaca, New York, the local people staged a successful campaign to prevent the construction of a giant out-of-town Wal-Mart. They also instituted what is now the largest local currency in the world – of which more anon.

Such approaches – and the fact that Americans vote for many more of their public officials than in Britain – allow individuals to reconnect with the notion of government – there is a much closer identification with local government in many areas. This civic spirit or connectedness is also seen in areas of life well beyond government. Freedland explains that 82 per cent of Americans belong to at least one association or group. Germany stands at 67 per cent, and Britain at only 54 per cent. Americans get involved in an incredible range of community groups, sometimes simply to pursue a hobby, but often to carry out functions that in other countries are carried out by government – or are simply not done at all. Perhaps the most graphic example of this is that 73 per cent of American households give to charity, compared to only 29 per cent in the UK – and they give at much higher rates in the USA.

This is not to say for one moment that everything about American society is perfect. I find it obscene, for example, that in a society of such enormous wealth, millions of people live in constant fear of illness or accident because they cannot afford basic medical insurance.

Yet I still admire the get-up-and-go energy which I saw in America in the early eighties, and which exists there today. We have that spirit in the best of our entrepreneurs in Britain, but if Britain is to prosper in the century ahead, we need to foster more of that energy, enterprise and drive, and we need to apply it to the sections of our community where it is most needed. We have huge inventiveness in our country – but we seem far less able to make it work.

There are reasons for this. It is often said that the Americans lack a sense of irony, which may be true, but British irony seems – in the booms and slumps of the last twenty years – to have turned in on itself, and what we have in its place is cynicism. Cynicism, disillusionment, and a belief that people who try to change things are misguided zealots, that too much damage has been done in the past for our country to have a future.

There is also a very British fear of failure which dogs the efforts of individuals and communities to work together for the common good. It originates, I believe, in a combination of British reserve – a fear of losing face in front of our peers – and the market-driven culture of the eighties. We are over-eager to set people up and then knock them down. I am pleased to live in a thriving market economy, but less pleased that we are living in a market culture, in which value means the same as money. In the voluntary sector, people are valued in terms of the time they give over to a project and the skills they can bring to it. I want to live in a society where the idea that a person's worth is related to what they do for their community, not how much money or purchasing power they have, is a core value.

To bring this about, there has to be a turnaround in our thinking. For community initiative to flourish – whether in tackling crime or homelessness, or in providing opportunities for youth – people need the room to experiment, to innovate, to take risks *and to make mistakes*. There needs to be a new culture of community and self-reliance, in which individuals feel confident enough to take a stand for or against the issues that matter to them, and to band together to make changes, to challenge government when they need to, and to know that their voices will be heard.

Examples of individuals and groups effecting real change on their communities are much vaunted in the press, but mainly because they are rarities. On a problem estate in northern England, parents organized a rota to ensure that all schoolchildren were safely escorted home in the dark winter months. In London, older West Indian men are recruited by schools to befriend boys from their community who lack the influence of a father figure in their lives. On the island of Eigg, off the coast of the Scottish West Highlands, crofters kicked back against a string of controversial landowners and abortive attempts to secure the title to the land, creating their own trust, bidding for ownership and achieving this in 1997. I don't wish to understate the bravery and determination of the people responsible for these initiatives, but I want to see a society where these things are not news, but the fabric of daily life. That's a true democracy.

This kind of local activity outside the economy is absolutely essential for making society function, just as the work parents and communities do to bring up children is vital to all of us. The author of *Future Shock*, Alvin Toffler, used to ask senior executives what it would cost them in cash terms if none of their employees had ever been toilet-trained. The truth is, business depends on parents, and parents depend on active communities.

Let's get some brains together, along with community leaders and voluntary workers, and think creatively about ways in which we can foster a civic society, in which everyone feels they have a part to play. For example, in an age when more and more school-leavers are going into tertiary education, why do universities only look at A level results when selecting candidates? There could be a points system for community action and voluntary work, which they could take into account alongside academic achievements.

I am also in favour of a JFK-style Peace Corps, to involve young people in a range of community projects. I have no interest in using this as a threat over the unemployed. A person's benefits should stay the same whether they joined Charles Kennedy's Peace Corps or not, but if employers were encouraged to recruit within the ranks of this corps – or if points earned counted towards academic qualifications or student loans – then unemployed young people would have a clear incentive to get involved.

People's 'outside' activities should be encouraged wherever possible. If a low-paid mechanic spends his weekends teaching underprivileged kids to play football, he could accrue credits, which in turn entitle him to have his roof repaired by another volunteer. With people living longer than before, retired people, who often have more experience and patience than their younger counterparts, are an under-utilized resource. Their involvement in the community could be exchanged for similar credits, or even for credits which they could pass on to their working children or grandchildren, so, in return for helping a neighbour's child with her schoolwork, an elderly person could be entitled to weekly lifts to and from the shops. They wouldn't have to rely on charity or hand-outs, they would earn the lifts themselves.

The idea of using time as a kind of money has proved popular on a global scale. Time exchange schemes are especially successful in the USA and Japan. In Washington DC, 300 residents of a problem housing estate performed 79,000 hours of voluntary work in 1997. By working, each person earned a fictional currency – time dollars – which could be exchanged with other residents for services they needed. The name of the currency illustrates the principle of the idea perfectly – in this case value has got nothing to do with money, it's about the time a person is prepared to give over to helping others. In New York state, one college allows its students to pay off their student loans in time hours – that is, by doing voluntary work in their local community.

'Let us give generously, in the two currencies of time and money,' said Tony Blair in March 2000, but he hasn't understood the implications of this. The point is that we can all see around us the enormous amount of tasks that need doing, even if the government doesn't consider that doing them constitutes a 'job'. Society apparently cannot afford to pay with money for all the old people who need help, the schools who need volunteers, the neighbourhood watchers and the youth leaders. We spend much time in politics worrying about scarce resources and cutting budgets, and assuming there isn't enough to provide for what we need. Yet all around us there are enormous untapped resources, of which older people – with their wealth of knowledge and experience – are only one. The old and the young, in particular, both wish to make a contribution, and we need to find ways of using these forgotten resources and directing them at society's intractable problems. We should encourage people to earn time credits through time banks, and then recognize them, for example by letting people buy recycled computers with it, as they do in the USA.

There are other kinds of exchange schemes all over the world which help people buy the basic necessities of life in local currencies. In Ithaca, New York state, the community where they saw off the Wal-Mart, a local currency was created, based on the mutual exchange of goods and services between local people within the scheme. It has been so successful that the organizers calculate $1.5 million dollars have been created in local trade in five years, and around 300 businesses in the town are within the scheme – helping many local businesses, such as struggling organic farmers, find a market. The federal government has decided to let it carry on without interference.

In areas of high unemployment and poverty, people's skills are quite literally going to waste alongside their communities. Local exchange schemes help people keep their skills fresh, as well as develop new ones. The isolation that often goes hand-in-hand with joblessness is tackled into the bargain.

There are currently 400 Local Exchange and Trading Systems (LETS) systems operating in Britain, involving around 35,000 people. Groats, reeks, bobbins, bricks and concrete cows may not be quoted on the stock market, but these unofficial currencies are doing much to improve individual quality of life and revive communities across Britain. Over 100 local authorities are now funding the development of these systems as a means of tackling social problems. Hampshire and Surrey use them as a means of getting people with mental health problems back into the world of work, while Bristol and Gloucester are linking them to local allotments, so that fresh fruit and vegetables can be given to people in exchange for their services.

In this country you tend to hear about schemes like local currencies and credit unions on the sort of day when there hasn't been much news and the *Independent* is short of something to fill its column space, but anyone registering as unemployed in New Zealand is automatically advised to join their local green dollar scheme, and governments in Australia, Ireland and Holland have ruled that participation in local exchange schemes does not affect people's entitlement to benefit. Their relative obscurity in the UK is undeserved.

The culture of British government has always made it reluctant to think laterally about social problems. For too long, people have thought in terms of two models: tax-and-spend or tax-concessions-and-huge-dole-queues. But there are alternatives. Voluntary organizations and local exchange schemes – whether they are exchanging time or local currencies – can and do have a real impact on society, by fostering and developing the skills and habits of public involvement.

Schemes like these are of particular importance in harnessing the enormous potential of our ageing population. It is a paradox that while we live in an increasingly ageing society – one where people survive to increasingly greater ages – we seem to attach less and less respect to the aged, and more and more to the young. The term New Labour is itself very telling – it suggests that, behind the nomenclature, there is a value system at work. Old equals bad, new equals good. We also see it when William Hague has a fashionable haircut and sports a baseball cap – as well as saying to the young, 'I want your vote,' he is effectively saying to the old, 'I'm not so bothered about yours.' Of course we must endeavour to engage the young, because they are the future – the disillusionment of young people with politics is an issue of particular concern to me – but we must not advance the values of youth at the expense of the elders.

I am keenly aware of this for two reasons. My parents are now both in their seventies, and far from being on the scrap-heap, they lead lives which are in some ways more full and active than when they were at work. But they have numerous advantages: they live in a small and close community, they have made adequate provision for the future, and they have a network of friends and relatives close by. I am fully aware that the same is not true for many people of the same age.

The importance of the silver vote was also made clear when I visited Miami for the Democrat primaries. There, every morning, the candidates hosted huge breakfast meetings in order to rally support. These were sell-out events and, understandably in a retirement state like Florida, dominated by people of retirement age. They formed a vocal, powerful and formidable body and the US politicians knew only too well that their success depended on securing their support. Politics has to take greater cognizance of the specific needs and concerns of the elderly. I think it telling that Tony Blair has given us a drugs Czar and a Heart Czar. Drugs and heart ops are emotive subjects, a gift for the press. The needs of the elderly are no less urgent, but they are, clearly, less fashionable. That's why we probably won't, under the present government, be seeing a Pensioners' Czar.

The elderly and the young alike find themselves excluded when it comes to the new credit economy. Between six and nine per cent of the UK population have no bank account, and therefore no access to small loans, other than by turning to loan sharks who charge exorbitant interest – sometimes even up to the equivalent of 6,000 per cent APR. The disappearance of so many bank branches means it's hard enough for many people, especially in rural areas, even to get hold of cash.

Credit unions allow people to help and be helped at the local level: people band together to save small amounts, and they can also borrow from the fund when they need to. They have their roots in the old friendly societies, which by the nineteenth century were an unofficial welfare state for over half the British workforce. Currently, we have around 400 in the UK, and under half a million people are involved, half of those in Northern Ireland.

Measures like these are more important than ever. New forms of money, such as credit and debit cards, smart cards, telephone and Internet banking are creating an electronic economy where money is invisible. All of this is exciting for society, and for those of us with secure incomes and bank accounts, but those on low and insecure incomes are being more or less excluded from this new economy, and need help if they are to become engaged.

Credit unions not only extend credit to disadvantaged people, but they also provide a range of financial advice and services. They need a new infrastructure to back them, to enable them to provide access to anything from small loans for the micro-businesses that provide much of Britain's employment, to mortgages on hard-to-let properties. This new generation of self-help financial services should also go hand-in-hand with measures to make sure the big banks lend their far larger resources in a fairer way. We should, perhaps, shame banks into ending their refusal to operate in some neighbourhoods with a Bill along the lines of the highly successful US Community Reinvestment Act, which forces banks to reveal their lending patterns, and has levered over $1 billion in investment into poor neighbourhoods during the past twenty years.

An area where community input is particularly valuable is in the fight against crime. Crime, and the fear of it, touches every person and community in Britain – although certain groups are disproportionately likely to be victims. Those who serve their communities are at particular risk. This was brought home early in 2000 when Liberal Democrats in Cheltenham lost an invaluable friend and dedicated party worker, Councillor Andrew Pennington. Andrew had gone to the aid of Cheltenham MP Nigel Jones, as a man wielding a sword attacked him in his constituency office.

Such high-profile cases are outnumbered by the thousands of other violent crimes committed every year. Total recorded crime doubled in the eighties and early nineties. While some property crime declined in the late nineties, violent crime continued to rise. And now the *overall* crime rate has risen again. In the year to September 1999, recorded crime in this country rose by 2.2 per cent – the first in five years. This general figure masked especially large rises in certain sectors. Most worryingly there was a 6.3 per cent rise in violent crime, and robberies were up by 19 per cent.

There is undeniable evidence that the bulk of crimes are committed by those with the least opportunities: men and women from the most disadvantaged sections of society. It follows that a major weapon in the fight against crime is the pursuit of equality, but we must also not forget the victims. The justice system should always serve the victims' rights: rights to medical help, counselling, financial compensation, and

welfare and legal services. Victims have already suffered at the hands
of a criminal. At present, too many go on to suffer at the hands of
the system.

When a mugger is sent to prison, he may, arguably, be repaying
his debt to society, but he is not, in any sense, making amends to the
person he mugged. Even worse for victims is the fact that many
offenders are not given any kind of sentence at all. Around three in
five young offenders are given a police warning or a caution.

That is why I strongly believe in restorative justice programmes.
They take a variety of forms: there is usually a meeting between
offenders and victims, but only if victims agree to take part. The aim
is to confront offenders with the consequences of their actions, and
to make them see the impact they have had on the lives of their
victims.

Thames Valley Police have been one of the leading innovators in
this area. A couple of years ago they ran a pilot restorative justice
scheme in Aylesbury, focusing particularly on young offenders committing shop theft. They held almost 170 restorative cautions or conferences involving the offender, their family and the victim. The initial
results were telling. Re-offending fell to 4 per cent, compared to 35
per cent in other parts of the country. Equally importantly, the scheme
was popular with people who had been the victims of crime.

The well-worn cry for 'more Bobbies on the beat' still rings true,
but it only provides a partial solution: it is not, and never has been,
a panacea for reducing crime. Nonetheless the role of the police is
vital. That is why Labour's promise to be 'tough on crime' rings so
hollow now. In opposition they pledged more police officers. After
three years in power there were 1,600 fewer police on the beat than
when they came to office. That is a dreadful betrayal of the promise
they made to the British people.

Police forces also need to be linked more closely to the communities
they serve. The restorative justice programme is one way in which
police forces can meet community needs, but there must also be
more community input on the strategic direction of policing. Local
representatives should be consulted when it comes to deciding police

priorities, and to do that we need to have more elected members on police authorities. The people who suffer from the effects of crime are best placed to guide the police, particularly when it comes to targeting problem neighbourhoods. We must also not ignore the insights and expertise of the 'shop floor'. During a visit to Colchester police station early in 2000, where I saw a fine example of community policing, one long-serving officer in particular impressed me with his detailed knowledge of the community and his impassive attitude to crime and its causes. He made the apt observation that community out-reach projects and various other flashily named directives were just a repack-aging of something that all good police officers had been doing since time immemorial. As in other public services, we need to recognize professionalism in all ranks of the police force, and make sure that future policy on crime takes full stock of what they have to say.

Conclusion

With a crisis in political involvement in Britain, it is vital that we examine all the ways in which civic society can reconnect with the people. This is something that I care passionately about, and I am determined to make it a priority for the Liberal Democrats. We can only do this as part of a broad movement dedicated to building power-ful communities – this is a road which politicians and the voluntary sector must walk hand in hand.

Britain will never have the vigorous voluntary sector it needs until individuals are made to feel that their contribution is both vital and valued. In many ways, this is as much an issue of culture as of policy. Just as the policies of the Conservative government in the eighties fostered a 'Me, Myself, I' culture, the policies of future governments have the ability to create a civic culture in which community pride, concern for the young, the poor, the homeless and the elderly go hand in hand with the optimism that things can be done, and in which, eventually, this attitude becomes an instinctive part of being British. Government must take the reins to ensure this happens.

Politicians cannot ignore the pensioners who write to me every day, complaining that Labour's extra 75p a week was an insult, nor can we ignore the body of statistics that prove social divides to be a lasting feature of Britain's geography. New Labour has not narrowed the gap, but the time has come to stop pointing the finger, and examine the ways we can change things. Instead of pledging higher, or lower, public spending to please various sections of the electorate, we need a rationalized, streamlined system of taxation to target the funds directly to where they are most needed.

At the same time, a responsible government is one which fosters a culture in which people think and act for themselves. Encouraging that spirit in our citizens is a duty every bit as vital as ensuring equal access to education and health. The power of government, in short, should be marshalled into giving power to its citizens.

Chapter Two

FREEDOM TO BREATHE:
THE GREEN FUTURE

'We have the knowledge and technology to solve many of the environmental ills facing our planet. What we need now is political will.'

KLAUS TÖPFER, Director of the
United Nations Environment Programme

I became involved in politics because, like many others, I wanted to 'do something' when I was growing up. I wanted to make a difference in areas that mattered personally to me. Being a Highland Scot, the question of devolution was high on the agenda, and as someone who remembered going to bed early in the dark due to the power cuts of the early seventies, the question of trade union power was very important in my eyes, when I came to realize why the power cuts had happened. Having rather alarmed my parents by rushing home from school to catch the updates on the Watergate Congressional hearings, issues of public accountability and political integrity were also strong motivating factors in my decision to join the milieu. Looking back, man in space and my childhood fascination with the Apollo moonshot programme stimulated the imagination as well. At that age, with the fine night skies which are common in my homeland, such things can but encourage your dreams.

There was little room in my conscience for matters such as pollution and global warming. I was aware of them, but they did not feature on my personal agenda. How that has altered! In 1999, during the Liberal Democrat leadership election, at a hustings meeting in Launceston, I was asked on what issue had I changed my mind most over the past ten years. I was then approaching my fortieth birthday, so my first response was to say that, a decade ago, I thought forty was old, but I had recently started to revise my opinions. But I also gave a more serious answer. Because little more than ten years ago, I could never have imagined how much environmental concerns would come to be at the heart of my own politics.

Like many people, I grew up taking certain things for granted. Perhaps most obviously, growing up in a crofting community in the Highlands, I took for granted the natural environment around me: the beauty and sheer physical presence of the mountains and glens; the fresh air; the clean water of the lochs and streams, and the quality of the life I had. At the same time I understood, from an early age, that the natural environment demands respect. At times it was harsh and extreme, and when the elements chose, life could be a bleak experience indeed.

There were some harmonious and idyllic aspects to life on the croft. I remember, for instance, that my grandfather ploughed the fields with a sturdy, brown shire-horse, who went by the name of Nellie. I also remember how little shop-bought produce we consumed, and how much we relied on home-grown, home-reared foods, which without doubt tasted superior.

At the same time, many of the people living closest to the land did not respect it. The hills around Fort William were always dotted with the rusting hulks of abandoned cars, seeping their toxic residues into the ground and the water supply. I recall interviewing the personnel manager of the paper mill in Fort William for a school project, which was investigating the possible causes of pollution in the loch, so it might be said that, even, or especially, growing up where I did, I had an embryonic green conscience.

It took time, however, for this awareness of the environment to transform into political awareness. That was partly forced on myself, and on all Liberal Democrats, by electoral disaster. At the European elections of 1989, we came fourth, behind the Green Party. That forced many of us to sit up and think – and to look at the state of politics. Everyone in my party asked themselves some hard questions, and I was asked some hard questions by others, too. I participated in a TV programme with Mo Mowlam and David Icke at the time of the election: Mo urged me on air to cross the floor and join Labour. If ever there was a time to do so, that would have been it, but the thought never crossed my mind. Call it Highland stoicism, but I have always believed that disasters can be turned into valuable lessons, if we are prepared to look long and hard at the causes, and see what changes need to be made.

I asked myself, along with the rest of my party, why people had voted Green in such dramatically large numbers. Traditionally, people who were disillusioned with the two largest parties had voted for us. Why were we now so unattractive? The answer, partly, was that we no longer treated the environment as a priority. A subject which, following the work of groups such as Friends of the Earth and Greenpeace, and even a speech given by Margaret Thatcher to the Royal Society in 1988, had become of great concern to huge swathes of Middle England. 'Maggie – Green Goddess' announced the tabloid headlines. The drastic events that occurred at the Chernobyl nuclear power station also served to heighten public awareness over the environment, even to whip it into hysteria. I recall a farmer in my own constituency, put out of business because nobody was buying his formerly popular goat's cheese, fearing that the 'Chernobyl cloud' had rendered it unsafe.

Our defeat was especially difficult for us to swallow, because we hadn't so much missed the boat as found that the boat we had built was being skippered by somebody else. For although we seldom gave environmental issues a high priority in our election manifestos, since the seventies we had produced many policy statements on the environment in an attempt to place environmentalism on the policy agenda. Our belief was that people who understood environmental issues and cared about them, would vote for us, because we felt the same. That led to a degree of complacency.

There was also, strange though it may sound, some internal hostility to the whole issue. When, in 1986, Davids Steel and Owen worked together on the book *The Time Has Come*, it included a section on 'green growth' which was written and eventually included despite some amused cynicism from David Owen, who felt that it was politically expedient to placate the more 'open-toed sandals' Liberal wing of the Alliance.

There were plenty of practical political reasons for us to start talking more about the quality of our environment: it was actually our territory in the first place, and we forgot that at great peril. There was also a wider political issue. I firmly believe that politicians should engage with people on the issues of public concern. One of the great failures of the Labour Party in the eighties was that it talked to people about politicians' issues, such as nationalization or unilateral nuclear disarmament, rather than people's issues, such as education and health. In the words of Nicky Hutchinson, the young radical in the BBC drama *Our Friends in the North*: 'People can't see how the big issues connect with their lives.' Labour lost support precisely because of that, and it damaged the whole political process, because people came to see politics as irrelevant to their daily lives. Today, if political parties do not talk about environmental issues, then people will disengage from politics and will instead get involved in pressure groups that do speak up for their concerns. Friends of the Earth, Greenpeace, the International Fund for Animal Welfare and the RSPB will all, rightly, fill a void surrendered by political parties.

Air, Sea and Land: the Facts about Pollution in Britain

This is not simply an issue that politicians have to discuss because people want them to. The environmental challenges we face today are as great and as real as the risks posed by nuclear arms and the Cold War between the forties and the eighties.

Take global warming: the Intergovernmental Panel on Climate Change predicts that if no action is taken to limit greenhouse gas emissions, temperatures will rise in the range of 1–3.5°C by the end of this century. This would be a faster rate of warming than at any time since the end of the last ice age, 10,000 years ago.

Stuck in traffic a while ago, I tuned in to a local radio show. The presenter was asking 'What's so bad about global warming? If we end up having summers like they get in Ibiza, I won't be complaining.' Being a Liberal Democrat, I have sufficient faith in humanity to assume he was talking tongue in cheek, but he may not have been.

The consequences of global warming will not, sadly, be to turn Northern Europe into the Côte d'Azur. The consequences will be almost entirely negative and disastrous: rising sea levels due to the melting of the polar ice caps, changes in rainfall patterns, violent storms and a growth in the expanse of deserts. All of these will impact on the life of everyone on the planet, affecting food production, buildings and the spread of disease. In Britain, 26 million people live on or near the coastline, around 40 per cent of our manufacturing industry is on or close to the coast and nearly 10 per cent of our best agricultural land is also less than five metres above sea level. Those figures alone indicate how vulnerable Britain is to the consequences of global warming.

We are also at threat from rising levels of pollution in our atmosphere, water and soil. Every year, an average 353 kilotonnes of sulphur are deposited on British soil as a result of industrial emissions. More than half of it comes from sources within the UK itself. The Department of the Environment, Transport and the Regions estimates that acid concentrations in soil and water supplies have been steadily increasing over the last twenty years. Areas of high rainfall such as Cumbria, Galloway and Snowdonia are particularly severely affected.

The impact of industrial emissions is proving particularly worrisome to the villagers of Weston, on the Wirral, where it has emerged that a deadly gas called HCBD is leaking from a nearby ICI chemical dump. Exposure to the gas may cause reproductive problems, along with foetal abnormalities and disturbed behaviour, and is believed to cause kidney and liver cancer. If ingested, it concentrates in the kidneys. Over the dump's fifty-year history, ICI has – quite legally, it should be added – also deposited mercury, perchlorethylene, carbide and lime slurry. The jury is currently out, but ICI may have to pay out millions in compensation to the villagers, and, if the worst predictions come true, much of the village might have to be demolished. According to Friends of the Earth, ICI Runcorn is Britain's second worst polluter of the environment with cancer-causing chemicals, trumped only by Associated Octel in Ellesmere Port.[1]

Small wonder that few people nowadays consider putting anything more than their toes in the waters surrounding our island. The decline of the British seaside holiday resort is in my view only partly due to the increased availability of cheap package holidays abroad. It is also due to a series of environmental disasters and scandals, from the Torrey Canyon oil slick onwards. Britain's record for clean beaches is very poor.

Family legend has it that my maternal grandmother, who always took her seven children to the Ayrshire coast for holidays, insisted on returning to Glasgow with a pail of sea water. She believed that it had multiple therapeutic properties, and, according to my mother, she was far from the only person on the train struggling to juggle a sloshing bucket along with children and luggage.

How differently we view the sea now, and with what good reason. In July and August 1999, eleven people became ill after visiting a beach in East Devon, and one girl died. Experts believe that they had contracted the bacterial strain *E.coli 0157* as a result of coming into contact with raw sewage. Pressure groups such as Surfers Against Sewage regularly report high levels of illness and skin irritation among those coming into prolonged contact with UK waters.

You do not have to be a surfer to come into contact with toxic chemicals. Surveys of oysters and whelks off the British coast found that they were suffering from various abnormalities, and in some cases females were developing male sex organs. Along with fish, they were found to have unacceptably high levels of tin and mercury in their systems. Seals in the Irish Sea – who not only live in the polluted waters but also, like us humans, eat the fish caught there – have been found to suffer from reproductive disorders. How long before similar effects are found in humans?

Anyone concerned about social justice has an automatic duty to care about the environment. Recent Friends of the Earth figures indicate that pollution hits the poor hardest: 662 polluting factories in the UK are in areas with average household incomes of less than £15,000, while only five such factories are found in areas where this figure is £30,000 or more.

The consequences for public health are obvious. The Global Environmental Change programme found that children needing special education and those with mental difficulties are more highly concentrated in urban polluted areas. Europe-wide, figures for asthma, bronchitis, emphysema and rhinitis – all pollution-related conditions – have increased over the past few decades and, unsurprisingly, they affect the poor in disproportionately high numbers.

It's not just a question of what we are putting into the environment, but also what we are taking out and *not* putting back. Current UK use of natural materials is completely unsustainable. Irreplaceable fossil fuels are being consumed for energy at ever faster rates, and while we produce vast quantities of waste, only around 8 per cent of it is recycled. Over-fishing has led to the depletion of stocks and a crisis for the fishing industry. Large amounts of UK paper are still produced from unsustainable forests. The only reason I stop the list here is because I want people to read on: the future is only bleak if we do nothing.

Who's NOT Doing What

I cannot charge the present government with doing nothing, but Labour's record is poor, particularly in the areas of transport and housing. One of the most important things it could do to make a difference is to provide decent public transport, so people get out of their cars and on to trains and buses, but House of Commons Library figures show that government spending on local and public transport is due to decrease in real terms by over 7.5 per cent by 2001–2 compared to when Labour came into office in 1997–8.

Labour has also abandoned its plans to set national targets for reducing overall traffic levels. All it is now aiming for is a reduction in the rate of growth of traffic, which amounts to little more than a clever spin on the statistics. Recent government figures show that traffic could rise by as much as 35 per cent between 1996 and 2010 – but as long as the *rate of increase* can be shown to be decreasing then the government can claim to be fulfilling its promise. This volte-face is effectively an admission that John Prescott has failed. He said himself just after the last election, 'I will have failed if in five years time there are not far fewer journeys by car.'[2]

Equally disappointing is the government's record on greenfield building – that is, construction on land that has not previously been built upon. It has made some welcome moves on this area – high-density housing is certainly the right way forward – but it remains the case that building on green land is effectively concreting over the countryside. This spreads pollution and threatens the natural habitat of indigenous species. Over 100 British species have become extinct in the past century, while others, such as the corncrake and the peregrine falcon, are in danger. Far from addressing this issue, the present government is set to exacerbate the problem.

The June 1999 report of the government's own Urban Task Force concluded that the government was set to miss its target of building 60 per cent of all new homes on previously used land: so-called brownfield sites. Instead, it will be building over 200,000 houses more than planned on greenfield sites. This might be understandable, if Britain did not already have 750,000 empty homes, which the government is doing nothing to fill. Many of these are in areas where people do not want to live – usually due to combinations of high crime rates, high unemployment, poor transport and pollution.

So surely, rather than write this huge resource off, government needs to think more holistically about housing policy? The answer is not just to build more houses, but to rescue the dying communities in Britain where housing is still in plentiful supply. Ensuring that our cities are green, attractive places in which to live will, as a direct consequence, protect the countryside.

If directing money to deprived urban areas can act as a carrot to prevent greenfield building, there also need to be some sticks. Government needs to discourage developers from encroaching on greenfield sites by imposing a tax on their profits – but so far, we have seen no action on this front. The problem is already too serious for complacency or half measures. The only way forward is a radical stance: *no* building on greenfield sites for ten years, or even more.

Current measures do not seem to take the urgency and the immediacy of the problem into account. It is as if, because we are talking about the *future* of the planet, governments believe they can just do a little gentle exercise for the time being, prepare the ground without too much disruption, and leave the real action to people in the future. As Eastern Europe copes with the consequences of yet another major chemical spill, and Mozambique is submerged due to yet more freak weather, it is clear that environmental collapse is not what *may* happen, but a menace we have to halt in its tracks.

The Liberal Democrat Approach

Sustainability is at the forefront of the Liberal Democrat approach to the environment. The principles of sustainability are simple. You take nothing from the environment that cannot be put back. You put nothing into the environment that harms it. You make nothing that cannot be put to another use after it has served its initial purpose.

In many parts of the Highlands, the earth has been farmed in the same way for generations, and hence people are accustomed to looking at the bigger picture. Many crofters see the environment – or at least their own small bit of it – as a precious inheritance, which is often all they have to pass down to their children. That attitude has made me realize that the environment is not merely something you inherit from your parents. It is something that you preserve for your children and grandchildren. This is as important for an urban population as for a rural one – I do not forget that Britain is predominantly and increasingly urban. Whether you live on a croft or on the fourteenth floor of a tower block, you are a steward of the environment on behalf of future generations – and it is the role of government to make every man, woman and child conscious of that responsibility. All our efforts will be fruitless if we do not hand on a living, breathing world to our children's children. So where do we begin?

The Road to Wellville

There is no point in a government issuing a single mission statement about the environment, or in instituting a single measure to cut global warming or reduce pollution, if it does not make a cohesive stand on transport. Transport policy may not sound terribly interesting, or grab many headlines, but it is the bedrock upon which a nation builds its whole environmental battleplan. Without an enlightened attitude to transport, you have, quite literally, a sick, disjointed nation.

Transport is a massive contributor to national pollution. Most significantly, cars – which transport relatively small quantities of people and goods – are responsible for huge emissions of carbon monoxide into the atmosphere. Car ownership is rising steadily, leading to increased road use, congestion and pollution. Increased pollution in turn leads to a rise in incidences of respiratory diseases and heart problems. It is a terrible indictment of this country that asthma is becoming more common among children.

There are three main ways of dealing with this problem: we could build more roads, to cut congestion we could use road pricing or tolling to reduce demand, or we could provide attractive choices, with better rail and bus services, and safer cycling and walking. A combination of the last two approaches is most efficient. Roads should not be priced until there are attractive alternatives, but when, and only when, decent public transport is available we should price roads to encourage people to use it. Major road-building programmes might improve congestion, but they will also encourage car ownership, and thus lead to further increases in carbon monoxide emissions.

My priority is to get people out of cars and on to public transport wherever possible. To do that, we need to provide a public transport system in which people have faith. An American visitor told me that, after a year spent in London, she concluded that the weather was not, as legend has it, the Brits' chief grumble. It was the buses and trains. I also find it very telling that, when putting my weekly schedule together, my team have to include slippage time in their calculations – an admission that public transport just cannot be trusted.

Improving public transport is not a particularly esoteric undertaking. There are some very simple measures that can be taken. At the moment, transport is deeply confusing to most people. Even on a simple journey, from one city to another, the average passenger might use a train owned by one company which runs on tracks owned by another. We need an integrated public transport system: one number, one website, so people can find out how to get to their destination – by rail or bus – and purchase their ticket for the whole journey. We also need integrated timetables. If most people on the bus to S. are using it to catch the train to L., then the train should leave after the bus. That's simple logic, but you would be surprised to see how rarely it prevails across the nation. Indeed, when a colleague recently missed a connecting train because the first train was late, he was brusquely told, 'There's no such thing as a connecting train any more.' Legislation should ensure that operators negotiated with each other to ensure that their services worked in tandem, but rather than strait-jacketing private enterprise, this integrated approach would maximize the number of potential customers.

Of course, with regards to private rail and bus operators, there is a major issue of quality. The media is constantly replete with horror stories about various rail companies who, in spite of huge profits and bonuses for their bosses, offer a desultory service to passengers, who in many cases have no other option.

The number of passengers carried each year by bus is now static, following a long period of decline. Fares have risen faster than inflation and it is increasingly difficult to recruit bus drivers. Unreliable, expensive bus services do not seduce motorists away from their cars, particularly as both are equally likely to get held up in rush-hour traffic jams, but giving buses priority on congested roads would make them a reliable, efficient and attractive alternative. Governments should reward councils who make public transport a priority by establishing and enforcing bus lanes.

Cycling and walking should also accompany decent bus services, as they provide non-polluting local transport. They could be the ideal means of making short journeys such as getting to school, to work and to the bus or rail station, but such journeys are often unsafe, and train stations and other destinations offer no proper storage place for bicycles. Britain is far behind Denmark and Holland in the use of the bicycle. In these countries, there are safe cycle routes, even in city centres, whereas in Britain, the routes often disappear at roundabouts and dangerous junctions. The Danes and the Dutch provide plentiful lock-up facilities in town centres and at rail and bus stations, and there have even been some highly successful borrow-a-bike schemes, which encourage city commuters to hop on a free bike and then leave it at their destination for someone else to use. Admittedly, the latter scheme is open to small-scale abuses (the canals in Amsterdam are often the resting place of abandoned bicycles!), but it provides an excellent example of innovative thinking in the transport sector. In Copenhagen, the authorities have side-stepped the problem of free bicycles being stolen by using a very distinctive kind of machine which is unavailable elsewhere. Solutions are available – a major effort to change the culture here could have a radical effect on traffic levels.

That is, ultimately, the challenge: without a green culture at the household level, government will legislate for ever in vain. Nobody should think that changing a culture is impossible. Look at the way seat belts are now routinely worn by 95 per cent of front seat car users – was that the case twenty years ago? Or was drink-driving considered to be as unacceptable as it is now? Meanwhile, recycled newspaper collection, something few people even considered in the past, is now so popular that the supply has swamped the industry's capacity to use it.

None of this is to say that I am anti-car. One of the most important points to recognize about cars is they are primarily a problem in urban areas, where public transport should exist, giving people alternative travel choices. Anything we do to get people out of cars must focus on urban areas, because in rural areas, a car is usually a necessity rather than a luxury. Nobody needs to tell that to somebody who has represented Britain's largest constituency, in the Highlands of Scotland, for eighteen years. I remember well the excitement with which my family piled into my father's first new car in the sixties, just as I recall the mobility and convenience that it gave to us. Owning a car is the aspiration of many, and motor cars are a tremendously liberating force. Although we have to look for new alternatives and support those that exist, I accept that no amount of legislation is going to prevent people from owning or using cars.

This makes it all the more pressing for us to encourage the use of fuel-efficient vehicles. Mentioning no names, a number of manufacturers now list environmental friendliness as a selling-point and, where this is genuine, governments should be nurturing it. We must abolish car tax (vehicle excise duty) for the most fuel-efficient cars. Companies who own fleets of cars could be encouraged to purchase fuel-efficient models, by similar tax breaks, financed with a tax on road fuel, which would make people much more aware of the real costs of each journey – as long as we find ways of protecting the needs of rural drivers for example, by supporting rural fuel stations. Some people say that such a measure will ensure that the roads are only accessible to the wealthy – those who can afford to pay the fuel tax, but that shows how many are out of touch with the realities of transport. Only around 70 per cent of the country has access to a car – around one third of the population, usually the poorest, are not able to use a car. Anything that encourages people out of cars, reduces pollution, and increases the use of public transport, will help the poor, not hinder them.

I own a car myself, a Toyota Corolla, but I must admit that I do not particularly enjoy driving it, partly because I much prefer to travel on trains. Not only do they give me a chance to think, read, write and even relax, but I also find that I get a very different perspective on the shape and structure of a community on arriving by train – a perspective that seldom comes when I am stuck cursing in ring-road traffic jams.

The car adverts invariably depict the latest model cruising down open roads, creating an image of space, comfort and freedom. Images totally at variance with the stressed-out, smelly, gridlocked reality. A quick straw poll among a few of my parliamentary colleagues revealed the same thing, over and over again. *Top Gear* enthusiasts excluded, very few people use the car because they want to, but because there is usually no alternative that is anywhere near as convenient.

If people felt confident about letting children walk or cycle to school, or if it was easier to share a car, then congestion would lessen – as it does in most towns and cities during the school holidays. Various councils have introduced 'School Safe' routes as part of their environmental programme. In these schemes, parents and grandparents take turns to police routes to school on a rota basis, so that children are able to walk to school or use public transport in safety. A friend in north London is involved in such a scheme, which arose partly out of a fear that while routes to school are dangerous, children are sometimes too pampered by their parents, and have very little freedom.

'School Safe' routes have many benefits. They can be part of a virtuous circle where congestion eases as the result of people's free choice and where road pricing or tolling is used only where road capacity is so limited that it is impossible to satisfy everyone. In such places, the proceeds of road tolls would go directly into providing subsidized light rail networks and prioritized bus lanes. That way, those who don't want to pay the toll have a choice, as do those who are adamant about staying in their cars.

The Warming World: Causes and Cure

With a forward-looking transport policy in place, we can then move on to tackle other key environmental problems, such as global warming. The Liberal Democrats want the UK to play its part in limiting global climate change to 0.1° C per decade. This translates into a UK target for reducing emissions of carbon dioxide (the main greenhouse gas that stems from human activities) by 30 per cent by the year 2010. It is an ambitious aspiration, and doubt has recently been cast on Labour's intentions regarding emissions.

At the Rio Earth Summit in 1992, Britain agreed to reduce its greenhouse emissions to 1990 levels by 2000. This has been achieved, and at the Kyoto Summit in 1997, John Prescott agreed to reduce British emissions by a further 5.2 per cent over the years 2008–12. Following Kyoto, Mr Prescott also pledged to reduce carbon dioxide emissions by 20 per cent by 2010, but this pledge has now become only an aspiration – familiar shift by New Labour. It shows the timidity with which it approaches the issue. Its chief instrument in enforcing these ever-shifting targets is the climate change levy, a tax on businesses whose emissions are deemed to contribute to global warming, but so many businesses are exempted (for instance, hauliers and all other operations whose chief emission is carbon monoxide from the use of vehicles), that the tax only targets a fraction of those who are pumping dangerous emissions into the atmosphere. Businesses for whom transport is a major concern should not just be taxed, they should be given incentives to adopt more efficient practices such as logistical planning, which can be used to reduce the number of journeys a vehicle makes empty, thus cutting emissions while reducing overheads.

There's a kind of international defeatism that tends to be trotted out by governments whenever pressure groups and scientists talk about the need for tough environmental measures. We all share the same air, rivers and seas, so the argument runs, therefore action on a national scale is futile if our neighbours aren't doing the same thing – the 'you make the first move' syndrome.

Climate change is a problem that pays no respect to national borders, so there needs to be an international regime, established and enforced by bodies like the EU and UN, with stiff penalties for offenders. It is true that the worst culprits in terms of greenhouse emissions and pollution are generally developing countries. It could not be any other way, when you consider all the other problems that developing nations have to contend with, but the situation will never improve if their developed neighbours have no consensus on environmental behaviour.

There is, however, a great deal of action that the UK can take on its own, both to set an example, and make a difference. The figures for energy wastage in the UK are shocking, and, unfortunately, no amount of cute advertising or public education can reverse this trend. It is vital to make some headway by reducing energy consumption, and the best way to do that is to introduce a carbon tax, on all fossil fuels, which would make it more expensive, and so less attractive, to burn precious resources. Fossil fuels are the polar opposite of sustainable – their extraction and production causes continual damage to the environment, as does their use – and they are running out. We should be moving away from them and looking for new ways to power the planet. This tax would be phased – that is, get higher gradually. If consumers, designers and manufacturers all understand that energy prices are going to rise and keep on rising, then they have a strong incentive to start using, creating and purchasing energy-efficient machines, appliances and buildings. Taxing fuel might seem to be an unpopular measure, but it would not have to increase the burden upon individuals, because we could use the revenue to reduce tax in other areas.

In addition, energy supply companies could be forced to invest in conservation projects, and we could raise energy efficiency standards for buildings, machinery, appliances and vehicles. We could provide additional support for sources of renewable energy, so that, year by year, the percentage of UK energy coming from fossil fuels is gradually reduced, and we could invest more in planting trees – forested areas act as a sink for the deadly emissions and thus help to reverse the trend.

In the cinema, when the globe faces disaster either from meteorites or despotic aliens, there is no-one to turn to except Flash Gordon or Superman. The same cultural perceptions seem to apply to global warming. It's something, so the thinking goes, that's happening inexorably, something – in the absence of caped crusaders – that we are powerless to prevent. Not so. There's something every single person can do to halt global warming, and I want everyone to be made aware of this. My notion of democracy is not just about everyone having rights. It's also about everyone having *responsibilities*. That's as valid for the environment as it is for law and order and education. Power is increasingly breaking away from the centre and settling in the hands of smaller and smaller groups of people. It's a trend I support wholeheartedly, but we must not forget that power carries duties as well as opportunities, and we must make certain that everyone knows what their environmental duties are, and is given strong incentives to fulfil them.

Green Stuff: Environment and the Economy

A healthy environment is an essential part of the Liberal Democrat aim of ensuring that individuals and communities realize their talents and take control of their destinies, but modern economies ignore the damage they cause to the natural environment. The real costs of energy use, for example – climatic change or the worsening of local air quality – are not reflected in the prices paid by households or businesses for the energy they consume.

I want us all to create a different framework, one in which individuals, businesses and governments *gain* by protecting and improving the environment. This approach has three major benefits: an improved quality of life, with lower pollution and protected landscapes, townscapes and natural habitats, a dynamic economy which uses resources efficiently and sustainably, and a decent inheritance for future generations, avoiding global pollution and the depletion of natural resources. Governments have a responsibility to make sure environmental costs and benefits are fully reflected in every relevant decision.

It also means working with industry to set minimum standards for products and activities. We can use the purchasing power of government departments to build markets for sustainable goods and services by buying them where possible. The environmental costs and benefits can also be reflected in the prices charged, as a result of taxes on pollution. The products and services that are most damaging to the environment would become the costliest. If we start to do that, we can alter the framework within which markets operate, so that we *promote* sustainability, instead of penalizing it. At the moment, going green is all too often an option only for those with money to spare. You only have to compare the relative costs of a plastic-wrapped, mass-produced sliced loaf from the supermarket with a freshly baked organic loaf from the local health food store. That needs to change – once organic producers can offer products at competitive prices, even people on the lowest incomes will have a choice.

Government also needs to promote investment in research and development for new, more sustainable technologies, and this has to be underpinned by tough pollution targets for businesses. It means working at a European and global level to build strong, effective environmental laws, and setting good examples nationally to encourage other countries to join and comply.

A Liberal Democrat government priority would be to pass an Environmental Responsibility Act. This would encourage government, businesses and households to act in an environmentally sustainable manner, to establish a new sense of environmental citizenship. The Act would have three key points. First, there would be a requirement for all levels of government to set, monitor and report on targets for environmental improvement. At the UK level, this would include publishing a comprehensive Green Chapter in the Budget statement – much more detailed than the current government's gesture. At the local level, all councils would be required to establish an environmental action plan and, more importantly, to get on and fight the battle.

Second, there would be a similar requirement on businesses to set and fulfil their own environmental targets. At present, every UK company registered under British law has to file an annual report. By law these reports would have to include an environmental audit stating what the company had done towards fulfilling its targets. I hope that the independent Company Law Review will take up this idea when it reports in 2001. Some individual companies have already taken up the gauntlet in this area: in 1994, The Body Shop committed itself to a programme of integrated ethical auditing. Since 1992, it has published an independently verified statement, confirming that the Body Shop fulfils all the requirements of European Union environmental legislation. Their profits with principles charter includes a range of environmental mission statements: for instance, to use sustainable resources wherever possible, and to screen and investigate the ecological credentials of all their finished products, ingredients, packaging and suppliers.

Thirdly, the Act would enshrine the citizen's right of access to environmental information. It would extend labelling and other information schemes, such as energy and efficiency ratings for domestic appliances, so that consumers could make informed choices. In shops and in advertisements, products are frequently labelled 'environmentally friendly' as a selling point, but all too often, consumers are provided with scant information about what that means, or whether their choice of purchase really contributes towards a healthier world. Labelling should not just cover products such as food and detergents: it has to be extended to cover *every* substance that poses an environmental risk, either in being produced or disposed of – for instance, trainers, food packaging and children's toys that contain PVC.

We have to fight the presumption that good environmental practice is a burden on industry. Certainly, creating pollution and then cleaning it up can be expensive, but an approach based on eco-efficiency, using materials and utilities effectively, minimizing the production of waste and reusing or recycling waste, is not only environmentally desirable, it's usually more profitable. The most progressive companies already understand this, and their best practice needs to be implemented across industry.

A good example is that of the multinational Interface, Inc., which manufactures commercial interiors, including carpets and other floorings. After coming across Paul Hawken's *The Ecology of Commerce* by chance in 1994, the CEO of Interface unleashed a sweeping seven-point programme of environmental reforms upon his company, which has outlets on four continents and over 7,000 employees.

Measures taken by Interface, Inc. include setting targets for the elimination of waste. Although zero waste might be many years away, it will never happen at all if we don't try to change the way we work. Interface, Inc. found that by establishing a goal of zero waste, and starting initiatives in all of its outlets, it saved $113 million in the last six years. It has also adopted the principle of zero emissions, and is developing a 100 per cent biodegradable carpet, whose creation and destruction leave no harmful emissions or residues.

Interface, Inc. has also committed itself to using renewable energy sources, rather than fossil fuels. In its two Yorkshire factories, it now uses 100 per cent renewable electricity. In the manufacturing processes, it uses renewable materials wherever possible – some of its plants actually take recycled carpet off-cuts to create new materials. When it comes to delivery of its products, the focus is on efficiency – it has cut its UK lorry fleet from fifteen to nine vehicles, simply by cutting down on packaging, and cutting out the wasted journeys.

Perhaps most innovative of all is its concept of redesigning commerce. When an office buys its flooring from Interface, Inc., it does so for life – or at least, for as long as it pays a monthly fee. Rather than ripping the carpet up and throwing it away when patches of it become worn, Interface continually restores and maintains the product, keeping it clean, durable and free from damage.

It's worth noting that Interface, Inc. is not some homespun green company, founded and administered by veteran eco-warriors. It is a multinational business with sales offices in 110 countries, twenty-six manufacturing sites on four continents and annual sales of over US $1 billion. It became green, quite simply, because its Chairman, Ray Anderson, perceived the damage that business was doing to the environment, and realized that, if industry was part of the problem, it could also be a major part of the solution.

Far from taking a business risk, Interface, Inc. has benefited from its green agenda by a significant reduction in overheads. Waste reduction measures in the UK alone have saved it over £500,000 a year. It has lowered its costs by £15,000 a year simply by requesting that its suppliers use the same sized pallets as it does, and by using thinner material in the 1 million boxes it sends out every year it has saved another £100,000 a year.

When businesses adopt green practice, they don't just improve our environment, they become sleeker and more competitive, thus stimulating trade. And as companies such Interface, Inc. and The Body Shop put a lot of money and effort into developing new, eco-friendly products and processes, they encourage the production of environmental technology and services. British business is currently losing out on this front. For example, we have the best wind resource in Europe, but we sold our last wind turbine manufacturer to Denmark in 1998. Now, 90 per cent of the world's wind turbine manufacturers are in Continental Europe, producing some 800 megawatts of power, worth around 900 million ecus – none of which flows into British coffers.

Energy: Conservation and Generation

Turning a blind eye to the potential of clean energy sources is dangerous. This is a subject close to my heart: my father was a draughtsman for the North of Scotland Hydro Board, which harnessed hydroelectric power to provide electricity for the Highlands; in the twenties, my grandfather worked on the vast tunnels which made the whole scheme possible.

Today, energy use is the cause of the most serious pollution problems, including climate change, acid rain and poor air quality. We are also consuming fossil fuels at unsustainable rates – oil reserves are likely to face exhaustion within the next century. At the same time, half of the energy currently consumed in the UK is wasted, and it could be saved using existing technologies. Prices for energy have never been lower, thanks to the liberalization of the market, and improvements in production and distribution, but while the consumer profits from this in the short term, lasting damage is being done to the environment as a direct result. Britain, lamentably, is at the bottom of the European league for the use of clean, renewable sources of energy. Government needs to create a framework in which households and businesses are given incentives to conserve energy, and to use clean instead of polluting energy sources – both essential if we are ever going to reduce the rate of global warming. The phased carbon tax on fossil fuels described earlier would be an important part of any such framework.

The average home is a site for massive energy losses every day. Every time you leave your television set on standby instead of switching it off at the mains, electricity is wasted. Some tvs, videos and stereos on standby use as much as 80 per cent of the energy that they do when they are on, so it would make sense if TV sets included the technology to turn themselves off or the TV networks reminded people to switch off at the mains when they finished watching. (They would obviously have to be able to retain dates and setting to make this acceptable.)

The loss of domestic heat is another major contributor to national energy wastage. That's why I want to institute a National Homes Insulation Programme to improve the currently poor levels of domestic energy efficiency and end the preventable phenomenon of fuel poverty – where people cannot keep warm in their homes because of the poor energy efficiency of the buildings, which literally leak heat. The government has made a start, but it has shown a poverty of ambition in this area and could do much more.

An estimated 10.7 million people are living in fuel poverty, and have to spend more than 10 per cent of their disposable income on heating. Not surprisingly, it is the elderly and those on low incomes who suffer the most from this phenomenon and its consequences. Every winter, at least 30,000 more people die than in the summer months – it was around 45,000 in 1999–2000. Every winter – as we saw with the 'flu crisis' in January 2000 – hospital admissions for cold-related illnesses increase sharply. Yet these deaths and epidemics do not occur in colder countries like Sweden and Finland, for the simple reason that their homes have adequate insulation. We need action on a national scale to ensure that every household in Britain has the same: it is already a legal requirement for all new homes. Insulating older properties can be costly, but the burden on individual homeowners could be lifted if the energy suppliers were given incentives to make the necessary technology and services available to their customers. In return for insulating homes, they would be assured of long-term supply contracts and favourable pricing rules. The people who would benefit the most would be the 10.7 million living in fuel poverty, for whom anything that brings down their overall fuel costs is a major benefit.

The benefits of this type of action spread beyond the environment. Carrying out energy conservation work for half a million households a year could generate up to 60,000 extra jobs. This growth does not have to occur at the expense of others. To encourage people to conserve energy government could reduce VAT on all energy-saving materials to 5 per cent, the same rate of tax currently charged on energy supply.

CHP – combined heat and power – is another way the average household will be able to contribute directly to an improved environment in the future. In CHP technology, fossil fuels are used to power combined boiler and generator systems. These systems operate much more efficiently compared to power stations and heat-only boilers, and waste far less energy – they directly help to reduce the amount of fossil fuels being used. Existing models are not small or flexible enough to meet the needs of the average household, but it is only a matter of time before we will see them in the home. A government that truly cared about the environment would be funding research to enable family-sized CHP units to be installed in every UK household.

In February 2000, I went to Taunton to look at a new project developed jointly by the borough council, a regional housing association and a local building contractor. This was the Eco-House – not only built from environmentally friendly materials, but also constructed so as to use minimal energy and produce minimal waste.

The timber used in the house came only from managed and sustainable forests, and the insulation material was manufactured without using CFCs. There was low-energy lighting and double glazing throughout, thus reducing heating and electricity bills. The plumbing made use of grey water recycling – a polite way of saying that the loo is flushed by dirty bathwater: totally safe, hygienic and it reduces water bills.

What impressed me was the ease with which eco-living can be incorporated into the modern home. The Eco-House did not look different or special from the outside – just an ordinary three-bedroom detached construction. It was not developed by some specialist team of eco-experts, flown in from Holland or further afield, but by local architects and builders, and although it is an experiment, it was not developed at huge cost. It was built for only £47,000. Furthermore, the young family moving into the home in March were delighted to learn that, thanks to the numerous energy-saving measures, they could expect their household bills to be significantly smaller.

Everyone involved in the Eco-House hopes it will teach them a great deal about sustainable living – as it assuredly will. It's still a one-off experiment, but there is no reason why these houses can't be built everywhere. It won't happen until government starts to provide an incentive to developers and builders.

There is also much that government can do to promote the development of renewable energy sources. There are a number of different options available including biofuels, solar, wave and tidal energy and the use of wind turbines. There is no reason why we could not use these to meet 20 per cent of UK electricity demand within fifteen years.

Of all these renewable sources, wind offers the most persuasive alternative. Wind power currently contributes only 0.15 per cent of all energy generation, which on a perpetually blustery island like Britain amounts to a criminal under-use of resources. The major complaints about the use of wind power are simply not justified. It is said that wind farms would be an unsightly blot on the landscape, but surely no more so than electricity pylons, of which there are around 22,000 across the UK, and which are now such a familiar sight that no-one comments on them. (People make far more fuss about mobile phone aerials, which are much smaller, as I recently found out when I visited a housing estate in Newcastle where local people are up in arms.) It is also said that wind farms are noisy, but they are generally situated at least 400m away from human habitation, and at this distance it is difficult to hear them. The risks posed to wildlife are insignificant compared to the risks posed by power stations. Indeed, the RSPB is so taken with wind power that it is considering installing turbines at its HQ. Unlike power stations, wind farms can also be dismantled and taken away, leaving no trace of their existence on the surrounding habitat, and no pollution for future generations to cope with.

Since we are an island, there is nothing to stop us minimizing the already minimal disruption to the natural habitat by building wind farms at sea. Off-shore turbines can be three times the size of land versions. They are also far more productive and efficient – off-shore winds can be up to 20 per cent more powerful, which, together with their increased size, means that the power yield can be up to 70 per cent more than on land. Using off-shore wind power, we could feasibly generate three times as much electricity as we need. Denmark has two fully operating off-shore wind farms, which will deliver 4,000 megawatts of power over the next thirty years. Wind energy is also cheap, or at least, it has the potential to be, once properly developed. In Denmark, the price per unit is set to fall from 5 US cents to two-thirds of a cent over the next five years. Currently, the UK has no off-shore wind farms, although an experimental installation is due to be completed in 2000, at Blyth in Northumberland.

We can learn a lot from the Danish example. Denmark currently has 4,900 wind turbines, providing 7 per cent of the country's electricity. This alone has helped Denmark to reduce its carbon dioxide emissions by 3 per cent. We need to do the same. In Denmark, ownership of turbines is mostly private: individuals or special co-operatives who live locally purchase shares in a facility which entitle them to purchase their power from it at a certain rate. The scheme was originally underpinned by hefty subsidies from the government, and is protected by a series of energy laws passed in the Danish Parliament. As wind power has become commercially successful, the government has gradually withdrawn its subsidies. In Britain, all that's required is an initial leg-up from government, and we will have a cheap, clean and everlasting source of power.

Conclusion

I am used to people asking me, 'What are your policies on the environment?' I always find it difficult to answer, but not – as this chapter has demonstrated – because we have little to say about the harm being done to the planet and the steps we can take to reverse the trend. I hesitate because I don't believe it is healthy to talk about an environmental policy as something separate and unique. The issue of how our planet is affected by our actions cuts across *every* area of life – education, culture, health and defence. By talking about environmental policies, we risk isolating the issues and losing public interest.

We need a totally joined-up approach to the environment. At the moment, efforts on the individual and institutional level are too disconnected: the government does a little here, the community and concerned individuals do a little there. The results of this are plain to see. Consider the fact that we currently throw out five million working computers every year. Most of those go into landfill, while our schools and colleges are desperate for IT equipment, and whole swathes of the population remain outside the new electronic age because they have no access to a computer. The waste is not just one of the equipment, but of the skills, talents and experiences of the young, the old and the unemployed. With the right approach, we can unite resources with needs.

Just as, on an international front, even the greenest nations suffer as a result of the irresponsible policies of their neighbours, the same is true within our borders. A forward-thinking company introduces energy and paper-saving measures in all its offices, for example – but how are its employees travelling to work? Where does its heating come from? Its employees buy their lunch from a neighbouring sandwich chain. The sandwich chain takes great pride in its all-organic ingredients and its dolphin-friendly tuna, but it hands the sandwiches to customers in plastic bags, whether they ask for them or not, and loads them up with paper serviettes, which mostly get thrown away. There are numerous examples like this. It is currently impossible for any individual or community to be completely green because, as Donne says, 'no man is an island'. I am all for individuals making a stand and setting an example to others, but without the clout of government behind them, individuals tend to become disillusioned. Support for green issues might dwindle to a core of die-hards, as – in spite of worsening climatic and pollution conditions – people find a fresh focus for their discontent.

We cannot risk that happening. That's why we need an integrated approach to saving the planet. Liberal Democrats don't believe that a fair and healthy society can be achieved either by governments forcing individuals to change – top down – or individuals forcing change on the government. The only sensible vision is of a model where the two interact continually with each other.

How can we achieve this when current responsibility for the environment rests with the DETR (Department of the Environment, Transport and the Regions), tucked away as an additional responsibility for the Minister for Transport? Future governments need to recognize the pressing need for reform – and the only way to achieve this is to have a Minister for the Environment. That way, there would be a green influence within the Cabinet, and no law could be passed or revoked without the environmental impact being properly considered. A Ministry of the Environment would have the freedom and the flexibility to liaise with all other government departments, to assess how little or much was being done by them to protect the planet and, where necessary, apply pressure to bring about changes.

In conclusion, we need to clear out the cupboards and get rid of some old preconceptions before we can make a start on improving the environment. We need to get the message across to individuals, communities and businesses that green politics are not part of the fringe – they are the only way to halt the global crisis that is already well underway. We need to make people see these survival strategies in terms of gain, not pain, and make people understand that their actions count as much as their opinions, and that the household is one of the most important sites for radical action.

I am optimistic that all this can happen – not least because I know that today's young people are very different from their parents. Even very young children have a level of environmental awareness that is awe-inspiring. That, in turn, means that the Parliaments of the future will be forced to stick to the green road by a new generation of politicians, for whom the planet is a precious inheritance.

Chapter Three

FREEDOM FROM GOVERNMENT:
PEOPLE AND THE STATE

'My fellow citizens of the world: ask not what America will do for you, but what together we can do for the freedom of man.'

PRESIDENT JOHN F. KENNEDY,
Inaugural Address, January 1961

What is a Liberal?

I am often asked the question 'What do you believe?' or, more frequently, 'What do you Liberal Democrats believe?' I never have any trouble answering that I believe in liberty, but I find it telling that people have to ask the question. As leader of the Liberal Democrats, one might suppose that my own and our beliefs would be self-evident, but it's as if, in today's political arena, beliefs and the boundaries between them have become blurred. It is not merely a question of the Left moving into the space vacated as the Right veers off into jingoism. It is more that the various political creeds, and their stand on certain key issues, have become less delineated. The 'Butskellism'[1] of the Fifties – where Labour and the Conservatives reached informal rapprochement over the central tenets of the modern welfare state – has found a contemporary equivalent in the ideological flux which followed the demise of Communism. In certain respects, particularly with regard to issues of law and order and personal freedom, the 'big guns' are now finding common ground, and, accompanying the death of party ideology, we have seen the birth and growth of pressure-group politics.

By contrast, when I came into Parliament in 1983, there were clear ideological divides in British politics: for instance, over nuclear disarmament, which saw members of the Labour Party and the Alliance at loggerheads with their own colleagues. Another was the more clearcut left/right divide over the economy. Margaret Thatcher's Conservative Party was pursuing a programme of privatization – selling off the family silver, according to Harold Macmillan – opposed at every turn by the Labour Party. It is hard to believe now that Labour could oppose the right of council house tenants to buy their own homes, but in the early eighties, Labour believed the answer to Britain's economic problems was more nationalization, not less.

In the last two decades, this devotion to ideology has often been a byword for sectarianism – on both sides of the House. In the early days of my career as an MP, I went to see Macmillan speaking in the Lords on the subject of the miners. He was appalled at Margaret Thatcher's recent description of them as 'the enemy within'. In his memorable oration, he pointed out that these men, 'the enemy', came from the same families which had fought two World Wars on our behalf. Leaving the Lords, another old-style, paternalistic Tory, the late Robert Rhodes James, MP, turned to me and said, 'I am so pleased. That speech has reminded me why I am still a member of the Conservative Party.' Men like Macmillan and Rhodes James found their balanced, 'fair play' conception of Conservatism squeezed out by the ideological extremists who gained sway under Thatcher.

In one sense, I am glad the boundaries are more blurred nowadays. Wherever extremes of doctrine flourish, democracy loses out. I became aware of this during the 1983–7 Parliament, when the SDP–Liberal Alliance succeeded in getting the House to debate the contentious subject of the political levy (whereby the Trade Unions funded the Labour Party). To say Labour were furious with us for raising the subject would be a gross understatement. They resorted to some distinctly un-parliamentary behaviour: David Owen was not allowed to sit down in his usual place, as Labour left-wingers had occupied the bench where the few SDP MPs sat. He responded by marching to the despatch box, only to find his passage physically barred by a very angry John Prescott. In the end, the uproar was so great that the sitting had to be suspended. It was depressing. The whole affair demonstrated the extent to which Parliament was still dominated by almost visceral, class-based attitudes. Other Labour MPs were so entrenched in their ideology that they were prepared to be threatening towards people who were not even their natural enemies, but had merely shown the audacity to question a key Labour principle. And the Conservatives kept laughing all the way to the next set of ballot boxes.

In spite of my instinctive opposition to sectarianism, I nevertheless believe it is time to make a stand, to state our own ideology, in clear distinction to the messages being sent out by the other two parties. The last Conservative government did great damage to the cause of freedom. Michael Howard and David Waddington were incredibly illiberal Home Secretaries, and Anne Widdecombe would be even worse, but we must also recognize the failings of Labour in power.

Labour's party HQ at Millbank tried to stop Ken Livingstone from standing for London Mayor. The government issues a blanket refusal to debate the decriminalization of cannabis, even when medical experts and the Police Federation are urging for a rethink. Jack Straw pushes through a restriction of the right to trial by jury. The word curfew enters the conventional political vocabulary. These sound like the actions of a right-wing, reactionary government. It might be fair to conclude that, if the boundaries between Labour and Conservatives are blurred nowadays, it is because the two parties have reached a kind of consensus: both are guilty of pandering to public prejudices and restricting the freedom of the individual.

The late Robert Mackenzie once observed that the more convergence between Labour and Conservative on fundamentals, the greater the rhetorical sound and fury on matters towards the political margins. Mercifully, there are still differences between the two, and the Conservatives still manage to find new extremes, as we saw on their approach to asylum seekers in April 2000. But, worryingly, where the civil libertarian agenda is concerned, too much overlap is painfully apparent. If the Liberal Democrats did not exist today then there would be a need today to invent us – if only to ensure that the voice of political conscience was not drowned out by the increasingly strident and competitive authoritarian cacophony on offer.

It is a matter of urgency for Liberal Democrats to make their voices heard. It should be no surprise that a party with the word 'liberal' in its name should step into the breach at a time when freedom is under fire – the liberty of the individual has always been a fundamental belief of ours.

The Origins of the Liberal Agenda

I would be betraying the party's roots if I were not committed to freedom. The very word 'liberal' comes from the Latin root *liber* – meaning free. Ramsay Muir, one of the twentieth century's most important liberal thinkers, defined it in 1935:

> The Liberal desires that every man and woman, and every natural and spontaneous group, such as nations, churches, or trade organisations, should be free to make the most and best of their own powers in their own way, so far as this is compatible with the exercise of the same freedom by others.[2]

That is not to say that Liberals are opposed to the state. Far from it. To quote Muir once more: 'The primary purpose for which the state exists is to secure and preserve peace, justice and the reality of liberty for its citizens.' Freedom, for a Liberal, is something that can only exist within a state, and under shelter of its laws. So it follows that the pursuit and preservation of liberty is part of our political agenda. It is, if you like, the only ideology to which I subscribe.

This is not solely a twentieth-century idea. John Stuart Mill (1806–73) is regarded as one of the founding fathers of liberal thought, and the freedom of the individual was at the core of his thinking. His most famous work, *On Liberty*, stated exactly that: 'Over himself, over his own body and mind, the individual is sovereign.' Mill abhorred what he called 'the tyranny of the majority' and celebrated the importance of originality and dissent. An MP from 1865, Mill's liberal philosophies were in a sense his undoing. He violently opposed the repressive rule of the white minority in Jamaica, and as a result lost his seat.

Thankfully, though, Mill's work continued to flourish, influencing political philosophy to the present day. L. T. Hobhouse, the first Professor of Sociology in Britain, wrote the seminal *Liberalism* in 1911, a work which owed a clear debt to Mill, but at the same time added a social dimension to his understanding of liberty. Like Mill, he felt the main duty of the state was to maximize liberty, but he also maintained that liberty was only possible if the state provided certain basic benefits, through taxation. 'Liberty without equality is a name of noble sound and squalid meaning.' A philosophy I wholeheartedly endorse.[3]

Less commonly associated with politics, but still a key figure in the pantheon of modern liberal thinkers, is Isaiah Berlin (1909–97). He has profoundly influenced political philosophy as a whole. His most significant theory was that different value systems can and do exist in parallel: if this is the case, and since mankind possesses such a variety of ideals, it follows that utopia is unattainable. In fact, people only subscribe to a belief in utopias because it offers them freedom from the burden of moral choice. This understanding led Berlin to condemn all utopian ideals – whether they be Fascist, Communist or Thatcherite – as leading only to suffering and conflict. In the final analysis, he argued, the only rational solution to all political problems is to allow individuals the maximum degree of choice and freedom.

I first read the likes of Berlin, Hobhouse and Mill when I was at Glasgow University, largely because they were on my reading list. But as I did so, I realized that the views I had held privately ever since I was old enough to have an opinion were not exclusive to me, or my family. I realized that there was a word for people like me. And that word was liberal.

In liberal thought, equality and freedom are inseparable goals, on the grounds that nobody can experience liberty unless they have equal access to certain basic human rights such as education, housing, food and health care. My upbringing prepared the ground for this by imbuing me with a strong sense of the importance of equality. While we do not have an entirely classless society, people in the Highlands place far more emphasis on what a person *does* than what a person *has*. A person's identity and their worth rest upon what they contribute to the community around them. My grandfather was a highly respected figure in the area, as were his two brothers, and this was due, in no small part, to their outstanding athletic achievements at the Highland Games, where they excelled in events as diverse as the long jump, high jump, shot-put and caber-tossing.

To some extent, geography is responsible for this. The Highlands are both a beautiful and a harsh environment. It makes sense, in a region where communities are separated from one another by huge distances, to co-operate with one's neighbours, rather than waste time trying to stay one rung ahead on the social ladder. In my grandfather's day, for instance, one bull, common grazing land and one grinding mill were shared between several families. In a region where extreme weather conditions can make daily life a struggle against the elements, co-operation is far more important than striving for status.

When I went to Glasgow University, I was surprised to see that Labour did not share my views. Socialism, particularly in the Glasgow of the seventies, seemed to be just as obsessed with the class hierarchy as the Tories it professed to oppose. The class struggle was fuelled by antipathy, rather than the ideals of equality and liberty for all. It became very clear to me that the choice was not between three parties but two sets of principles: equality and freedom or hierarchy and stagnation.

The names Hobhouse and Mill are not exactly on the tip of the public tongue these days, but as we see in the press practically every time the present Home Secretary opens his mouth, the words of Gilbert and Sullivan are just as relevant today as they ever were:

. . . every boy and girl
that's born in the world alive
is either a little Liberal
or else a little Conservative!

It's clear which side of the fence Mr Straw comes down on, and I am often depressed that this is the case. It is a shame that he hasn't learnt more from Roy Jenkins, who as a great liberalizing Home Secretary in the sixties gave us a much better example of how a centre-left Home Secretary should behave. Looking back to the night of the 1997 general election, I don't think I ever imagined that individual liberty would be such a pressing concern under a Labour government. I have been appalled by the extent to which Labour has disappointed Britain with its actions. From day one, it has behaved in a profoundly illiberal manner. Let's examine some of the evidence from recent years.

Faith Under Fire: the Labour Assault on Liberty

In February 1999, the Home Secretary began to speak about new measures in relation to people with severe personality disorders. It is true that there is a small number of individuals in the country who pose a grave threat to the public, but cannot legally be detained. In such cases, preventive detention may be the only answer, but liberals everywhere grew concerned, because it seemed that the government was creating legislation whereby the mentally ill could be detained indefinitely, without review, and without having committed any crime. This is a serious breach of individual liberties: preventive detention cannot exist without safeguards. The decision to detain someone must be subject to regular review, and detained individuals must have the right to institute such reviews. Proposed legislation has yet to take account of these basic safety measures. Mental health organizations, the Law Society and numerous professionals have attacked the proposals as inhumane.

In March 1999, when pressed in Parliament, the Home Office

Minister Paul Boateng admitted that the present Labour government has no commitment to ending discrimination against homosexuals, or to achieving equality for homosexuals when framing legislation. The government was, in fact, forced into altering the age of consent for gays by the European Court of Human Rights.

I applaud Tony Blair's efforts in trying to scrap the draconian Clause 28, which forbids the 'promotion' of homosexuality in schools. It is clear that such a clause only perpetuates prejudice, exclusion and inequality. If children are to be taught that there is a hierarchy of human relations, in which the marriage of a man and a woman stands at the top, it follows that everyone from other backgrounds is held to be somehow 'less' than ideal. This includes homosexual teachers, who are banned from ever mentioning their own background or lifestyle in front of their pupils for fear that it may 'encourage' them to follow suit. (If this is the case, are we also to assume that openly heterosexual teachers promote heterosexuality, and if so, why have people with such teachers ever grown up to be gay?) It also undermines the sizeable and growing body of children whose parents are not married, and those with gay parents. Last, but not least, this furthers prejudice against youngsters who are themselves gay, believe themselves to be gay, or are believed to be by others. In all respects, Clause 28 engenders a culture of intolerance.

As I write, it looks likely that, due to opposition from the Lords, Labour may have to abandon its plans to scrap Clause 28. It seems unusual that a government with a record for pushing through unpopular legislation should be so easily defeated. Perhaps we are to assume that the promotion of equality is no longer a key Labour principle?

May 1999 saw the publication of a draft Freedom of Information Bill. It looked encouraging in the early stages, but the draft showed just how little this government is committed to the principles of freedom. Public authorities have the power to withhold information for up to forty days, or even to restrict it altogether, on the pretext that they are doing so 'in the public interest'. A nebulous term, not defined, which basically gives public bodies free rein to flout the Bill. The draft Bill also excluded various categories of information altogether, such as that relating to government policy, to the police and to accident investigations. Many were left wondering how, with those restrictions in place, anyone could talk about freedom of information at all. 'Freedom from information' might be a more accurate description.

Despite sustained pressure from Liberal Democrats and others, the situation was not much improved in the late 1999 draft. The proposed Bill suggested that the Information Commissioner could *recommend* the disclosure of information, if it was in the public interest and did not cause 'substantial harm', but recommending is vastly different from insisting. Effectively it meant that, in certain cases, the decision of the Information Commissioner could be overruled. The government also refused to allow a more rigid definition of 'substantial harm', – giving those who want to withhold information a perfect get-out clause.

The proposed Bill also allowed government departments discretion over whether or not to release background information on policy issues, which would entitle the government to withhold factual information on subjects such as BSE and GM foods. Yet the public, beyond doubt, has a legitimate interest in such issues. Any society which is genuinely open and inclusive should, by definition, welcome citizens' enquiries. One which recoils from them is neither liberal nor democratic.

In October 1999, the government issued proposals which would have given the police, the security services and some dozen other government departments the right to intercept and decode private and business e-mails. These proposals found legislative form in the Regulation of Investigatory Powers Act. Throughout its passage through both Houses of Parliament Liberal Democrats sought greater safeguards for civil liberties in a Bill which had worrying implications with regards to the burden of proof and access to private and personal information.

The Bill finally became an Act with a number of key safeguards conceded. However, this exercise serves as a reminder of the tendency of this government to reach for authoritarian solutions to questions of law and order, and to put expediency before civil liberties.

In the Queen's Speech in November 1999, we saw proposals to take away up to 40 per cent of benefits from offenders doing community service, if they fail to show up or otherwise to fulfil the conditions of their order. The people most affected by this measure will be those who have drifted into crime precisely because they are deprived. Cutting money, without any provision to enable these people to live, simply creates a cause for yet more crime. It seems faintly perplexing that Jack Straw and his advisers do not see this. And what happens to the dependants of these offenders – their wives and children? They suffer because of someone else's crime, the poverty in which they are forced to live forces them into crime themselves, and so the cycle is repeated across the generations. It is the politics of despair and self-defeat.

The Queen's Speech also included proposals for mandatory drug testing of the half million people arrested every year. Even from a government that announced itself 'tough on the causes of crime', this draconian measure seems astonishing. Quite how police officers, their budgets already stretched to the limit, are expected to drug test every single detainee is not explained. Nor is there any logic in denying bail to anyone found to have class A drugs in their system. Drugs such as ecstasy and amphetamines are, regrettably, taken by large numbers of young people. They are class A drugs, with very real risks, but unlike heroin and crack cocaine, users are rarely in such a state of dependency that they have to steal or rob in order to purchase them. Denying bail to these users is not addressing the crime rate.

The reasoning behind locking up addicts is continually questioned by the police themselves. Arrest referral schemes are in operation in various London boroughs, whereby people committing crimes due to a drug habit are referred to a rehabilitation programme as a part of a non-custodial sentence. These have made great strides in getting offenders away from drugs and consequently from reoffending. Sending people straight to jail, where they will not receive the help they need, and in some cases find a plentiful supply of drugs, simply exacerbates the problem.

The above two proposals have all the hallmarks of Jack-Straw-style legislation. If you imagine the proposals as a tabloid headline, then they have an immediate and apparently persuasive logic. 'Axe Benefits for Thugs Who Won't Say Sorry', for example. Or 'Sweep Junkie Muggers Off Our Streets'. The average person, seeing Labour's policies reduced to statements like that, will probably have no argument with them. Until, of course, the proposal becomes law, and the consequences begin to appear. Many offenders denied benefits will drop out of the welfare loop altogether, reoffending and becoming homeless. People who steal property to feed a heroin habit will find themselves waiting six months on remand, their habit untreated. And what happens when they are released – where will they find the money for the next fix? Suddenly, we will find social problems are multiplying again, all because of legislation that seemed quite attractive when it was a newspaper headline. Labour's priorities veer too much towards this kind of punitive populism which does not treat the causes of crime or safeguard the rights of the individual.

New Labour does not seem to understand that its policy of appeasing Middle England at the expense of the poorest sections of society is going to backfire. Poverty breeds crime, and, as crime rates rise, those with the most to fear will have to spend the most protecting themselves. If taxes are low, they will turn to elaborate security in their houses, high insurance premiums and even private security patrols. All of which means less freedom, less free income and, ultimately, less enthusiasm for Labour when it comes to the next election.

By focusing on draconian measures to deter and punish offenders, rather than addressing the causes of offending and re-offending, Labour is neglecting its commitment to look after the most vulnerable in society. Much was made, early on in its term of office, of its policy on noisy neighbours and other social nuisances. Yet human rights lawyers have pointed out that government plans for anti-social behaviour orders (ASBOs) violate the European Convention on Human Rights in certain key respects. For example, the proposals allow a local council to impose an ASBO on flimsy grounds that would have no standing in a criminal court. Equally, there is very little individuals can do to interrupt the proceedings once an ASBO is on-course. They can be fined, evicted and stuck on council housing black lists with very little opportunity to defend themselves or present their case. Local government does need to be able to tackle noisy neighbours, to protect the rights of those around them, but ASBOs are the wrong way.

Hardly a week goes by, it seems, without yet another outburst from the Home Secretary. I am still amazed at the broadside he let loose in January 2000. After proposing to restrict the right to jury trial, he then accused opponents of this move of being 'woolly Hampstead liberals'.

This is political opportunism at its worst. Apart from the recent spooky suggestion to DNA test everyone arrested, guilty or not, the plan to restrict jury trials represents New Labour's most serious assault on the rights of the individual. More than any other minister in the Labour government, Jack Straw has opted for simplifications where rational debate is required. Instead of debating the threats posed to basic rights by limiting jury trials, he dismissed principled people in a way unworthy of the minister who should be defending liberty, not attacking it. When a key Labour figure can use the world 'liberal' as a pejorative, it is clear that his party is renouncing its former ideals. I have no claim to being a 'Hampstead liberal', having never lived in that district of North London, but I am certainly a Highland one, and not ashamed of it.

Juries are a cross-section of the community. They are chosen by lot for their age, gender, ethnic background, religion and qualifications. A diverse community needs such diverse representation, which avoids domination by the prejudices of one group or class. Guided by a professional judge, so that they work within the framework of the law, jurors can make decisions in a fair and balanced way that no other system offers.

Contrast that with the magistrates' courts. At the end of 1999, in a debate in the Lords, my Liberal Democrat colleague Lord Thomas of Gresford, took us back to the days when his father was a prosecuting police inspector in Wrexham. He said that then, 'it was extraordinary how the magistrates' courts were run by the great landowners and coal-owners of the district'. Thankfully we no longer face that situation, but it remains the case that magistrates are still predominantly white, middle aged and middle class. They are certainly not noted for their understanding of ethnic minorities, gay people and the young.

There is much else wrong with magistrates' courts. Advice on legal matters is not given to those who find themselves up before the magistrate, and in such trials, there is no obligation on the prosecution to disclose anything to the defence. Recent surveys by the Bar Association and the Law Society have turned up cases where highly important evidence was held by the police, not shown to the defence, and subsequently a miscarriage of justice took place. The reforms that have been made in the Crown Court after serious miscarriages of justice have passed the magistrates by. These are real issues that affect real people – not the hobby-horses of so-called liberal fanatics and egghead lawyers.

I might be accused of overstatement when I say that there is a sinister edge to much of New Labour's legislation, but I stand by that comment. Everything we have looked at so far raises a wider issue – the extent to which this government is increasingly seeking to restrict liberty of the individual. Why is it doing it? The answer is partly that this is where Labour politicians judge the votes lie. And if, as I believe, the party leader is uncertain as to how far he can trust his own party, it follows that he extends this level of mistrust to the wider populace.[4] Labour's very method of government predetermines illiberal outcomes. Until they control less and trust more, the situation will not change.

I believe that this is a profound miscalculation, which will ultimately have dire consequences for New Labour. Put simply, the government has misjudged the mood of the nation. As a report by the Future Foundation, *Britons on the Verge of the Millennium*, showed at the end of 1999, 'an unprecedented period of peace and plenty has helped to create a new liberalism, as far as different behaviours and lifestyles are concerned'. The government has missed the boat on this agenda.

The catalogue of measures above sheds light on the soul of New Labour – bossy and authoritarian, talking about devolving power, but actually keeping much to itself. We have seen this at a local level for many years, where the tone of councillors in traditional Labour fief-doms often leaves much to be desired when they are dealing with individual rights on housing, planning applications and education. It is now clear that the Great Reform Act of 1830 only temporarily abolished rotten boroughs – they have re-emerged under a Labour banner. In early February, an Ofsted report revealed that Leeds council-lors were able to channel thousands of pounds' worth of funds into schools in their own wards – one school received £45,000 to improve facilities, while other schools received nothing at all.

The trend toward authoritarianism has also manifested itself on a national scale. We saw it in the way ministers cut benefits for lone parents in a bid to force them into work. It was evident when Millbank tried to manage the selection of the party's candidate for the mayor of London, excluding Ken Livingstone. Excessive and counterproductive interference also occurred in the Welsh Labour party – Tony Blair decisively gave his backing to Alun Michael as candidate for the First Secretary of the Welsh Assembly, even though Rhodri Morgan was the popular choice. This tinkering decisively backfired in February 2000, when Michael resigned. At least, subsequently, the Prime Minis-ter has had the good grace and good sense to concede that he simply got it wrong.

I am in regular contact with the Prime Minister, and we get on well, but he would not be surprised to find me saying that we have very different ideas about running a party – although admittedly we have very different parties to run. That became very clear on two occasions: concerning tuition fees in Scotland and the resignation of Alun Michael as First Secretary of the Welsh Assembly. Both times the Labour instinct was to dictate a solution from London. The Liberal Democrat instinct was to let Scotland and Wales decide their own course of action. That is the point and purpose of devolution – that power be exercised where it is at its most effective. Whether those with the power do what Westminster approves of, and whether they triumph or fail, is beyond Westminster's remit.

Recent political history can explain this state of affairs. In oppo-sition, Labour kept tight internal control, by painting those who veered from the party line as jeopardizing its chances of election success. The likes of Tony Blair and Gordon Brown were schooled in this atmosphere of control. This approach, entirely necessary in opposition, has been translated into government with unnecessary zeal. I do not subscribe to the view that Tony Blair is a control freak, but his estimation of his own party can impel him into acting that way. In my various dealings with him, I have gained the impression of a politician who cannot fundamentally trust the political organization which he heads. He is probably justified in this, but this attitude regrettably spills over into policy, and there I am bound to oppose him.

This is especially true for Scotland. The government gave the Scottish Parliament the power to raise its own taxes, but then announced that no Labour First Minister of Scotland would be allowed to raise income tax by more than 3p in the pound, or alter any other tax. So, effectively, Tony Blair remains in control of Scotland.

At the moment, the Scottish Parliament is funded by the block grant – meaning that London disperses an annual sum, thereby retaining control of the purse strings. A far better system would be for the Scottish Parliament to assume responsibility for all those taxes which are raised within Scotland, and then transfer to London the required sum for those services which are provided on a UK basis, such as benefits, defence and overseas aid. This would not result in less cash for Scotland. Instead, Scots would be given the right – and the means – to raise money according to their own specific needs. The 'subsidy-junkie' jibe is as inaccurate as it is offensive – and this approach would effectively put that myth to the sword. A government which is allowed to spend, but not raise its own revenue is likely, if not forced, to be financially irresponsible. The same is true for the new mayoral London. It is absurd that a capital city, with an electorate of five million, will lack the powers of a parish council to raise its own revenue. The reason for this attitude is paranoia – Labour does not trust its own activists not to be spendthrift.

Labour deserves great credit for having harnessed a non-Conservative majority, in the Commons and in terms of public opinion. But its strength is also its weakness – for that majority is both broad and shallow. People voted Labour for a wide variety of reasons, and the party cannot hope to secure their continuing support with a narrow set of policies. Restricting liberty – for individuals, for regions and for nations – will only alienate those whose votes Labour is trying to court.

Liberty vs Libertarianism: What Can Governments Do?

The role of government, and what it should do to advance the cause of liberty, was a matter of raging debate when I was elected to Parliament in 1983. Then, one of the voguish ideas in town was libertarianism, which motivated a generation of excitable Young Conservatives to 'roll back the frontiers of the state'. In my view, we as a country need to rediscover some of that scepticism about government, and revisit that libertarian agenda, but we need to do it in a very different way from the libertarians of the eighties, and we should certainly reach some different conclusions. Then, libertarians rightly wanted a market economy, but they wrongly wanted a market society, in which the cash bottom line counted above all else. In their emphasis on the mantra of 'society is dead', they did tremendous damage to civic Britain, and though they spoke the language of individual rights, they were profoundly hostile to policies that would promote alternative lifestyles and diverse cultures. In contrast to that libertarian agenda, we need a *liberal* agenda, where government refuses to interfere in the lives of individuals, but plays a very active role wherever it can advance liberty for everyone.

The liberal agenda has four key principles:

1 Government cannot solve all problems, and sometimes does more harm than good.

2 Some problems are best left to government. It is far more

able than the private sector to deliver health and education services that successfully tackle inequality.

3 Where government does act, it needs to do so differently: we need clearer rules defining what government can and can't do, and many decisions need to be taken at a different level of government, for instance at the local and regional levels, rather than in Westminster.

4 Central authority should be used to stamp out inequality rather than enforce conformity.

Put simply, my philosophy of government is that it should do less in a few areas, do more in others, and do different in most. There is a curious assumption that individual freedom means the withdrawal of the state, and that taxation is a form of state control. The opposite should be the case. Efficiently gathered and spent taxation is not a curb on personal freedom. It is the means to achieve it.

Traditional right-wing thinkers make much of the right to choose. They equate the profusion of private services with freedom, but this is the same as saying that a chronically short-sighted person has the 'freedom' to go the cinema. Without spectacles, it's no freedom at all. For people to enjoy freedom, government has, in a sense, to provide the 'spectacles' through taxation. Providing opportunity, in essence, through health care and education, gives people true freedom.

Imagine a situation where government did virtually nothing to provide these services. It is not difficult, as it is there in the history books of our own country, and many of our grandparents have lived through such times. Was the bulk of the population more free or less free when schools provided only rudimentary education? Did they have more opportunities, or less? Were people more free or less free, when only the better-off could afford a doctor? Were the starving poor happy to know that, while their children might die, at least they didn't have a portion of their meagre earnings taken by the state? The nineteenth-century Liberal activist and philosopher T. H. Green was wise to the shaky logic of right-wingers, arguing that there was no such thing as freedom for 'an untaught and under-fed denizen of a London yard, with gin-shops on the right hand and the left'. Green was a passionate teetotaller – a philosophy I cannot quite bring myself to endorse – but the core of his message is just as true today.

Doing Less

When power is exercised exclusively at the centre, rigid rules and alienation of the people subject to those rules result. This does not apply simply to the way Westminster retains control over the Scottish Parliament and Welsh Assembly, but also to questions of lifestyle and parenting.

New Labour needs to realize that family life and the way we raise our children are private matters. In its policies we have seen, for example, serious attempts to discourage lone parents from staying at home with their children. Measures such as the New Deal and the Working Families Tax Credit encourage parents into an inflexible model where the only way they can stay above the breadline is to work from nine to five, regardless of the individual needs of their children. This is grossly out of step with modern values. In a 1999 survey by the National Centre for Social Research, the majority polled felt that mothers of pre-school children should be free to decide for themselves, and those who felt that mothers should stay at home far outweighed those who felt they should be obliged to go out to work. If New Labour is the party that cares about public opinion, then it has a strange way of showing it.

Government also needs to maintain a sense of proportion over the question of drug use and abuse. It is becoming increasingly clear that cannabis offers pain relief to sufferers of multiple sclerosis, and for that reason its medicinal use should be legalized. There is also evidence that its properties may be of benefit to people with other conditions, such as arthritis and glaucoma. At present, government has issued a blanket 'no', not just to the question of medicinal legalization, but even to debating the subject seriously. Although many magistrates and judges have thrown such cases out of court, and there have been successful appeals, in numerous instances people growing cannabis plants for personal, medicinal use have been arrested, prosecuted, fined and even imprisoned. Furthermore, this is a situation that the police are unhappy with. The Police Federation have argued that precious time and resources are being wasted arresting people for the crime of possessing small amounts of cannabis. There are even those making the case that hard drugs such as heroin ought to be available to registered addicts on prescription, thereby removing the need for them to finance their habit by crime, and also cutting organized criminals – who have traditionally controlled the drug supply – out of the loop. I am not arguing for an immediate 'free drugs' policy, far from it, but it is clear that we need to debate the issue urgently. All the while the government refuses to reconsider its stand, it is restricting both the liberty of the individual and the liberty of the community in which that individual resides.

Over-legislation and bureaucracy create problems where they do not exist, and no government body is more notorious for it than the Department of Trade and Industry. There are numerous DTI regulations that are burdensome, unnecessary and undesirable, heaping complicated paperwork upon citizens, burdening them with a plethora of restrictions, which are enforced with the full force of the law when they are inadvertently infringed.

For instance, the so-called 'tea bag tax' forces employers to quote any free tea and coffee they lay on for employees as a taxable benefit in kind. This is often impossible to calculate, but in one notorious case an employer was fined £6,000 by the Inland Revenue. Providing sandwiches can also be dangerous, since current legislation classes it as a taxable benefit as well as one which attracts National Insurance. Under such excessive legislation, employers find themselves with an incentive not to provide anything for their employees.

Section 9 of the Conservative government's 1996 Immigration Act is no more forgiving. It makes it the duty of employers to police the visas and passports of their employees, threatening them with hefty fines if they allow people without the correct paperwork to continue working. This does not deter illegal immigrants from seeking work, since they are not penalized, but it does deter employers from hiring anyone foreign, out of the fear that they might land themselves in trouble. Under the Parental Leave Directive, employers who grant paternity leave, whether paid or unpaid, can find themselves subject to criminal proceedings if the Inland Revenue judge their record-keeping to be sub-standard. Rather than spend time making certain their records are in order, many companies choose to avoid the risk by simply not granting paid paternity leave.

What is the solution, other than purely scrapping the legislation? One answer would be to establish an inter-party Jargon and Regulation Taskforce, with a role similar to the Plain English Campaign. Like the Social Justice Audit, such a body should contain representatives from both the public and private sectors, as they are equally affected by over-legislation. Their duty would be to examine existing and pending legislation, to ensure that it was clear, precise and above all else minimal. Government bodies with a record for over-legislation would be put on notice to improve. In cases where it was decided that rules were badly worded, over-complicated, or simply needless, the committee would have the power to order an immediate redraft, with another vote in Parliament to follow. By publishing its findings and its achievements every year, such a committee would become a powerful force in changing the culture of government, so that those in charge of the rule book understand that less equals more.

Within the public sector government needs to start respecting professionalism and to curb its desire to overwhelm people such as teachers and nurses with paperwork and excessive regulation. In my travels across the country, speaking to numerous teachers and nurses, I am consistently struck by the sense of mission they have about their work. They have not embarked upon their professions for the money (hardly likely that they would, given the pitiful level of nursing and teaching salaries) or an easy life. Any teacher will tell you that the much-vaunted long holidays are significantly occupied by marking, preparation and responding to the latest directives from the government. They report being unable to plan lessons with any degree of creativity, because they are too bound up with form-filling. Lord

Haskins, Chair of the government's regulation taskforce has reportedly described the Department of Education as 'the most Stalinist department in Whitehall'.[5] The amount of paperwork that a teacher now has to process has multiplied over the last decade as have the number of rules governing the level of permissible contact between teachers and their pupils. The biggest challenge facing education and nursing is to encourage more people to join the profession, but cash sweeteners are not the sole solution – young people are reluctant to join these professions because they are not sufficiently respected in society. Over-legislation is a telling feature of the lack of respect which lowers the status and morale of those within these professions.

Government is also seeking to subject the civil service to a similar level of interference, as we saw in the publication of plans by Sir Richard Wilson, head of the home civil service. Wilson wishes to improve managerial effectiveness within the service by adopting the principles and practices of the private sector. The aim is to give 'incentives to people to seek more challenging responsibilities, develop their competences and demonstrate leadership'. In effect, civil servants are to be made individually accountable for delivering specific targets – just as in the business world.

This level of government interference in the civil service is not only unnecessary, it is in direct contradiction to Tony Blair's own much-publicized policy of joined-up government. Joined-up government is all about shared responsibility. It is designed to deal with intractable social problems, like social exclusion, drugs and community health by re-creating social capital and restoring communities. Success in such an endeavour is likely to be a long-term affair – and it is not reasonable to make it subject to any regime of 'incentivizing' or performance-related pay because it is actually very difficult to measure performance in any meaningful way.

Bodies such as the Institute of Chartered Accountants, the Institute for Fiscal Studies and Oxford Economic Forecasting have also criticized the government for over-legislating when it comes to taxation. When Labour came into power, tax was charged at fifteen different levels. The Budget of March 2000 took that figure to thirty-eight. There used to be three rates of income tax – now there are five. There were three levels of capital gains tax – now there are twenty-one. This situation provides the very opposite of transparency for the average citizen. It is very difficult for people and businesses to know how much tax they owe, and why. To quote the Liberal Democrat Treasury spokesman, Matthew Taylor MP, 'There is very little evidence that the government's complications produce any economic benefits and plenty of evidence that they confuse people, increase bureaucracy and waste money that could be used to lower the burden on businesses and ordinary people.' This proliferation of taxes also provides a smoke-screen, whereby New Labour can claim to be helping people, but hits them by less obvious means – so-called 'stealth taxes'. The Treasury even claimed that the tax burden on the 'average family' has fallen to its lowest level since 1972, but it only takes a little analysis to see that this 'average' family would have to be non-smoking, non-drinking, never fly abroad on holiday, not pay a mortgage and not pay council tax.

These tactics simply serve to undermine public confidence in the government, and the end result will be further alienation. The cynicism and disrespect with which people currently view the government is a worrying sign that Labour is already losing the support it coveted for so many years, precisely because it is now holding on to power so tightly. Restricting the freedom of individuals, pinning businesses and professionals down with legislation and befogging them with stealth taxes engenders a culture where government is viewed as an obstacle to success, not an aid to achieving it.

Doing More

People are only truly free when they have the means to exercise and enjoy their freedom. That is why, in certain areas, government has a duty both to stay involved and to do more towards ensuring that every citizen has equal access to the benefits of modern society. It needs to ensure a decent education and comprehensive health care for all citizens, for nobody is better equipped to provide these than central government, and without them, nobody can be free.

Labour recognizes this, and in its general election manifesto it promised to raise the proportion of national income spent on education. Not only has this figure not increased, it has actually *fallen* since Labour came into power. Real spending per pupil in secondary schools is now at its lowest level for ten years. In 1990, spending per pupil was £7,167. In 1998, it was £5,812.

In July 1998, Gordon Brown announced 'that for the next three years, additional expenditure will total £19 billion'. This was a very substantial commitment, when you consider that the total education budget at that time was £38.3 billion. Nor did he, as Tony Blair did, then claim this was an aspiration. Labour politicians have repeatedly spoken since then of 'the £19 billion' as a very real entity.

Yet the *Guardian*'s research into education in March 2000 revealed that, with only one exception, every local authority has schools whose budgets are in severe deficit. It might, in a mood of goodwill and optimism, be possible to assume that 'the £19 billion' is just not getting through – it is tied up, taking time to filter through to the areas where it is needed.

Sadly, the truth is more alarming. As Nick Davies wrote in the *Guardian*,[6] the '£19 billion is largely composed of magical money, literally billions of pounds which have been conjured out of thin air by trickery – double-counting, treble-counting, several different book-keeping manoeuvres and a steady stream of fundamentally misleading public statements.'

The mathematics are not hard to understand, even if the motive is. If you add £3 billion to your education budget one year, it then becomes a permanent part of the budget. So if you add another £3.5 billion the next year, that £3.5 billion is the total increase for that year. You do not count the extra £3 billion you stuck in the year previously.

But this is what David Blunkett has done. In year one, he had a rise of £3 billion. In year two, he had a further rise of £3.5 billion. But because he was now also paying in the extra £3 billion from last year's increase, he counted the two together, and said that £6.5 billion was now going into education. Then, in year three, he was given another £3.2 billion. But he added this to the £3 billion that appeared in year one and the £3.5 from year two, and said it was an increase of £9.7 billion. And then he added the whole thing up – £3 billion plus £6.5 billion plus £9.7 billion – a grand total of £19.2 billion. My colleague Matthew Taylor, Liberal Democrat Shadow Chancellor, has rightly dubbed this 'funny money'.

The Treasury Select Committee – which has a majority of Labour MPs – spotted this very swiftly and delivered a highly critical report, which received very little public attention. Personally, I would not care so much about mathematical chicanery if Labour were palpably delivering its promises on education, but class sizes have not decreased – many have got bigger. The average secondary school class size is at its highest for twenty years. Class sizes for eight to eleven-year-olds went up in the first two years of the Labour government. British pupils are, on average, in far larger classes than their European counterparts. Meanwhile, recruitment figures for teachers are falling across the board, and in some cases are at a five-year low.

The start that anyone has in life is the most important determinant of their life chances. A good start, through a good education, will open doors and maximize freedom, yet our schools and colleges are under-resourced – higher expenditure on education is so essential. The challenge is how to provide the best possible quality of education for everyone, including that fifth of the school population which leaves school poorly qualified and ill-fitted either to get a job or undertake further training. Getting class sizes down and providing schools with the books, equipment and staff that they require must be our priority. We need to double spending per pupil on books and equipment – nothing less will do to repair the damage of the preceding years. There must also be national standards for class sizes. None of this can be enforced when tax cuts are a priority for government.

Early years education should be a special focus for concern. It is still commonplace for educational difficulties, such as dyslexia, to go undiscovered into adulthood. In smaller primary classes, teachers would have more time for each pupil and thus any problems could be identified and redressed at the earliest stage.

This issue is of particular importance to me because, in a sense, I owe my political career to having attended a small primary school. It was there that my teacher identified a mild speech defect – I had problems with my pronounciation of 'th' and 's'. I went on to receive one-to-one speech therapy, and though it was only for a short time, I still have vivid memories of these sessions, saying 'this thing' and 'that thing' until I was blue in the face and playing a lot of snakes and ladders.

The treatment corrected the defect and, to this day, I am grateful to the teacher who spotted it. I suspect that, had we lived in a larger community, and I had attended a larger school, the teacher might well not have had the resources to take such a personal interest in her pupil's welfare, and I might have been stuck with a significant personal handicap. Focusing spending on early years education makes economic sense, because it is much easier and far less costly to address difficulties in younger children.

In further and higher education we must make it as easy as possible for all students, whatever their means, whatever their age, to undertake the studies of which they are capable. That means no tuition fees up to and including undergraduate level, and making it easy for students to repay their maintenance costs. The coalition agreement (which established a committee that subsequently proposed the abolition of tuition fees) in Scotland has provided part of the UK with its first opportunity to tackle this problem – thanks to the Liberal Democrats.

We must also be clear what we are educating people for. We can't be satisfied simply by turning out students with a good grounding in core academic subjects, important though that is. We must also do more to prepare young people for a swiftly changing job market, to nurture communication skills, enquiring minds and creative thought – the traditional ideal of a liberal education. Modern employers have no need for the fact-based, rote-learned education of the past. They need people who can solve problems, just as society needs people skilled in self-help. We need to teach people independence and interdependence at the same time.

Schools need to enlist wider resources in bringing this about.

Rowntree Foundation studies have shown that schools which enlist the help of parents and non-teaching professionals achieve positive results. In France, the USA and Sweden, the school is not just the site of compulsory nine-to-four learning, but the hub of a range of child-centred community activities, including after-school, weekend and holiday care. These have the added advantage of drawing children and their parents into community life. In France, schools are seen very much as a means of inducting children – many of whom come from Arab and African backgrounds – into French citizenship. Our schools need to reshape their roles along the same lines, but without seeking to iron out cultural differences as some see the French system doing.

It makes no sense to have a building, stacked with resources, which is only used for eight hours a day, five days a week and nine months of the year, but that's what happens to most schools. It would make economic sense to open schools up to the wider community – for adult literacy, for evening classes or for community meetings. Education still has an aura of elitism about it in this country, that leaves parents feeling alienated from those who are in charge of their children's education, and renders many adults reticent when it comes to going back to education and developing new skills. We need to break down these attitudes by throwing school doors open. The same is true of further and higher education institutions, many of which are richly endowed with sporting and learning facilities which are only in use for part of the year and are restricted to students and staff. If we can break down some of the barriers, then education and the professionals who provide it will start to be valued by the whole of society.

Schools and colleges can accrue revenue from providing wider services, but the bulk of educational reform will cost money, not create it, and it can't come out of thin air. A recent survey by the *Times Educational Supplement* showed that 83 per cent of parents don't believe the government is spending enough on Britain's schools; seven out of ten would be prepared to pay more tax in order to see improvements in education. New Labour has misjudged people's attitudes to taxation and the state. Today's voters are very sophisticated – they understand that you can't have a fair society for free. More than that, they are prepared to pay for it, when they can see that their money is going to be spent effectively.

The NHS is equally in crisis. In its election manifesto, Labour pledged to cut NHS in-patient waiting lists by 100,000. At the time of writing it had almost achieved this, but at the expense of out-patient waiting lists, which had *risen* by 248,000. Even before the flu 'epidemic' of January 2000, there were far more people waiting for attention in the NHS than when Labour came to power.

In response to huge pressures in the House and a vigorous campaign in the national press, in March 2000 the government suddenly announced massive additional spending on the NHS, in order to bring health service spending up to a par with European levels. Yet I had asked the Prime Minster only the week before if he would reverse his decision to cut income tax by a penny and put the money into education and health. He said he would not. Labour's volte-face seemed tailored for the front pages, and given Mr Blair's attitude just a week beforehand, it seemed to be a move developed on the hop. It has not yet become clear whether this announcement will be translated into effective policies. Shortly after making this 'promise', Mr Blair then claimed it was merely an aspiration, and one dependent on economic growth. Possibly because Gordon Brown had pointed out to him that, under current rates of spending, Britain would not be on a par with its European cousins until Mr Blair was drawing his pension! I find it deeply ironic that Tony Blair always quotes Nye Bevan as one of his heroes. It's unlikely that the feeling would be reciprocated – particularly when you consider that Bevan quit the Cabinet over prescription charges. Given Bevan's feelings about the NHS, it's fairly unlikely that he would have been invited to join Tony Blair's Cabinet.

Equal access to a top-class health service is vital for securing individual liberty, and, contrary to eighties thinking, the private sector is inefficient at delivering health care, because it has to spend valuable resources on advertising and public image. As the health insurance sector is profit-driven, no private health care package is comprehensive

– people with HIV, diabetes or mental illness find it difficult and sometimes impossible to get cover. The weak remain at a disadvantage.

Doing more does not involve the interference and excessive legislation of the Nanny State. It is the rationalized use of power – deploying the might of government to ensure certain universal rights for all its citizens, rights which would otherwise not be available equally to all.

Doing Different

Government needs to rethink its role in the twenty-first century. It is not solely the protector and preserver of contracts, nor the guardian of morality, but it is also the promoter of liberty. This last duty has two implications. Government has to let go of powers which could be best exercised elsewhere; particularly with regard to local and regional government. By contrast, in other areas, government has to forge the path: this is vital in areas such as sexual and racial discrimination, where without tough and concerted action, equality and thus liberty will remain compromised.

If government is to promote liberty, then creative solutions are called for. That is appropriate – the world already views Britain as a creative nation, both in terms of commercial inventiveness and in design, the arts and music. Nurturing this creativity makes economic sense and gives power to individuals in itself.

Because creativity places so much emphasis on individuals, government can only further it through a highly decentralized approach, in which the can-do mentality is encouraged in both the public and private sectors. Devolution to Wales, Northern Ireland and Scotland, and the creation of a London Assembly, as well as Regional Development Agencies in England, will loosen the Whitehall straitjacket and give a tremendous boost to local economic initiatives, by ensuring that the power to stimulate local economies does not rest solely in the capital.

The original Highland and Islands Development Board (now Highlands and Islands Enterprise) has made tremendous progress within my own constituency. I remember its former Chairman, Robert Cowan, a former merchant banker, arguing that the Board was a far preferable alternative to borrowing money from the banks. Banks, he felt, had a culture of cowardice when it came to backing small, local initiatives whose success was far from guaranteed. As a result, innovation and originality are rarely encouraged or rewarded.[7]

Devolved bodies help to produce a co-ordinated, joined-up approach to training and support for small businesses. Their economic development strategies can build on local strengths – offering training, for example, in the jobs in which that region has a strong tradition. This approach should mean that an unemployed person, via the New Deal, would get the training and support they need to get a job with prospects, whatever age he or she may be, and that someone with a good business idea could secure the support and funding to get it off the ground.

Locally directed initiatives can get to grips with the micro-processes of local labour markets, in a way that centrally driven policies cannot hope to. A report by the Joseph Rowntree Foundation last year found that policies to tackle unemployment were only proving effective for between 20 and 25 per cent of people targeted.[8] Those least successful were the most vulnerable groups: poorly qualified men, single parents with young children and people with a history of previous unemployment. It also found that the most effective unemployment schemes were those which took full account of both individual circumstances and local conditions.

Labour has not realized just how much devolving political power can contribute towards the fulfilment of Britain's economic potential and enhancing the quality of life for individuals. The Regional Development Agencies still lack many of the powers they need, notably control over the Training and Enterprise Councils, and so long as the government refuses to give local councils a power of general competence (the authority to do any task unless it is specifically prohibited from doing so), and (except in Scotland) baulks at proportional representation for local councils, then people will not be able to implement innovative local solutions to local problems.

Once again, this is not some new, fashionable concept. It is at the roots of Liberal thought. Like John F. Kennedy, I believe 'political action is the highest responsibility of a citizen', but we cannot expect people to act when they are unable see any evidence that they are achieving anything. Back in the 1880s, T. H. Green argued for greater power at the local level, stressing that this was the only way to make political participation solid and tangible for the average citizen – the only way, in essence, to achieve a true democracy.

My thinking owes a debt to other great Liberals as well. In the Thatcher years, it became fashionable to say that the economist Keynes was outdated, yet when I first read Keynes, it struck me as both common sense, and sheer decency, that government should co-ordinate the nation's resources, particularly through investment, to provide work when markets fail to create the jobs that are needed. I remain persuaded that it should be within the remit of government activity to intervene where markets fail or exploit. Without such inter-vention, the world will be dominated by Microsoft-like monopolies, and it will be impossible to meet needs such as health care and edu-cation for all, that cannot be met by markets alone.

Keynes also had a belief, which we can learn much from, that society is basically wealthy and that we have the resources – if only we can access them – to build the communities we want. In 1933, he wrote:

> London is one of the richest cities in the history of civilisation, but it cannot 'afford' the highest standards of achievement of which its own living citizens are capable, because they do not 'pay'. If I had the power today, I would surely set out to endow our capital cities with all the appurtenances of art and civilisation on the highest standards ... convinced that what I could create I could afford – and believing that money thus spent would not only be better than any dole, but would make unnecessary any dole. For what we have spent on the dole in England since the war, we could have made our cities the greatest works of man in the world.

Of course we need to adapt Keynes to the modern age – markets are more global today – but there is a vast range of options still available for a government that wishes to think creatively. Keynes was co-author of the 1929 Liberal manifesto. His basic principles have a central place in Liberal Democracy, and they will always inform my views on the potential for government to take an imaginative role in the economy. They are a major weapon in the fight for social justice, and thus in the fight for liberty.

Keynes believed that economic stability is a fundamental requirement of liberty, and that, as it is a basic right, responsibility for delivering it rests with government. But the wild fluctuations in prices, interest rates and exchange rates in recent decades have made a mockery of even the best-laid plans of governments, individuals and firms. This is a key reason for supporting membership of European Monetary Union. Membership of the Eurozone will bring lower inflation and interest rates and reduce risk in our trading relations with Europe. It will also give our entrepreneurs a domestic market of over 370 million people, and so make it easier to turn a good idea into a commercial success. The result will be a healthy economy and greater opportunity for all.

Even with a stable and thriving economy, and power devolved wherever possible, some individuals will experience compromised opportunities, until government takes tough action to tackle inequalities of gender and race. I have declared myself an opponent of bossy, authoritarian government, but it does need to flex its muscle to protect its citizens from discrimination. This calls for just as much creative thought as the devolution of power, for issues such as race and gender equality have been on the agenda for decades, and decades of legislation have not solved all problems. Government plainly needs to 'do different'.

In 1911, Lloyd George famously said, 'You cannot trust the interests of any class entirely to another class; and you cannot trust the interests of any sex entirely to another sex.' Gender inequalities in our country are much less pronounced than they were ninety or even twenty years ago. Since the introduction of universal suffrage, equal pay and sex discrimination legislation, women's rights have improved vastly: there are more women in paid employment, there is less of a gap between male and female earnings and there are more women in Parliament than ever before, but those advantages have tended to extend to women who are white, well-educated and in the middle-income bracket. A disproportionate number of women still suffer conditions of poverty in the UK.

Much of my personal interest in this issue is due to Nancy Seear, a lifelong champion of equality. In the 1987 election, as the SDP's spokesman on Social Security, I learned much from Nancy, who was leader of the Alliance Social Security team. She was known for her unshakeable feminism, but far from being intimidating, I found her to be totally engaging, inspirational, and serious fun – as her widespread popularity across the parties testified.

Under the influence of Nancy Seear I learned the importance of examining all statistics twice, to see how they are affected by gender. For example, in 1995 the great majority of those earning less than half the national wage were women. Ninety per cent of single parents were also women. It is estimated that 62 per cent of single-parent households had an income of less than half the national average. Unemployment is a major contributor to single-parent poverty. Equality is equally in crisis in the working population. Women comprise 44 per cent of the workforce, but only 20 per cent of managers, and 2 per cent of senior executives were women in 1995. By 1998, the proportion of women in managerial and administrative roles was still only 32 per cent.

Before the last election, Liberal Democrats argued that Labour's plans to establish a Ministry for Women were misguided. It smacked of tokenism, and risked marginalizing an overarching concern, but it turned out, no such ministry has been created. Margaret Jay, current Minister for Women, works out of the Cabinet Office and heads the Women's Unit – amongst her other duties as Leader of the House of Lords.

Many of Labour's moves are, however, welcome: maternity leave has been extended, and women are entitled to additional leave after one year's employment rather than the traditional two. Similarly, the government is committed to ensuring that 50 per cent of all public appointments are filled by women. Measures to strengthen rights for part-time workers also favour equality for women, since they are disproportionately confined to the part-time sector.

The New Deal, by contrast, is proving highly unpopular with women. It marks a significant departure from traditional Labour thinking, as it involves cutting benefits for lone parents and replacing them with a scheme that 'encourages' them into work. Subsidized childcare is still far from universal – rural areas and deprivation pockets in the inner cities are particularly poorly provided for – and, as a result, many working mothers (and fathers) find themselves worse off than they were on benefits. As well as being an economic issue, this is also one of personal choice: mothers do not want the state telling them they should be going out to work, when it may be better that they remain at home with pre-school children. In its promotional literature, and its championship of the New Deal, the Women's Unit makes much use of a MORI poll conducted in 1999. Paradoxically, this poll concluded that young women were less concerned that they faced unequal opportunities in employment, and more concerned that they be given the freedom to live their lives as they wished. Hardly what the New Deal is about.

The New Deal is all about getting people into work, and while that is a very pressing issue, the needs of women extend far further. Forty-three per cent of working-age women in the UK have dependent children. In a society where women are still disproportionately burdened with the responsibilities for childcare and the care of sick and elderly relatives, simply propelling people into work is not a cure-all. A recent study by Bristol University's Institute of Child Health also indicated that 17 per cent of mothers who returned to full-time work after having children switched to part-time jobs within two years, and 19 per cent gave up work altogether – such are the problems of balancing child-rearing and employment. The situation is exacerbated by the outdated attitudes of employers to childcare. In 1998, an estimated – and derisory – 2 per cent of employers operated crèche schemes, and only 10 per cent of public sector organizations offered practical assistance with childcare. Recent findings by the Institute for

Social and Economic Research indicate that families with children are still not finding their way out of poverty, and that women find it disproportionately difficult. Whereas fathers tend to secure employment based on standard economic criteria, like experience and qualifications, a mother's ability to find work depends on factors like the age of their children.[4]

Labour's commitment to a National Childcare Strategy is welcome. It aims to set national standards for childcare quality, and to ensure that more families are able to afford it, but their intention to fund over half of its estimated £300 million costs from the National Lottery is plainly misconceived. Statistics show that the bulk of money going into the lottery comes from the poorest sections of society. Single mothers with children – those the strategy is supposed to be helping – make up a sizeable part of that body, so the most disadvantaged are paying for a scheme which is supposed to make them better off. This is the very opposite of what should happen in a just society, where the strong take responsibility for the weak. A Social Justice Audit would bring the National Childcare Strategy to book for this, and seek alternative ways to fund it.

In June 1999 the government introduced a code of practice relating to age discrimination in employment. This is an important issue for women, as they are far more likely to suffer from it than men, but in its election manifesto, Labour made no clear pledge to enshrine this in legislation, and it hasn't done so since. Instead, it has promised to review the situation in 2001. One of its chief arguments against full legislation seems to be that employers will always cheat anyway: a thoroughly specious line which could be used to justify government abdicating responsibility in a variety of areas.

Government also needs to think differently about the whole question of women's empowerment. Crèches, assisted childcare and workplace legislation are only part of the solution. Every mother should be freely able to make the decision to have children and to remain with them until they are of school age. Government's role is to ensure that mothers can exercise that freedom, by making adequate welfare provision for the mothers of pre-school children, and by giving employers incentives to employ mothers returning to the workplace. Gordon Brown should be given credit for his plans, announced in February 2000, to give women the automatic right to return to part-time work after maternity leave, and also to offer up to £30 a week to mothers on low incomes who choose to remain at home with children after the statutory maternity leave has run out.

John Stuart Mill spoke out in favour of gender equality in 1869, in his essay 'The Subjection of Women'. In those days, it was a relatively unfashionable issue and it did him few favours in terms of public opinion. Today, our party's concern with equality for women has nothing to do with public opinion, and everything to do with the fact that, as Liberal Democrats, we support the pursuit of liberty and equality for all. We cannot accept a society in which over half of our population faces diminished opportunities.

Personally, I have changed my viewpoint, and now support positive discrimination to ensure that more women become part of the political process. The imbalances in all the political parties – not least the woeful percentage of women Liberal Democrat MPs in Westminster – clinched the argument for me. There is a genuine clash of principles here: interference, or at least a degree of political manipulation, versus the desirable principle of having more women at all elected levels. Ultimately, we have to apply Guy Fawkes' maxim, that 'desperate diseases require desperate remedies'. We cannot aspire to represent British society adequately if we continue so lamentably to fail to reflect it, and without equality in Westminster, we will never create equality across the nation. Simply deploying a system of proportional represen-tation in the elections for the Scottish Assembly produced a higher rate of women Members of Parliament than anywhere else in Europe – apart from Sweden and Denmark. When parties select one candidate they usually select the one that reaches the top of the pile quickest. Family constraints mean that women are often prevented from putting in the time to fight for the candidacy of a seat and so they miss out. By contrast, when a party selects a list of candidates for a single-transferable-vote election, it wants a list that represents the constitu-ency in a broad sense, and as an all-male list would look crazy to many, women tend to be chosen more frequently than under the old system. The Welsh Cabinet has a fifty–fifty balance of men and women – but much more still needs to be done. Within Westminster itself, there are still no crèche facilities – nor are there any on the sites of the Scottish and Welsh Assemblies. Working practices within these bodies – especially the late nights – do little to encourage those with childcare responsibilities to become involved.

New Labour made a public relations mistake in going for the 'New Lad' image: endless shots of Tony kicking a football, cracking open cans of lager to watch the match with Gordon Brown, and Peter Mandelson revealing a passion for Hartlepool FC. These stunts only reinforced the belief that government is male-dominated, and persisted in making women feel dissociated from the political process. The chauvinism of the gentlemen's club has simply been replaced by that of the terraces.

The images sent out are of vital importance, but less so than the measures actually instigated. Within the Liberal Democrats, there must be a thorough reworking of our internal selection procedures, to redress the gender imbalance. All-women shortlists (which are currently illegal) and the practice of 'zipping' – whereby you assure that nationwide, there is a fifty–fifty balance of men and women at first and second place on candidate shortlists – must be instigated with urgency.

A major advantage of zipping is that in ensuring an equal gender balance on shortlists, it is not seen to favour the interests of one gender over another, and therefore is not illegal. Strange as it may sound, outdated legislation in England still makes positive discrimination a crime. As yet, the Labour government has done nothing to change this situation, or announced any firm intent to do so. Even Harriet Harman, quoted in the *Financial Times*, has attacked her party's policy on the issue. This is yet another area where England lags behind the rest of Europe in terms of the opportunities it offers its citizens.

Labour's incorporation of the European Convention on Human Rights into domestic law is a welcome development, all the more so because the Conservatives would never have done it. This prohibits all discrimination on grounds such as sex, race, colour, language, religion, political opinion or membership of any minority. All existing legislation in these areas should be replaced with a stronger Equality Act, based on the twin assumptions that everyone has a right to be treated equally, and that to treat anyone otherwise is an offence. It would cover all issues of pay, harassment and discrimination, and would tackle gaps in the European Convention on Human Rights, for example on age discrimination.

The popular issues – nursery places for pre-school children, benefits for mothers who choose to remain at home as well as those who choose to go out to work, and equality in education and in the workplace – naturally deserve our intense attention, yet we also have to understand that the position of women has suffered because of strait-jacketed approaches which address the central issues but do not consider how gender cuts across every sphere of life. We need a different, innovative approach to address all areas in which women face inequality.

Take transport: as many as 45 per cent of women report feeling unsafe on public transport late at night. Inequalities of pay make ownership of cars more difficult for women than for men, but rather than simply encouraging private car ownership, we might look at forcing companies to institute car-sharing policies for their employees, if not to pay for taxis after a certain time of night, which at the moment is a matter of discretion.

Creative thinking on the subject of sexual equality also means taking account of changes in culture and social trends. We have to be aware that, in targeting the needs of women, we run the risk of ignoring another alienated and much compromised section of society – today's young men. Their fathers, entering the labour market in the late fifties and early sixties, usually found paid work, but as each generation has hit sixteen, the statistical likelihood of unemployment has become greater. According to a 1999 survey by the Rowntree Foundation, fewer young men are now entering paid employment and the proportion of young men with unbroken records of employment between the ages of sixteen and twenty-five has fallen sharply. Changes in the workplace, resulting in an increase in poorer-paid service industry jobs and a decrease in well-paid manual jobs, have offered opportunities for the employment of women, but left too many young men out in the cold.

There are fears that high unemployment among young men has also led to a rise in anti-social behaviour, family breakdown, even the emergence of an underclass. Thanks to the efforts of various feminist campaigners and thinkers, male chauvinism is now being tackled on a wide range of fronts, but, as roles change, many young men are confused about their position in society.

The Rowntree Foundation study reported that many young men felt ill-prepared by school for the new job market. Careers advice and the opinions of their fathers – who had seen a very different economic climate – were of limited value. School needs to prepare young men for a changing world. Many of those interviewed reported spending their final year 'waiting around' for exams they did not think they would do well in, which is why, as the report suggests, a 'school into work' programme would be of such value, enabling young men to spend their last year learning more about the workplace, perhaps even spending a portion of the time in it.

The report also found that too many young men embark on college courses for which they are inadequately prepared. In an age when there seem to be so few opportunities available for young people, it makes sense to go to college and get further qualifications, with a view to securing a better job, but many young men drop out within the first year and do not return. Part of the blame rests with traditional male attitudes, in which asking for help and admitting you have a problem are frowned upon, but part also rests with our educators, for failing to recognize those attitudes and to develop specific strategies for engaging with young men, so that further education is a productive experience, rather than one which diminishes their already low self-esteem.[10]

The New Deal is ill-equipped to address the problems faced by young men. They emerge from it and find work, but it tends to be of a low-paid, short-term and repetitive nature, such as working in supermarkets, fast food chains, picking and packing, and cleaning. This type of work does nothing to enhance self-esteem. Even though there is much truth in the adage that you 'have to have a job to get a job', such work is rated poorly by young men, and it is the type with which they are least likely to persevere. At the moment, once a young man gets a job, he becomes a success statistic and thereafter, those authorities previously concerned with his predicament tend to wash their hands of him. This has to be addressed – we need a support network so that young men in work can still receive careers advice and access to further training.

One idea of particular interest is the 'foyer', one of which I recently visited in Eastbourne. Based on a French concept, there are around 100 such institutions across the UK. These offer combined accommodation and training for sixteen to twenty-five-year-olds, thereby helping to break the vicious cycle of 'no training, no job, no home'. The young people joining the Eastbourne foyer sign up to a personal action plan and receive accommodation and training conditionally upon keeping to their side of the bargain. They have full access to counselling and advice facilities as part of their residency. Local businesses are closely involved, ensuring that the young residents receive appropriate training for jobs which actually exist nearby.

We also have to consider the specific problems of the ethnic minorities. A 1999 study by the University of Essex found that young Caribbean men are more than twice as likely to suffer from unemployment as young white men, and when they do find work, they can expect lower earnings. African men suffer particularly severe disadvantages in the labour market: in spite of educational success, an African graduate is seven times more likely to be unemployed than a white graduate. Future strategies must take account of this particular set of difficulties. In the public sector, targets for ethnic minority employment have been in place for a number of years, yet the problem is not diminishing. If we are to believe that a Drugs Czar and a Heart Czar can succeed where less identifiable bodies have failed, then we should certainly have a Race Czar as well, backed up by a team whose sole responsibility is getting more people from the ethnic minorities into full employment. Devolving more power to the regions will also help – the Asian community in Bradford has radically different needs from, for instance, the Afro-Caribbean community in south London, and initiatives to promote business and development are best exercised by those with an intimate understanding of local factors.

Just as the introduction of proportional representation would ensure that more women enter Parliament, by encouraging parties to select more representative panels of candidates, so it would ensure that more members of the ethnic minorities became integral to government. With more MPs from the ethnic minorities, the attitude of their communities on subjects such as the police, education and asylum, would be heard where it was most effective – within the House of Commons itself. Conversely, until the minorities are fairly represented in Parliament, we cannot claim to be operating a democracy.

Sociological studies performed in inner city America found that young men from poor Italian-American backgrounds were less likely to turn to crime or gang membership (which often amounts to the same thing) than young African-American men in similar economic circumstances. One reason cited was that Italian-American Catholic culture, with its extended family and array of immigrant networks, provided a safety net for young men – one which had been eroded among African-Americans because of their specific history. Even though young Italian-Americans might find themselves unemployed and without any close family to turn to, there were people looking out for them and people to whom they could turn *in extremis*. There was, in a sense, a community vigilance in place, whereby neighbourhoods looked out for all their members.

Vigilance is necessary, but not the vigilance of the Nanny State: citizens must start looking out for each other and safeguarding each other's rights and freedoms, while central government must police itself, to ensure that it retains no powers that could be exercised more efficiently elsewhere.

One key issue ties together many of the themes of doing different: health. Every single opinion poll shows that the state of the National Health Service is right at the top of the political agenda. It is usually the major concern of most voters, yet too often we seem to be stuck in old debates about how to improve the NHS. I am quite clear that one vital requirement of the NHS is more government investment – we have to be honest about that, but if there is any area which needs a creative approach it is health. How do we start?

One of the big problems with the NHS is its distance from the citizen. The April 2000 report of the commission on health chaired by Will Hutton highlighted the 'accountability deficit' in the NHS, which leads the public increasingly to use the NHS's 'undeveloped complaint mechanisms'.[11] The NHS is a vast bureaucracy, too often run from Whitehall, and unable to cope with local demands. It is also too often disconnected from other arms of welfare provision such as social services. Health policy should be one of the major responsibilities of regional government in England, which could take over the current NHS Executive Regions and establish greater accountability for all that the NHS does. This could be accompanied by widening the composition of Primary Care Trusts, so that local social services are tied in more effectively. We could also involve local authorities in setting Health Improvement Plans for their areas.

Doing different in health is not just about making the NHS more accountable: we also have to make sure that people understand their entitlements more clearly. To do this, we need National Health Service Care Guarantees, which cover the major medical conditions, and set down the minimum standards of care that patients should expect to receive. These could be drawn up by the Secretary of State for Health, in consultation with patient groups, health professional bodies and external experts. This would begin to enable everybody to understand what they are entitled to, and should be one of the major priorities in making the NHS more responsive to citizens.

Conclusion

The focus of politics has to shift, away from the old ideological struggles and to a new mission: that of advancing and protecting liberty. This is particularly vital if we are to engage with the young voters of the twenty-first century, who want a dynamic economy and wide-ranging liberties, bolstered by high-quality public services. At present, we have a neurotic government. After so long in opposition, it cannot quite believe that it is in power, and is terrified that it will lose it any moment. As a result of this neurosis, our government suffers from delusions. It believes, quite wrongly, that its success depends upon keeping tight control: control over the Celtic fringe and local government, control over party members who challenge it, and control over the liberty of its citizens. In reality, the future success of every government depends upon having the strength to let go, to redirect its energies towards realizing the liberal agenda. If New Labour are incapable of doing this, they will rapidly find that Britain becomes tired of being told how to live.

Chapter Four

FREEDOM TO INNOVATE:
SCIENCE AND DEMOCRACY

'Some men see things as they are and ask themselves: "why?"
I dream of things that never have been and ask myself: "why
not?"'

AESCHYLUS AND ROBERT F. KENNEDY[1]

Beyond Government: The Pace of Change

The spectrum of popular familiarity with technology ranges from the 'anorak' to 'can't program the video'. Most people under voting age are entirely comfortable with new technology. When I visit primary schools I am always struck by the fact that most six or seven-year-olds know just as much about laptops as I do. It is common for parents to ask their children to program the video recorder – I'm sure I would do the same, if I had any children.

In 1985 I bought what I then thought was a cutting-edge piece of technology – one of the early home word processors with a distinctive green screen. I battled with it for days, before abandoning it in a corner for several months. In the end, the exorbitant cost of the outfit preyed upon my conscience and forced me to sit down with the manual, cursing, until I had mastered the basic functions. I still keep this machine in my study for nostalgic reasons, but it has been a long time since I switched it on – and colleagues laugh at it now when they see it, such is my reputation for being a computer Luddite.

It is interesting to look back, though, at the state of basic home-use computers today, compared with fifteen years ago. I now own a laptop and a pocket organizer, which are far from advanced in today's terms, but can do so much more than my first word processor. I can fax, e-mail, create leaflets for community campaigns and buy products over the Internet from far away countries. That was not only impossible fifteen years ago, it was virtually undreamed of. We might understandably feel that we live in a time of revolutionary change.

It is easy to become carried away by the current enthusiasm and to imagine that we are the first generation to see such a change, but in fact, throughout recent history, certainly since the beginning of the Industrial Revolution, most people have seen their own time as an era of great technological, industrial and scientific advance. They would have been right to do so. The eighteenth, nineteenth and twentieth centuries saw a huge expansion in the sophistication and use of technology. In Britain, the Great Exhibition of 1851 – the Millennium Dome of its day – proudly displayed every kind of machinery and new technology which had transformed industrial manufacture: railway engines, steam ploughs, steamship engines, cranes, printing machines and much more besides. Scientific and medical advances such as the invention of anaesthetic, the discovery of penicillin, the sourcing of radioactivity, accompanied technological and industrial development.

The late nineteenth and early twentieth centuries also saw revolutionary developments in communications. The invention of the telegraph, radio wires, the telephone and Morse code completely transformed the world. Peoples around the globe who knew little or nothing of one another were able to communicate from country to country and continent to continent for the first time in history. Other inventions of the last 100 years have had an equally important impact on the social history of mankind: not just the television, but also labour-saving devices such as washing machines, vacuum cleaners and fridges, have transformed domestic life. Whatever the arguments about the importance to society of the technological revolution currently taking place, many would argue that the revolutions of the past 300 years had greater and lasting impacts on the peoples of that day.

Thinking about this on a more personal level, it is easy to see how more recent changes have affected my own family. I can clearly remember my grandfather coming next door to my parents' house, on the rare occasions when he deemed it necessary to use the telephone. I can remember our gentle amusement when he bellowed into the receiver, not quite grasping that the device was a little more sophisticated than a speaking-tube. When my parents were born, in the twenties, it was still a very rare thing indeed for people to fly. The newsreels that they saw in cinemas were replete with stories of the latest achievements in the air: continents and oceans crossed for the first time, records broken and human endurance pushed to the limits. Yet it is now commonplace for me to take a plane to Inverness, and for them to do the same when visiting me in London. Travelling back further to my grandparents' generation, we find them born into a world almost without cars, yet they lived to see men walking on the moon. Their parents and grandparents lived through times that were even more remarkable in many ways, as towns, cities and factories replaced ways of life that had been largely undisturbed for centuries.

It is perhaps human nature to believe that one's own generation is the most significant, or that one's own lifetime has seen the greatest advance, but the current *pace* of technological change does make this era exceptional. That is especially the case for computers: as their power develops, so do their uses. It is interesting to compare computers and other areas of technology: in 1900, top speeds of basic cars were seldom more than 30mph. By 2000, a very basic car could easily top 100mph – a three or fourfold increase. The rate of change in computers has been markedly different. A basic home computer in the mid-eighties had a 32k memory, whereas now we measure memory not in kilobytes, or even megabytes, but gigabytes. It is as if a 30mph car developed into one that could travel hundreds of thousands of miles per hour. With such an increase in speed, a car would no longer be a means of travelling from town to town, but from galaxy to galaxy. With this magnitude of change the uses to which computers can be put have completely changed. The same applies to many other aspects of technology. No arena of life, from religion to medicine, is untouched by the revolution, especially politics.

From a politician's point of view, one feature is missing from this scenario of rapid technological change. That is the role of government. Politicians may believe that government is the main co-ordinator of the nation's resources, and the driving force behind social change, but it can be argued that none of the major shifts in technology have taken place because of government. In fact, one might say that they have taken place *in spite* of it, entirely independently of the House of Commons.

The recent technological revolution has been driven, and continues to be driven now, by a mixture of a few large technology and computer giants such as Microsoft, and many small entrepreneurs. According to the *Economist* the current boom in European Internet and high-technology businesses is being fuelled by venture capital from the USA:

> Europe is awash with venture capital funds, many of them American in origin and many of them destined for new high-tech and Internet firms. Coupled with the growing influence of American methods of starting companies, this is having a profound effect on Europe's business culture. The money currently available for investment in European Internet and high-technology start-ups is estimated by venture firms at around $10 billion.[2]

The role of government in all this seems limited at best. The attitude of those entrepreneurs making the running in these industries is neatly summarized by Martha Lane-Fox, the co-founder of Lastminute.com who recently said:

> I think there are things [the government] can do with tax breaks, with options, with all sorts of things to encourage people to go into these kinds of businesses. But in the end, the Government can't make things happen. It's companies that need to change

the dynamics of how they work. It's up to companies to encourage little start-ups. And it's people that need to take risks and start their own businesses.

Ms Lane-Fox's virtual fortune may have dwindled, but her words are still poignant. The question is not whether government has played a part in innovation to date, but what it must be doing, and not doing, in the future. Should governments be increasing regulation, or reducing it? Should governments change the way they support research by giving more incentives to companies, or should they encourage more partnerships between universities and business? Can governments harness the new technology to further participation and democracy?

Enabling Not Interfering

Nowhere has the speed of the technological revolution been more apparent than in the growth and use of the Internet. The last decade has witnessed a huge expansion in the use of computers in the workplace, in schools and in private homes. The next generation of children will certainly suffer none of my own frustrations when they purchase a new PC. They will have become comfortably familiar with them at school: the average secondary school in Britain now has 101 computers. The number of people in the West who now have access to the Internet is staggering – some 102 million in the USA and Canada. While European countries are slightly behind North America, Internet expansion on this side of the Atlantic is nevertheless strong. In Britain, 12.7 million people have access to the Internet[3] of whom more than 6 million are home users.[4] As of last year, 93 per cent of secondary schools and 62 per cent of primary schools were on the Internet.[5] Europe-wide 2.2 million businesses are using the Internet, and this is predicted to rise to 5.4 million, or two thirds of European businesses, by 2004.[6]

The speed with which use of the Internet has spread is unprecedented, and WAP (Wireless Application Protocol) technology, which enables the Internet to be accessed via mobile phones, will make it spread even faster. The US Department of Commerce calculates that it took less than five years for the commercial Internet to have more than fifty million users in the United States. This compares to nearly forty years for broadcast radio, and over ten years for TV. Such widespread Internet use means that we now truly live in an 'information age'. Never before has it been so easy to communicate and do business on a global scale. As a result, electronic commerce is now growing dramatically, particularly in North America, Europe and Japan, but to varying degrees, in the rest of the world also. E-commerce is defined by the DTI as:

> the exchange of information across electronic networks, at any stage in the supply chain, whether within an organisation, between businesses, between businesses and consumers, or between public and private sectors, whether paid or unpaid

Much of the current public interest in e-commerce is based around the novelty of shopping on the Internet. Soon, it is said, consumers in the whole Western world will be able to purchase all of life's essentials, from food and clothing to cars and holidays, without moving from their computer screens, but this makes up only a small part of e-commerce. Most activity is business-to-business, involving electronic data and financial transactions. The Forrester Research Report (December 1998) estimates that in the United States alone, the revenue from business-to-business e-commerce will reach $1.3 trillion by 2003. The very nature of such electronic interchanges – immediate, cheap and secure – has enormous implications for companies around the world.

The recent government report *e-commerce@itsbest.co.uk* highlights the dramatic changes in business practice which the growth of e-commerce will bring, not just for those involved in high-technology industries, but across all of business. The main impact it will have is on barriers to entry: e-commerce demolishes many existing market barriers. For example, geographic boundaries: a product sold at one price in the USA may cost something different in Japan and a third amount in the UK. There is a variety of reasons for this, such as differing domestic tax rates and the imposition of import duties, but on the Internet, a product will have a universal price. This has important implications for government. If someone in Britain purchases an item over the Internet, from a site based on the other side of the world, it is extremely difficult for the government to collect VAT on the sale.

Aside from altering the tax system, government must do much more to ensure that the benefits of technology reach as many people as possible. In *e-commerce@itsbest.co.uk*, the government claims to have been going to great efforts, in tandem with industry, to prepare the UK to take advantage of the technological revolution. In the foreword, the Prime Minister wrote: '[The] Government cannot simply regulate to achieve its aims in this new global electronic environment.'

What government can do is to alert the wider business community to the dangers of being left behind by the new technologies. There is, the government contends, still a substantial number of businesses in the UK who do not use the Internet. More worryingly, as the government is keen to highlight, a survey of directors showed that only 2 per cent of UK board directors believe the Internet poses a serious competitive threat.[7] Our measures to address this would include government-led and sponsored education and training in Internet use for small businesses.

We should also be connecting businesses to universities, a model we see throughout America, but more rarely here – although the Cambridge Science Park is a pioneering example. Under such schemes, companies fund the research which they, in turn, benefit from. Great strides are also being made in Oxford, where the university has set up a company, Isis Innovation, to manage the transfer of new technology from its academic sources into commerce and industry. Co-operating with the university's own Research Services office, Isis aims to provide a seamless route to take researchers from A to Z, from the first stages of applying for a grant, right through to starting a small company and getting their product marketed. Partly as a result of this innovative approach, Oxford is now attracting record amounts of funding for research.

Oxford's Science Park, founded in 1991, may not be quite as well-known as its counterpart in East Anglia, but the university patents a new product every week. Meanwhile, just down the road from the Science Park is the Rutherford Appleton Laboratory, which formerly specialized in providing facilities for academics. Nowadays, it is attracting a number of tiny start-up companies. A prime example is Bookham Technology, which was created by a Ph.D. student, who originally used the laboratory for his academic research and then decided to work there on a commercial idea. Bookham manufactures components for fibre-optic systems, such as a revolutionary sensor device which monitors the pressure inside car engines and therefore allows the driver maximum control over engine responsiveness.

Across Oxford, academic research is being turned into commercial success. Biotech start-up firm Evolutec built on research begun by the NERC Institute of Virology and Environmental Microbiology to develop a ground-breaking anti-asthma drug. A researcher, Professor Patricia Nuttall, noticed that ticks and other parasites had a unique ability to prevent their hosts from experiencing an allergic reaction and therefore getting rid of them. Asthma attacks are triggered by responses from the body's immune system so, by studying the ticks' strategies, researchers were able to pioneer a drug which switches off the immune system's unnecessary reactions. Similarly revolutionary, and coming from similar academic origins, has been the development of a painless, infection-free injection system, which negates the need for syringes and needles by blasting a powdered drug through the skin using helium gas.

At least 45 per cent of these tiny start-up companies perish before their ideas ever become commercial reality, and government has a duty to do more where it *can*. One measure would be to copy the example of the Oxford Trust, founded by Sir Martin and Lady Wood. The trust provides incubator units designed to protect start-up firms from the ravages of the commercial world, until they can fend for themselves.

These units assist start-ups by providing low-rent facilities, flexible leases on property, and also free advice from accountants, lawyers and patent agents. Official estimates put the survival rate for start-ups 'reared' in incubator units at 85 per cent. Government could help to achieve similar results by diverting research funds away from military and defence-related projects (where the bulk of all government research spending goes), and into establishing a safe, nurturing environment for new technology start-ups. With this, and the decent-ralization of power that Liberal Democrats favour, local entrepreneurs and local governments would be able to work together to get projects off the ground and create local opportunities. This should be the defining characteristic of government's role in the technological revol-ution: not legislating, but *enabling*.

Technology has profound implications for the nature of society itself. Pundits are currently making a great deal of noise about e-com-merce and the way it will affect the high street. They are also predicting the death of the office, as e-mail and video-conferencing make home-working more feasible. The government has a duty to keep abreast of the social changes spelled by these new developments, but I believe that these Huxley-style visions of the future are exaggerated. I am reminded of those learned nineteenth-century gentlemen who opposed the steam engine on the grounds that travelling over thirty miles an hour would cause people to spontaneously combust. I daresay the wheel was greeted with equal despondency. Despite these gloomy scen-arios, it is not likely that communities will be destroyed by e-com-merce, because people need a spatial hub, and 'the shops' can provide exactly that. If anything, a nation that works from home will tend to make use of local businesses – it is when everyone commutes into cities and town centres that smaller local shops lose out.

I welcome the convenience that the Internet offers to consumers, but convenience is not the only thing a nation wants. A recent trip to Europe's largest outdoor market, in Walthamstow, east London, showed me just how many people were prepared to come from far and wide to get their shopping. They had huge supermarkets closer by, many of which offered an array of customer-convenience gimmicks, such as home delivery, courtesy packing, etc. Many market customers were both middle-income and computer-savvy, so there was, in theory, nothing preventing them from ordering their groceries over the Internet. It wasn't even as if the market stalls offered greater value or choice. The market was thriving precisely because it represented community. It was lively, loud, bustling and opportunities for interaction were everywhere. This is, in my view, a basic human need, probably a primordial one. So even if, in the nightmare scenario of the technophobes, the role of the shops is diminished, new forms of community activity will surface in their place – we've already seen that with the growth of interest group communities via mailing lists on the Internet, where people with shared hobbies or other interests are able to make contact with each other.

Besides that, I personally believe that traditional shopping will never go out of style. The connection between handing over one's money and receiving one's goods at the same time is a groove cut deeply into the communal consciousness and not, I think, one that can be erased. While I do not underestimate the power of technology to change society, we should also be cool-headed on the subject. The Internet and technology in general are changing the way we work, but they are not going to launch us into a frightening Brave New World – not if we treat them sensibly.

Ideal Partners: Technology and Democracy

Approached correctly, technology can mean greater opportunities of participation for everyone, for example, in terms of freedom of information, and learning new skills and languages over the Internet. The University of the Highlands and Islands uses the new technology to link campuses, students and tutors who are hundreds of miles apart. I recently dropped in on one class in the Highlands which was being tutored by a man in Aberystwyth!

The government has been laudably swift in seeing the implications of the new technology for democracy. It has already invested much time and money in creating user-friendly websites for every Department of State, and has made a pledge to conduct increasing amounts of its own business on-line over the next few years. As Bill Gates said in his second book – *Business@The Speed of Thought* – the digital revolution gives government the opportunity to 'reinvent itself around people'. From pensions right through to parking, governments throughout Europe are now going on-line, thereby streamlining administration and cutting costs. The US government aims to have information on all of its resources available electronically by the year 2004.

Electronic voting could be a major means to combat the problem of voter disengagement. Already, thanks to pioneering work by companies such as E-Vote, it is possible for company shareholders to cast their votes with a click of the mouse. This does not just make things more convenient, it results in greater democracy. The cumbersome and time-intensive business of voting on paper means that many shareholders tend either not to exercise their right, or hurriedly get it out of the way without full consideration. E-voting removes the hassle, and thus encourages informed participation. It does not take a genius to see that this technology could also be used to link governments and citizens, to great effect.

With the development of WAP phones it is possible to imagine a scenario whereby citizens could vote on the issues that matter to them simply by tapping a few buttons on their mobiles. With such a system in place, voting need not be confined to the four-yearly choice of government – there could be regular referenda on all the 'hot' issues. It would also be far easier for governments to take stock of public opinion on a continual basis, instead of relying on costly and lengthy surveys.

However, we must also beware of the shortcuts which the technology could tempt us into. Those who participate in on-line voting at present tend to be from a narrow stratum of society which is both computer literate and affluent. We must ensure that all citizens can access on-line voting systems before they can truly be considered democratic. The government may think that its ability to connect directly with citizens means that it no longer needs to bother with Parliament, which has traditionally been the conduit for bringing people's views to bear on government policy, but instead Parliament must adapt to the new technologies and reinvent itself as an informed, deliberative body which truly holds government in check.

The City of Sheffield, which has a Liberal Democrat council, is currently leading the way in the public provision of on-line services, by setting up twenty-five IT kiosks at key locations such as shopping centres, hospitals and bus stations. Financed by advertising, access is free and has been developed with the most computer-illiterate consumer in mind. By simply touching the screen, Sheffield citizens and visitors can access information on local travel, entertainment, shopping, jobs, council services – they can even enquire about benefits and pay their bills.

Across the Irish Sea, the town of Ennis, Co. Clare is also making unique use of the new information technology, and setting an example for the communities of the future. In September 1997, Ennis was designated the Irish Republic's official 'Information Age Town'. Fifteen million pounds was invested in the town, to give every business an ISDN line, to provide every school-age child with regular access to a computer, to put all public services on-line and to give the majority of households direct access to the Net. Ennis is a live experiment, set up precisely to see what happens when an entire community becomes 'wired'. A key feature of the programme is the use of technology to promote democracy and participation in society. Since the launch, seven training centres have been established to cater for citizens with special needs. Early school leavers and the unemployed have the opportunity to search the Web for jobs, and to use on-line learning facilities to improve their skills and qualifications.

At the same time as encouraging innovation and democracy, and encouraging ordinary people to make use of it, we also have a duty to protect people from being cheated in this new electronic marketplace. At the moment, this is very difficult, because countries can legislate as much as they like internally, or even with their neighbours, while their citizens can sit in their front rooms and deal directly with companies in the USA, Japan and beyond, not all of whom are bound by the same codes of practice.

Access to Technology

The first steps towards a global perspective are being made in Brussels, where the EC has set an end-of-year deadline for all legislation on the Internet, in order to help European countries catch up with the USA. The legislation includes directives on copyright, distance selling of financial services, and the settlement of on-line disputes. This will give European e-commerce a tremendous boost.

Without full participation in the European economic community, Britain does not have the power it needs to influence future legislation in favour of its own citizens, and without full participation by all member states, the EU will not have the clout it needs to influence global bodies like the World Trade Organization, whose own legislative processes are sometimes at the mercy of powerful economic blocs such as the USA and Japan.

The facility to transmit information across cyberspace has so many ramifications that it is often possible to ignore the implications of other technological advances. This is particularly relevant in terms of the recent development of smart cards. We have been used to swipe cards, with a magnetic strip down the back containing information, for several years. The smart card is its latest incarnation. While the magnetic strip on the back of your bank card can just about handle your PIN number, account number and expiry date (provided it doesn't get scratched by your doorkeys), the smart card contains a chip capable of storing much larger quantities of information.

This opens up the possibility of combining various functions, so that instead of having one card to get on the Tube, one to pay for lunch and another to get into the car park, everything – passport, Internet access, airmiles, banking information etc. – is contained on the one piece of plastic. The savings in terms of time and money would obviously be enormous. At the same time, condensing information on to a single card does raise questions about the rights of the individual to privacy. It might be feasible for someone – government, police or others – to track the electronic movements of every citizen, and that state of affairs would be intolerable. Future governments will have the weighty responsibility of promoting technological advances like smart cards, while at the same time safeguarding the rights of the individual.

We also have to ensure that technology is easily available to all. I welcomed Gordon Brown's announcement in February 2000, that he intended to find ways of co-operating with the major telephone operators in order to cut the costs of Internet phone calls. Major Internet service providers in Britain have now started to follow the American example, by offering unlimited free phone calls in return for a monthly subscription. These moves, combined with the expansion of the Net away from PCs and on to mobile phones, television sets and games consoles, will help to ensure more widespread usage of the Net. Cyber banking is on the increase, but what good is it to someone who has no ordinary bank account, or e-commerce to someone without a credit card? Technology is only an aid to progress when everyone has equal access to it.

We must also not forget the dictum about leading a horse to water. Even with more primary-age children skilled in using the Internet, and even with computer terminals available in more public places, there are still large numbers of citizens who are reluctant to make use of them. That reluctance increases with age, and with levels of poverty. Government has a duty to identify those groups who are at risk of e-exclusion. We have to start viewing basic Internet and computing skills in the same way that we currently view literacy. Tuition should be freely available to pensioners, those on benefits and on low incomes. This would not have to result in increased taxes – it would be funded by businesses, who have a vested interest in the end result. We should apply lateral thinking when it comes to providing access points. Plenty of people on low incomes never visit shopping malls or libraries. Terminals in doctors' surgeries, benefit offices, local Post Offices, even pubs, would help to engage a wider section of the populace.

The role of government in the on-line revolution is far from traditional, for it is being asked very clearly to stay out rather than legislate, to grant individuals and small companies the freedom to make full use of the new technology. This does not mean that government can simply bow out. Far from it – it must act as an enabler by locating those groups who have unequal access to the new technology and ensuring, through a variety of creative processes, that they are given the potential to make use of it. It also needs to remain vigilant about the potential for people to use the Net to promote, for example, race hate and child pornography. The internation nature of these problems makes an international approach all the more necessary.

Legislating In the Labs

The issue of government involvement in scientific advances becomes yet more cloudy in the areas of medical technology which have important ethical implications. As I write, the Human Fertility and Embryology Authority (HFEA) has just given the go-ahead for British women to freeze their own eggs and create children at a later point in their lives. This offers hope for women undergoing cancer treatment – since radiotherapy damages eggs, they now have the option to store them beforehand and conceive children after the treatment is completed. At the same time, fears have been voiced that women will simply come to view pregnancy as a consumer choice – those with careers will pick when to have their babies.

Fundamentally, I do not feel that governments should interfere with that individual choice. Surely it is better for children to be born into homes where their parents have the time and the resources to do the best possible job of child-rearing? However, there is an onus on government to prevent exploitation of the technology. There could one day be a trade in frozen eggs – women with eggs to spare, as it were, could sell them to those suffering from infertility. At present, the success rate for this treatment is very low, and its costs are very high, but this will not always be the case, and eventually the government will have to decide the question. On the one hand, as a Liberal

Democrat, I support the right of individuals to make their own choices, and do not believe that government can dictate to a woman when she should have her babies, or what means she should use to produce them, but my liberal convictions also mean that I do not want to see something as precious as the human embryo becoming a simple commodity. Nor do I want a society where disadvantaged women end up selling their eggs as a last-ditch escape from poverty. If we accept that the technology for freezing embryos is going to become more sophisticated, more efficient and ultimately cheaper, then we have to be one step ahead. Government has to look at ways that the technology can be encouraged, and at the same time institute codes of fair practice in discussion with the practitioners themselves. Counselling should be compulsory for everyone considering freezing their eggs, as well as for everyone donating them, so that the full personal and the wider ethical issues are properly understood. Checks have to be kept on the financial element, so that profiteers are heavily discouraged from either creating or entering a market.

We also need to be as informed as the scientists when it comes to understanding the implications of recent advances in genetics. The discovery of genes which predetermine certain terminal diseases can, of course, empower people to make informed choices when it comes to having children. Our understanding of genetics also helps oncologists in the fight against cancer.

But as our understanding reaches greater levels of sophistication, the risks also increase. It is far from infeasible that, one day, scientists could identify the genes that determine intelligence, physical strength, even myopia or musical ability. The designer baby is not that distant a prospect. Rather than swap ghoulish speculations with journalists, or dismiss the idea altogether, government needs to be in advance of the technology, but the need for prompt responses must be tempered by the need for careful deliberation. There are plenty of examples of government reacting too quickly to moral panics. The Dangerous Dogs Act was a particular case in point. It was a massive over-reaction, in response to tabloid-fuelled panic about vicious dogs. A more ridiculous example was the establishment of a Cabinet Home Affairs

Sub-Committee on fighting between Mods and Rockers in 1964 – some of our Honourable Members were clearly of the view that a few seaside skirmishes spelled the breakdown of Western society.

'Act in haste, repent at leisure' is an important principle which should determine the attitude of government to all technological and scientific advances. There needs to be a continual process of consultation with the people at the cutting edge, so that we understand the full implications, and can legislate accordingly. As with freezing embryos, the principle has to be this: people have the freedom to make their own choices, but they also have the right to a safe, secure, healthy and fulfilling existence where the value of equality and justice play a key role. A society where those with money and power can buy their offspring physical and mental advantages is far from a just society. Our legislation has to guard against such a possibility, and the commercial exploitation of the technology. That's why Liberal Democrats oppose the patenting of genes. We also intend to prevent insurance companies from making genetic screening a condition of offering policies, to ensure that all have access to insurance regardless of their genetic inheritance.

The law needs to make a clear distinction between those genetically inherited conditions which result in a seriously impaired quality of life for sufferers, and those which are merely inconveniences or acceptable characteristics. Certain genetic conditions result in terminally ill children being born, and it is fair to give parents the right to know whether they carry the gene for such a condition, but on the other hand, even if left-handedness might be a 'disadvantage', it is clear that nobody should be given the right to terminate a pregnancy on such a basis.

In other areas, I am inclined to be more dogmatic. Dolly the sheep awoke the world to the possibility of cloning. In reality, cloning is not some scary new technique but something that has been in existence for centuries: all identical twins are clones of each other, and when you buy a chrysanthemum, you are effectively buying a clone of some long-deceased ancestor bush. The word 'clone' comes from the ancient Greek word for 'twig'.

It is possible that, in future decades, our understanding of cloning could make it possible to apply the technique to humans. Infertile people might be able to clone themselves instead of reproducing, and people could perhaps have a copy of their embryo made and frozen as a form of insurance, in case their original child died. This kind of technology in the wrong hands could place us on the brink of a frightening future. Cloning does not necessarily mean making a replica. Nature and nurture both define character, but it's a frightening thought. Imagine if a Hitler, or a Saddam Hussein, had the ability to make clones of himself. Or, more realistically, let us imagine for a moment which groups in society would be most likely to make use of such technologies. As I write this, British newspapers are full of rather tongue-in-cheek reports about the development of commercial cloning in the USA, where people are now paying outlandish sums of money to have their pets' DNA stored. It will not be long before the same technology is on offer to people in Britain, and it is obvious that only the richest people will be using it. Once this kind of technology is extended to human beings, then we face a terrifying scenario, in which the privileged elites, keen to guarantee their own survival, use their increased economic power to buy themselves the greatest of evolutionary advantages – the ability to have offspring. All attempts by the state to achieve a just society would be rendered meaningless as economic superiority became wedded to physical and biological advantages such as longevity, intelligence and freedom from diseases.

I am therefore in favour of a permanent ban on human reproductive cloning for anything other than basic research. Just because we can do a thing, is not an argument for saying that we should – sometimes quite the opposite, as we saw in the development of nuclear technology at the close of WWII. Suddenly, as a result of technological advances, man was equipped with the capacity to destroy himself and the planet, and we live under that threat to this day. I am, however, equally opposed to the knee-jerk government reaction which assumes that all scientists are evil tinkerers with nature, or that *all* cloning is on a par with the seventies film *The Boys From Brazil*, in which crazed Nazi scientists created 'copies' of Hitler. I want a continual dialogue to exist between government and science, so that they inform one another.

There is a cultural misconception, throughout the Western world, that because a thing is 'natural', it is 'good', and conversely, that anything done in a laboratory is bad. This equation goes deep to the roots of the modern consciousness – we see it in the image of the 'mad scientist', Dr Frankenstein, who created a monster, we see its effects when people take the risk of childbirth at home, without painkillers or access to life-saving medical equipment.

Such distrust is not reasonable. Archaeology and anthropology make it clear that our ancestors, who lived much closer to 'nature' than ourselves, engaged in infanticide and other practices that we would consider repellent, and most of us owe our lives to medical advances which made childbirth safe and infections treatable. An irrational fear of science is far more dangerous than anything that science could create.

A full, balanced look at cloning reveals that the process has many uses, and does not have to result in the production of fully-formed creatures. Cloned embryos could be used for research purposes, provided they are not allowed to develop beyond the point at which the law considers an embryo to have become a human life. These embryos could be used simply to develop a few cells, which could then be used to produce human skin tissues, for graft operations, or to generate whole organs for transplantation. A blanket no to all cloning would outlaw many potentially useful avenues of research. That's why we need to be constantly informed, and take nothing at face value. We cannot use opinions derived from sci-fi films to determine our attitude to science.

The same is true for gene therapy and germ-line therapy. An instinctive response to these might be to assume that they are both suspect processes that should be banned – far from it. In gene therapy, DNA can be introduced into cells in order to correct disorders. It could be an extremely useful technology, for treating any disease where a faulty gene fails to function. Germ-line therapy, on the other hand, involves the genetic modification of whole embryos in order to correct defects. It may be desirable and in some cases necessary to correct serious inherited conditions – so it should certainly not be subject to a blanket prohibition. But it would be open to great abuses, if embryos were selected or rejected by parents for non-medical reasons – for example, intelligence or eye colour. It is very important for governments to understand the different technologies and their uses, in order to legislate fairly.

A classic example of an over-hasty reaction to scientific developments came in April 1994, when the Tory Dame Jill Knight pushed an amendment through the House, which banned the use of eggs or tissue from human foetuses for fertility treatment. Admittedly, the idea of 'babies from the dead' raises a number of ethical concerns, but Dame Jill's argument went thus: 'I want to send a message out to scientists that there is no point in spending any more time on research in that area, or in messing about with aborted mouse eggs, rat eggs or anything similar.' This 'messing about' encompasses the painstaking and costly process of research that gives scientists a better understanding of the causes of birth defects and miscarriage, and unwanted foetal tissue also provides the best material for research into a wide range of blood diseases and some cancers, such as leukaemia. Such research which is threatened by this kind of poorly informed legislation.

The hugely successful BBC 1 children's drama *Pig Heart Boy* dealt with another recent scientific development with its own particular set of pros and cons. Xenotransplantation – the use of animal tissues and organs for transplanting into humans – raises a number of ethical concerns, which have to inform our legal stance on the subject. There is a chronic shortage of available organs and tissues for transplantation, but at this stage, no-one knows the true consequences of, to put it simply, sticking a pig's heart into a human. Scientists have suggested that there might be retroviruses which, although dormant in a pig, would become activated when passed into a human, and that the only way to rule out this possibility is to try the process on humans and then monitor them for the rest of their lives – a tall order, if not an infringement of people's liberty. Before we can allow trials on humans, we have to look at the issues surrounding the procedure. Research should obviously be permitted and encouraged, but the possibility of retroviruses and their implications must be investigated before government permits anything so radical as a human trial. This is another example of the need for informed dialogue between the law-makers and the scientists.

The same principle governs my attitude to genetically modified crops. I represent a largely rural constituency, where many people derive their income from agriculture. The prospect of using science to create higher yields, hardier crops and larger, plumper vegetables is bound to seem attractive, but we need to recognize the high level of public concern about the subject, and we do not yet know enough about the effects of genetically modified foodstuffs to create fair legislation. There is a danger that policy will be dictated either by US commercial pressures or by eco-warriors. A quick response either way is not the answer.

Instead, we need time to research the long-term consequences for human health and the environment. For that reason, I want a temporary moratorium on the commercial growing of all GM crops on British soil, which will not be lifted until research has adequately demonstrated that the consumption of such crops is not dangerous. To allay public fears, we need food manufacturers to be 100 per cent honest about the ingredients going into their foods. This must also cover the ingredients *within* ingredients – for example, GM soya has now regrettably entered the food chain, and, as well as appearing in many products in the form of soya oil, it is also used in feed for many animals, such as chickens, which we then consume. Many food manufacturers are trying to play down concerns over genetic modification. I argue that if these concerns are unfounded, as the manufacturers claim, then they should accept full legal and financial liability for any adverse effects. That way, we would have a truly fair and rounded policy.

Of course, as with e-commerce, we can legislate until we are blue in the face, but it all becomes a mockery when someone can fly anywhere in the world for a few hundred pounds, and goods can be exported thousands of miles in a few days. In Canada, where testing for the sex of an unborn child is illegal, a steady stream of women catch a bus across the border into the States to have the test, and some of them, who don't want girls, then return to Canada and have abortions. In the global village, there is no point in passing legislation on the use of new technologies, if this is not done on a global basis, and there is no point in governments encouraging technological advances if we do not ourselves understand their implications.

Conclusion

I began this chapter by reminiscing about my first computer. I purchased it during my first term as an MP, and it often strikes me how much technology has altered the nature of my job. I hope that I have provided a balanced view of modernity in this chapter – on the one hand celebrating innovation, on the other hand arguing for government to have a clearly defined role when it comes to encouraging and regulating it. Many of the innovations I have mentioned are still only possibilities – perhaps inevitable, but still in the realm of *Tomorrow's World*. That makes it all the more important for politicians to prepare their stance in advance, because the rate of change forces us to learn to think on our feet. When I first became an MP, there was not only no Internet, there was no breakfast television, no televising of Parliament, no twenty-four-hour news channels and no Radio 5 Live. The profusion of instantaneous media makes it almost impossible for politicians to 'take ourselves off' and develop our programmes of action in solitude and quiet. We are often criticized by the media for speaking in soundbites, but this is in reality a consequence of heightened and continual media attention. It seldom means that there are no policies behind the slick wording, but that is exactly what government will be reduced to, if it does not keep abreast of new technology, because it won't be informed enough to make policy. I am proud that I made the effort to decipher the manual to my first computer, and proud that I have persevered, despite the jargon and the bewildering rate of change, in my efforts to understand the implications of technological progress. It means that, in my own small way, I am maintaining my commitment to those I represent, and my wider commitment to freedom and equality. Proud as I am, my efforts will be futile if politics as a whole does not follow suit.

It is vital that politicians do not throw up their hands when faced with technology and the moral issues that it often raises, but it is equally vital that they do not intervene on every occasion. When morality meets politics there is always more heat than light, and as a result, politics too often fails to deliver. Whenever intervention is in question, some hard questions must be asked. Is it necessary to disseminate knowledge about new technologies in businesses? Or is intervention necessary to stimulate innovation? If neither of these can be answered in the affirmative, then government should almost certainly steer clear. In areas of medical technology such as genetics, government needs to ask two simple questions. Is intervention necessary to prevent health risks? Or is intervention necessary to prevent exploitation of science for profit? Again, an affirmative answer to one of these is vital if intervention is to take place. All of that means keeping up with science. This warning, to remain in touch with the times, has been sounded frequently throughout this book.

Chapter Five

FREEDOM TO GOVERN:
THE GREAT DEVOLUTION DEBATE

'Which government is best? That which teaches us to govern ourselves.'

JOHANN WOLFGANG VON GOETHE (attrib.)

Although I was interested in British politics when growing up, Hansard was not exactly my choice of bedtime reading. The bedroom wall featured popstars, not politicians. Some of our other party leaders were politicians from cradle to grave, but not me.

Looking back, I can think of several reasons for this. Partly of course, other things took up my time as a teenager: friends, a passion for the music of David Bowie, TV shows like *The Man from UNCLE* and *Mission Impossible*, parties and even the occasional helping of school work. Politics seemed very distant. There were few young people involved, and those who did care about particular issues were more often members of pressure groups like CND, rather than political parties. More than that, politics seemed physically distant and Westminster-based to a youngster growing up on a croft in the West Highlands. There seemed to be little acknowledgement of, let alone respect for, concerns in parts of Britain beyond Westminster. There was little sense that Scots might have different opinions on some issues to the English, and there was certainly never any acknowledgement from Westminster that a Highlander might think differently from someone from Edinburgh. Politics was uniform, and it was dull. As people often said, it was difficult to tell the difference between Edward Heath and Harold Wilson – they were a Tweedledum and Tweedledee double act, equally weak when it came to controlling the Unions, equally keen to bicker.

While I had a keen interest in current affairs, it focused more upon events outside Britain. I was moved greatly by the 1968 assassinations of Bobby Kennedy and Martin Luther King; later, in 1973, I was passionately interested in the Watergate hearings. However, British politics became interesting to me when Prime Minister Heath and Foreign Secretary Douglas-Home prepared to take us into Europe.

I found the 1975 referendum fascinating, not least because it was an example of leading politicians, from different parties, standing together on an issue. Edward Heath, Roy Jenkins and Jeremy Thorpe made a particular impression; on the other side of the argument, Tony Benn, Peter Shore and Barbara Castle stood out. I began to realize where my instincts and inclinations lay.

That nascent political consciousness was given further encouragement by one of my secondary school teachers, Robert Dick. In my early school years, he established debating as a new, extra-curricular activity. In due course I found myself selected for our school team and we went on to participate in three successive finals of the Scottish Schools Debating Tournament (and never managed to win – a feat achieved at the fourth attempt, by which time I had regrettably moved on to Glasgow University). The tournament was the brainchild of the late Charles Graham, a long-standing and senior political journalist at the old *Scottish Daily Express*. He was an important teacher to me in his own right. His political experiences and insights, so freely given over the years, were an important part of my broader political education.

The fact that the tournament's final was always held in the debating chamber of Glasgow University Union, allied to long-standing family connections with the city, made this the obvious choice for my university education. By the time I went to university, my interest in politics was confirmed, founded in particular upon an enthusiasm for the cut and thrust of debate. Once I was based in Glasgow, the effects of Margaret Thatcher's policies became graphically evident. I saw too how Labour's alternative, founded, so it often seemed, on opposition to success and innovation, offered nothing better. I took part in a trip to Westminster, relished the debates, and resolved that I wanted to be part of all that, to speak on the issues that concerned me, and above all, to make a difference.

The issues close to my heart were very much the products of my background: the status of Scotland, social justice and inequality. My age and background meant that I felt something of an outsider in my early years as an MP, but I recognized that, while the situation was far from ideal, it was my only opportunity to change things. I remembered Harold Wilson's 1966 election victory surprisingly clearly – in particular the famous picture of him as a twelve-year-old on the steps of Number 10 that was regularly trotted out in the press and on TV as indicative of some kind of destiny. Curiously, I was not moved by the image at the time, but when I gave my maiden speech in the House, it helped me to feel less intimidated. Wilson had, on the picture's evidence at least, been just an ordinary child. So had I, and it meant that I had just as much right to be there.

Today, politics looks very different. Crucially, it is more diverse, even at Westminster, where more women and ethnic minorities sit than ever before, on benches that once seemed to belong to middle-aged, public-school-educated white men. It remains intimidating for newcomers, but less so.

There is also diversity beyond Westminster. The greatest political revolution of our times in Britain has been the establishment of the Scottish Parliament, and the assemblies in Northern Ireland and Wales. Having entered the nineties as one of the most centralized states in Europe, we have begun the new century as a country well on the way to giving its excluded nations and regions a clear voice. That voice for all was clearly lacking in politics when I was growing up, and was one of the reasons that politics seemed distant and unattractive. Now, the nations of the United Kingdom can have their say, in a way that I dreamed of upon entering Parliament in 1983, but thought I might never see.

I recall once travelling on a BA 757 shuttle from London to Edinburgh. As we touched down, the stewardess went through the usual litany about staying seated, not lighting cigarettes and flying with BA again. She concluded, 'Welcome to Edinburgh, where the local time is 3 p.m.' Her minor gaffe met with an array of reactions from the passengers. I found it funny. My neighbour, who was travelling on to his home on the Isle of Lewis, found it less so. 'It's already getting dark,' he said, looking out of the tiny cabin window. 'It's not getting dark in Naples, is it?'

Travelling through Edinburgh later that day, I remembered his comments. They seemed particularly poignant as I went past its numerous landmarks: the Castle, the Church of Scotland General Assembly Hall and the Old Royal High School. It was clearly the capital city of a nation with its own history, culture, law and traditions, distinct from those of its neighbours, but the key to genuine nationhood – control of its destiny – was missing. That was back in the eighties, and even if my fellow passenger is still campaigning for an end to Daylight Saving Time, it is clear that a huge measure of self-determination has been returned to Scotland.

Whither Britain?

Scotland may be experiencing a new dawn, but this development poses us, the British, with a problem. One of the concepts that used to bind the nations of the UK together was that of a single sovereign Parliament, based at Westminster. It had a single agenda, with parties which largely represented the whole of the country, and until those parties lost touch with parts of the country, it made people feel that they were part of a nation of 56 million people. Today, the situation is more complex. With a Parliament in Edinburgh, Scots think of themselves as a country, not merely when sports teams run out at Hampden Park or Murrayfield, but also through their politics. The fate of Scotland's schools and hospitals now lies in the hands of Scots. To a lesser extent, the same applies in Wales: with an Assembly in Cardiff, the Welsh now have more responsibility for their own affairs. In Belfast, at Stormont, where once there stood what Viscount Craigavon called 'a Protestant Parliament for a Protestant People', there is the potential for a diverse legislative assembly sharing power throughout Northern Ireland.

It can legitimately be asked, what's left for Britain? Is it possible to be British today? Why do we need the United Kingdom any longer? And what about England? Do the English not deserve their own Parliament? These are tough questions, for the English as much as for anybody.

Highland legend has it that a Spanish visitor met a crofter, and during their carousing, attempted to explain the meaning of the term 'mañana'. 'Surely', the visitor insisted, 'you have an equivalent in Gaelic?' The crofter thought about it long and hard and finally shook his head: 'Nothing expressing quite that degree of urgency.'

By the same token, there is, as far as I am aware, no equivalent in Gaelic, or for that matter in English, to the word Schadenfreude, a useful German expression meaning to take pleasure in the misfortunes of others. But it is not an emotion exclusive to the Germans.

Do I detect a certain Schadenfreude among Scots at the current turmoil being suffered by the English over their national identity? If so, it is given extra savour because that crisis of identity has been provoked, at least in part, by the creation of the Parliament in Scotland and the Assembly in Wales. Suddenly it is Scotland which is forging ahead in a grand constitutional experiment, and England which is contemplating its national navel and asking: 'Who are we ... and why?'

I welcome these changes to the political map of Britain, for they indicate that we are finally recognizing and celebrating diversity, but devolution clearly has serious implications for several areas of policy. In particular, Britain needs much clearer rules for regulating relations between the constituent parts of the Union. Liberal Democrats have long argued for a written constitution for the UK. Now, more than ever before, this is needed urgently, if we are going to cope successfully with the tensions that will inevitably arise from the existence of powerful bodies in Cardiff, Belfast, Edinburgh and London. At present, the government in Westminster is allowed to exert unlimited power, invariably on the basis of a minority of the votes cast in a general election. We need to set limits on what politicians are allowed to do, and those limits need to be set out in the kind of language everyone can understand. In the States, veneration for the US Constitution is such that most schoolchildren can recite it like the Lord's Prayer. This is perhaps a little extreme for British tastes, but a copy of the written constitution should go to every household in Britain, and every schoolchild should be taught what it means. The supposedly wise ruling the supposedly ignorant is not, in my view, any sort of democracy, but it is what we will have to tolerate until there is a written constitution.

It is worth noting that any of the government's far-reaching reforms – such as the creation of the Scottish Parliament, devolution of power to Wales, even the Good Friday Agreement – could be overturned, practically overnight, by a future UK Parliament. Effectively, Parliament can vote itself more powers, without the citizens having a say. This is the 'What Westminster gives, Westminster can take away' syndrome. While it may seem fanciful to imagine that any future House of Commons would vote to dispossess either the Welsh Assembly or the Scottish Parliament of their rightful democratic inheritances, we should always favour the history book over the crystal ball – dispossession is exactly what happened to Stormont. The only way we can protect these reforms, and the rights of the British people, is to establish a written constitution.

At present, devolution is an irregular and unequal process. The Scottish Parliament currently has greater responsibility and power than the Welsh Assembly. It has the ability to alter legislation on issues such as education, health, housing, transport and enterprise. That is why the Scots can consider abolishing tuition fees for universities, while the Welsh assembly has nothing like this level of legislative autonomy. It is not clear yet what New Labour really means by devolution. One is reminded of the line from Orwell's *Animal Farm*, often applied to Communist Russia. In the new Britain, we celebrate diversity. But some are more diverse than others . . .

Supporting diversity is not just a matter of devolving power to Edinburgh, Cardiff and Belfast. It also means taking action through a coherent race relations policy, and providing refuge for genuine asylum seekers. We should be proud of the heritage of our isles, but also that we are an innovative and resourceful people who are not restrained by tradition. The idea of Britain now encompasses the Londoner whose grandparents came to Britain from the Indian sub-continent, and the Welsh man or woman whose family has tended the same farmland for generations. We all feel at different times that we belong to different groups – as someone who feels himself to be a Highlander, a Scot, a Briton and a European, I am more comfortable in the new diverse Britain than I have ever been.

In the new Britain, we will all learn to be comfortable with different identities at different times. When am I a Highlander? Certainly when I am at home, at the foot of Ben Nevis, or with friends and family on New Year's Eve. The same applies in much of my work as an MP. I care fundamentally about the land and people of my constituency, and I will fight their corner whenever I can, but when the teams run out at Murrayfield or Hampden Park, then I know I am a Scot. I have the same feeling on Burns' Night, or St Andrew's Day.

When am I British? I always know that I am British at Prime Minister's Question Time, when I am pushing the government on their health and education policies, or on the issues of tax cuts and pensions, knowing that the problems faced by British people are so often the same across the nation. And when am I European? I might point to golf's Ryder Cup as one example, but more than that, whenever I have visited the European Parliament, and met fellow liberals from other countries, it is abundantly clear that beliefs in liberty, equality and community are shared across the Continent.

A diverse Britain can cope with all of this. There was much wrong with the old Britain. It was the most centralized democratic state in Europe; it assumed that there was little regional diversity within England; and it often left the non-English nations of the Union with a profound sense of being ignored. In the past three years, the sweeping away of that old structure has been truly a sight to behold.

Yet we must not lightly discard the idea of Britain itself. Historically and internationally, ours has been an outstandingly successful and harmonious exercise in political union and cross-country co-operation. There are several compelling reasons for maintaining Britain in its current form. It would be tremendously costly to break up the UK further, not least because of the sheer workload that this would necessitate. We must therefore be certain of the benefits. It is surely self-evident that there are some things we do better with others than we do alone, defence being the most obvious. The British military is not only one of the most effective forces in the world, but it is logical that the four nations of the UK, which share so many security interests, should pool their armed services. Then there are the benefits of a single market, a single currency, education systems that co-operate, a single tax regime, and even combined sports teams where appropriate.

There is something else, less tangible, but no less important. The diversity of the Union gives us many strengths. Centuries of success and innovation have shown the British together to be a resourceful, tolerant and open-minded people, with much to learn from each other, and much to give to the wider world. Michael Ignatieff recently argued that 'there is something intrinsically good about multi-ethnicity', and that this applied to the nations of the UK as much as anywhere else. 'Let us remain together,' he said, 'so that we can continue our argument together.'[1] There are certainly great arguments to be had within our own nations in the United Kingdom, and remaining together can ensure that those arguments are fruitful.

Small is Beautiful: An England of the Regions

Having decided that the Union is a concept worth maintaining, then one question remains unanswered. Because, having dealt with the Celtic mice, the English elephant now poses a considerable problem. It never has before. For many years, people born and brought up in

England used the terms 'England' and 'Britain' interchangeably. They understood the theoretical distinction between the two, but felt it scarcely existed in reality. It always used to amuse and annoy Scots to see how the English used the Union Jack at England-Scotland football matches. At one end of the ground would be the Scots with the saltire, and at the other end would be the English, with the Union Jack – which is just as much a Scottish flag as an English one. Jeremy Paxman, in his recent work *The English*, has pointed out that English fans at rugby matches tend to sing the American spiritual hymn 'Swing Low, Sweet Chariot'. 'Rule Britannia' celebrates the Empire, not England, while 'God Save the Queen' is a homily to our sovereign, not the land of England. The only difficulty we Scots have, on the other hand, is remembering the words to our numerous national songs.

There are some signs that this is changing. The cross of St George has replaced the Union Jack at football matches and many other places too. Once a flag rarely seen beyond Anglican churches and heraldic textbooks, its increased presence is a sign that the English are now more aware of their identity. Up to 50,000 people now buy St George's Day cards, a product only introduced in 1995.

Yet for all the signs of a sluggishly emerging identity, England has no representation as a political entity. There is no English Parliament. MPs from Scotland, Wales and Northern Ireland have an influence over English legislation in a way that is entirely unreciprocated, a phenomenon known as the 'West Lothian question', as it was first posed in the seventies by Tam Dalyell, then MP for that area. He pointed out that, should the Scots get their own Parliament, he would have the right to vote on matters English and Welsh, yet when it came to deciding what happened in West Lothian, his English and Welsh counterparts would have decidedly less power.

It is possible to overstate the problem. No English men or women are suffering the huge sense of injustice that the Scots felt over, for example, Thatcher's legislation of the eighties. In that decade, a majority of Scots had not elected Conservative MPs. Their votes had gone to Labour, Alliance and SNP MPs, but the Conservatives had massive majorities in the UK as a whole. The English MPs alone, with the support of the tiny number of Scottish and Welsh Conservatives, had the power to make laws for Scotland, and they did – the most notorious example being the Poll Tax.

Yet the reverse does not, and cannot, happen. The mathematics of Parliament are such that even if all the Scottish, Welsh and Northern Ireland MPs voted together, they would still need the support of a significant number of English MPs if they were to gain a majority sufficient to pass any legislation affecting England.

That said, there is discontent within England. Many English people have suddenly realized that England has no democratic structure of its own, and that its affairs are dealt with through a British Parliament, in which MPs from outside England sit. Some have argued that a separate English Parliament is the answer to the English question.

This is both an incorrect diagnosis and the wrong prescription. Under the current devolved framework, the Scottish Parliament has more powers than the Welsh Assembly, and they both have different powers from the Northern Ireland Assembly. This means that there are certain areas where Westminster legislates for England alone, but others where it legislates for combinations of England, Wales and Northern Ireland. To tackle this problem we might not need just one extra Parliament, but, conceivably, several, dealing with English, English and Welsh, English/Welsh/Northern Irish, and conceivably English/Northern Irish matters. Would this really make sense to the British people? Would it in any way reflect the identities of communities within the Union? The consequence, surely, would be a proliferation of bureaucracy, inefficient spending and the creation of a huge gulf between government and the governed. Instead of feeling that their identity was enhanced and protected by an English Parliament, it is just as likely that the English people would turn their backs on it altogether.

The second problem is that an English Parliament would do nothing to give voice to the serious regional differences within England. We can view the political map as being something like a water-bed. Apply pressure in one area and you will get a reaction somewhere else. We have devolved power to the Celtic fringe, and in consequence some regions within England are themselves now pressing for greater autonomy.

The regionalists have a strong case, not least because the population of England is vast compared with those of other parts of the Union. A national Parliament within the UK is all very well for the Scots with a population of five million, but will the forty-six million people of England really get a more accountable body than Westminster if an English Parliament is established? Moreover, would the people of Newcastle, Cumbria or Cornwall really feel that an English Parliament was more representative of their specific interests than the current United Kingdom Parliament?

A family friend of Kentish extraction, who did his National Service in 1946, tells me that regional differences within England were then so strong that he found it hard to understand what his Staffordshire bunk-mate was saying. There were fights between the Devonshire and Cornish conscripts, based not on any real causes, but on a centuries-old animosity.

I also remember being struck by regional differences myself at a young age. A curious consequence of growing up in the Highlands was that we often spent our summer holidays in Glasgow. I was especially impressed by seeing escalators and double-decker buses – phenomena completely unfamiliar to someone from my background. Nowadays, no Fort William child would be astonished by his or her first encounter with a double-decker bus – not only because we have them in the town, but also because they are a familiar sight on the ubiquitous TV. Regional differences have been levelled by the global media and business. Slang is more likely to come from MTV and NYPD Blue, than express regional differences. Many towns look the same: high streets dominated by McDonald's, Argos, The Body Shop. We go to similar cinemas, to see the same films. Cheap travel means we can all visit the same places, which our grandparents' generation would never have dreamed possible.

There are nevertheless huge regional disparities within the UK, and they are far from being nebulous issues of dialect or preference for a certain kind of ale. They are about money, and consequently, they are about people's opportunities and quality of life. The North-East, Yorkshire and Humberside have a per capita income 10 per cent less than the national average. Meanwhile London has a per capita income 41 per cent greater than the national average. The taxes taken from Londoners are estimated to provide the rest of the UK with £14 billion a year, but while some very rich people live in Chelsea and Mayfair, London also contains some of the poorest wards in the country, and its transport networks are for ever on the brink of collapse, permanently crying out for investment. Not surprisingly, some London politicians argue that local taxation might be the way forward, so that a greater proportion of the taxes coming from Londoners is spent in and on London. Certainly, many federal countries – like Germany and the USA – allow much more local autonomy over taxes, and they profit greatly from it. It does not, as anti-federalists claim, always result in higher taxation. Many federal countries actually raise less tax than the UK as a percentage of GDP.[2]

The West Lothian question might have troubled Tam Dalyell, but it does not keep many people in Liverpool or Redruth awake at night. Those in the regions of England are not particularly bothered about Scots and Welsh MPs voting on English matters. They are far more concerned about decisions being taken in London by people who seem never to have ventured north of Watford or west of Shepherd's Bush. And they are worried because, in an increasingly sophisticated and competitive Europe, they are seeing their communities lose out.

As the constitutional changes in Northern Ireland, Wales and Scotland take effect, these nations will acquire greater political might. They will be able to lobby hard on the issues that affect them – for instance, the proportion of centrally collected tax revenues they receive. The English regions will have their elected MPs of course, but they will not have strong bodies looking out for their interests in the way the devolved legislatures do.

It is difficult to envisage a future without regional assemblies. This trend is already underway in Europe. Increasingly, English regions are looking across the water, and seeing how they are losing out. Foreign-owned plants can be closed down and relocated with increas-

ing ease – and across the Continent, the regions with their own governments are becoming adept at competing to attract inward investors.
Already, the more powerful regions of Europe are becoming skilled at
lobbying in Brussels to alter the development of policy directly affecting
them. The English regions need support to enter the race with a chance
of winning.

There also is one major financial problem that needs solving – the
way we distribute money throughout the UK via the Barnett Formula.
In essence, the Barnett Formula is an equation used by the government
to work out how much extra money should be given to Scotland,
Wales and Northern Ireland. The amount of money they receive is
calculated in relation to population, not factors such as health and
education needs, and although it takes account of the differences
between London and Glasgow, it doesn't tackle the further variations
between Liverpool and London. We need to ensure that future funding
arrangements respect the regional make-up of England. Clearly, areas
such as the North-East and South-West have varying spending needs,
and we should address that regional disparity through a new formula
that reflects the different requirements of the different parts of the
UK much more effectively. With equality of opportunity for every
citizen, the liberty of individuals will be enhanced. This, in turn, will
invigorate the political process.

Lessons from Europe

In recognizing the needs of our regions, we must not forget that we
are a United Kingdom. In a Union of English, Scots, Northern Irish
and Welsh, the 'English question' is itself misphrased. Surely we should
instead focus far more on a new British question – how do we create
fluid structures which allow new relationships to develop between the
different nations and regions of the Union? Instead of assuming that
cities such as Bristol, Leeds and Newcastle want to look towards
London for their next level of government, we should be much more
imaginative. If you live in Bristol, it is far more easy to reach Cardiff

than London. If you live in Newcastle or Sunderland, your nearest capital city is Edinburgh, not London.

We need, in other words, to rethink the idea of Unionism, so that it is no longer associated with the Conservative Party, or one particular community in Northern Ireland. The New Unionism in Britain should not be about treaties between capitals and crowns, but about establishing practical relations between the regions of England, and the other nations of the UK, in which the North-East works with the Scots, and the South-West works with the Welsh, and both work with Europe as much as with London.

How might this be structured? Firstly, we need to have regional government in England for the regions that want it. As a recent Centre for Reform study showed, several other countries use models that we could learn from.[3] Even though some have relatively inflexible structures, in which each state or region has similar powers, they are often allowed to vary the rates of tax that they levy, giving them a significant degree of autonomy. That allows them to set levels of spending on public services that reflect different attitudes, aspirations and needs in different areas. For example, in rural areas such as Cornwall, poor public transport is causing the break-up of communities, so transport is a key issue there. In densely populated Merseyside, this might be less of a priority, but inner-city initiatives, which provide job training and childcare, might be more important.

The most appropriate system would be one that is as flexible as possible. If we look at the North-East, or the North-West, we can see some fairly distinctive regions which would want significant powers. On the other hand, it is difficult to see the South-East as a distinctive region, and, given its proximity to Westminster, it may feel that it does not need its own level of government. That probably rules out some of the more rigid systems, such as that in Germany, where sixteen states or *Länder* all have the same powers over a range of policies.

There is another model that might well work for Britain: that of Spain. That may sound surprising, as we haven't often drawn political lessons from Spain, but Spain has had experiences of regionalism very similar to our own. Just as Londoners are likely to have less antipathy to a Westminster government than Tynesiders, the Spanish have had to deal with markedly varying attitudes to regionalism in different parts of the country. Their solution has been flexibility. Under the Spanish constitution, the national government retains exclusive control of thirty-two clearly described areas, such as defence, foreign trade, monetary policy and banking, but with the agreement of local government in regions, regional governments can take control of all other areas if they wish. Distinctive regions may take significant control of their own affairs, and they can do so on a timescale that suits them. It's possible to imagine Tyneside, Yorkshire and Merseyside opting for regional government very swiftly, and this would probably spur the regions to the South into joining the scheme, as the benefits became apparent.

Of course, we already have local governments, and we need to establish very clearly how these would interact with regional government, but there is no reason to assume the relationship would be anything other than beneficial. Take the example of Leeds, which is keen to win the status of a world city. To do so it needs to present itself as the capital of an attractive region – attractive in terms of economic resources and thriving business, and in terms of its cultural life and the provision of entertainment. Co-operation between regional and local government is the only method of achieving this. Local government has knowledge and expertise acquired through decades of practice, while regional government will be new to the game. Conversely, we would expect the regional assemblies to have more clout when it comes to dealing with Westminster and effecting change at a national level.

Last year, I visited New York for the first time in many years. I was impressed by the extent to which the leadership of Mayor Giuliani had reinvigorated politics in the city, giving it a new sense of purpose and involvement. New York used to be a filthy city, but the streets were visibly cleaner, thanks to a concerted policy on waste disposal and litter. They were also palpably safer, and no longer emptied after nightfall. There are aspects of his programme that I disagree with, but in many respects modern-day New York provides an example of what regional government can achieve, and how it can reinvigorate a community.

Opponents argue that regional government will simply create a proliferation of bureaucrats. But at present a system exists whereby the various Regional Development Agencies are being advised by Regional Chambers. These Chambers are far from solely composed of politicians – they draw a significant contribution from the voluntary sector, the business community and the Church. There is no reason why these people should not be included within the new regional assemblies, when they are created. Meanwhile, any new regional bureaucracy would lessen the need for bureaucracy at a central level. The result would be increased democracy.

The first steps towards a Britain-of-the-regions came about, curiously, as a consequence of the 1997 Good Friday Agreement, for it created the British–Irish Council, more commonly known as the Council of the Isles. It is a multinational body, including as it does representatives from two nation states: the United Kingdom and the Republic of Ireland, but it is about far more than London–Dublin relations. The UK is represented in all its diversity, with representatives from not only the Westminster government, but also from Cardiff, Belfast, Edinburgh, the Channel Islands and the Isle of Man. Its brief is to promote harmonious relations among all the people of the British Isles.

The British press has largely greeted the Council with a mixture of cynicism and diffidence, but given that the Good Friday Agreement talks about the 'totality of relationships', why couldn't the Council have a key role in the politics of the future, directing the partnerships between the three nations of mainland Britain and the two parts of the island of Ireland?

Currently, it has a limited remit, and acts largely as a talking shop, but it provides an existing structure under which co-operation between the regions could be enhanced. The Council could potentially direct the gradual devolution of England into self-governing regions, and provide a framework within which England could relate to all the other parts of the new Union.

Imagine Cardiff, Dublin and Belfast working together over pollution in the Irish Sea, an important issue given that the Irish government has appealed for the Sellafield nuclear plant to be shut down because of its environmental record, or Belfast and Edinburgh liaising over communications and transport between Scotland and Northern Ireland, regions with strong community links. A powerful North-West assembly would also have a clear interest in both of these issues.

The Council of the Isles would also help to regularize our relations with the Republic of Ireland. The Irish Republic is our closest neighbour in Europe. It is the only country with which we share a land border. There are nearly 5 million people in Britain with at least one Irish parent, who thus qualify themselves for Irish citizenship. An estimated 5 per cent of the Irish population lives in London.[4] For all our historic differences, there is probably no other country in Europe with which we have so much in common. On average, some 24,000 people cross the Irish Sea in one or both directions every day. Given the strong body of shared interests between the UK and the Republic of Ireland, it is logical to suggest that, in time, these numerous civic links could multiply and develop, under the auspices of the Council of the Isles, into a more stable political relationship.

We need a body like this because national identities have never been so diverse and complex. The 1991 census revealed that nearly 20 per cent of the population of Wales, for instance, was born in England, as was nearly 8 per cent of the population of Scotland. Meanwhile, nearly three-quarters of a million Scottish-born people were living in England, and over half a million Welsh-born people. It makes sense, politically, culturally, and in every way, to talk of us having a mutual British–Irish identity, in the same way that the Danes and Swedes share a Scandinavian one.

A working precedent already exists in Europe: the Nordic Council, which represents the common interests of Norway, Sweden, Finland, Denmark and Iceland. Recently, a number of academics and politicians have suggested that the Nordic Council offers a useful model for the way the Council of the Isles could operate. The nations making up the Nordic Council share common historical and political experiences (in their case, Lutheran monarchism and social democratic governments), in the same way that Britain and Ireland have a common heritage. For example in 1721, Finland – along with Estonia and Latvia – was part of the Swedish Empire, and Norway was part of the Danish Empire, while Britain and Ireland were both part of an Anglo-Scottish Hanoverian kingdom.

Our image of Scandinavia may be one of liberal, peaceful Lutherans, but in recent centuries it has been far from stable. The Danes and the Swedes have waged various wars against one another, while in 1809 Sweden gave Finland to Russia, and as a result many Finns took part in the 1905 Revolution. The Norden association was formed in 1918. It was basically a loose citizens' movement which sought to promote co-operation between all the Nordic peoples. After further common experiences in the Second World War, the Nordic Council put things on a more formal basis in 1952. In 1971, they added a Council of Ministers, with their own budget.

Far from being a symbolic talking shop, the Nordic Council has made substantial contributions to the stability of the region. It has successfully resolved the dispute over the Åland Islands, whose inhabitants are Swedish-speaking, but belong to an autonomous region of Finland. It has also helped to mediate in the conflict between Denmark and Norway over Greenland, and negotiated an equal share of oil resources in the region. Rather than being another bureaucrats' gravytrain, the Nordic Council is extremely streamlined. It has a workforce of eighty people and costs £60 million a year, which in governmental terms is extraordinarily cheap, particularly when you consider the potential cost of severed relations.

Whether or not the Nordic Council eventually acts as the template which enables the Council of the Isles to live up to its promise, one fact has to be faced. Not all of our relationships with Europe have to go through Westminster anymore. Many argue that the discrepant sizes of the EU member states is what currently prevents them from working as an effective federation. If Europe is to work effectively, it will do so as a Europe in which regional diversity is given greater recognition. In other words, it will be a Europe of regions more than one of nations.

Several years ago, I spent a stimulating Monday afternoon in the Bonn office of Chancellor Helmut Kohl, along with Sir Russell Johnston, MP, in his capacity as a UK Liberal member of the Council of Europe, and Graham Watson, MEP. Helmut's company was fun (more than one bottle of wine was consumed) and his working environment fascinating, dotted with fish tanks, various rock collections and many pictures. He waxed lyrical about how Europe had to develop along federal lines, by which he meant with more localized structures and direct lines of communication between the regions of Europe and Brussels. His view was a million miles away from the warped image peddled incessantly by Euro-hostile sections of the British media.

Two of his pictures caught my attention. One was of Adenauer, the other of Mitterand – and personally inscribed to 'Mon Ami, Helmut'. As we were leaving, I could not resist asking why he had no picture of Margaret Thatcher. The Chancellor practically doubled up with laughter – not an insignificant reaction for a man of his dimensions. It was a reaction that also spoke volumes about the regrettable gulf between Britain and Europe.

For many European countries, becoming a federation of regions is a natural step. The Germans, with their strong regional bodies, have no problem with this, and nor do the Spanish. Throughout their history, different parts of their countries have related to other parts of Europe in different ways. The same can also be said of Britain, but all too often we do not appreciate this sufficiently.

What we *do* recognize, increasingly often and with mounting gloom, is that English identity is in crisis, and not just over which flags to wave and which songs to sing at football matches. It is also about a reappraisal of England's colonial past, which has made many English people ashamed of their forefathers' strident nationalism. That embarrassment may be justified, but it nevertheless has a damaging effect on English self-esteem. That said, the English are becoming morose without reason. We are increasingly learning from Europe that strong regional identities are refreshing and sustaining the economic, social and cultural life of their nations. As a recent research paper from the think tank *Catalyst* argues, Britain, with its patchwork character, could be in a uniquely strong position in this regionalized Europe of the future.[5]

Pride in being English can return, if regional pride is accompanied by political clout. As Jeremy Paxman puts it in *The English*, this renewed sense of pride is 'less likely to be based on flags and anthems' and more likely to be 'concerned with cities and regions . . . in an age of decaying nation states, it might be the nationalism of the future'.

This returns me to my concept of democracy, and the fact that we cannot truly claim to live in one when so many of our citizens feel that their opinions and actions are of no consequence. If people feel that their vote counts, then they have a stake in their society. A regionalized England is the only way this can come about. If power is kept close to the area upon which it is being used, the result is a more efficient use of that power. Things get changed, and people start to see how their region is improving, feel that they are responsible in part, and as a result have a renewed sense of local and civic pride. This is the future for national identity.

So what of Englishness if this came about? Scaremongers argue that some centuries-old tradition would be destroyed, but this need not be the case. There is nothing to mourn, precisely because England has always been an association of diverse kingdoms. The Romans created the notion of a single England, because it was administratively simpler, but the regions have always had their own relationships to each other and the rest of Europe. People in the North-West of England have the strongest cultural ties to northern Wales and Northern and Southern Ireland. East Anglia, on the other hand, has a long tradition of exchanging goods and people with the Low Countries. Before the Isle of Man became a self-governing dominion of the English crown, it was ruled first by Norway and then Scotland. Berwick-on-Tweed belonged to Scotland until the seventeenth century. (Its local football team still plays in the Scottish league!) Much of the centralizing of power around London, and the emergence of the South-East as England's richest and most powerful region, began with the Tudors, themselves a Welsh dynasty.

If we go back even further, we see that the Angles and Saxons were from the region currently covered by Germany. They were invited here, and given land, by the Celtic king Vortigern, because he was worried about the intrusive raids by the Picts. There are thousands of similar examples, but the message remains the same. Regional England is not a new or unfamiliar concept. It is very much a feature of our shared British national history.

There have always been common interests and co-operation between all the constituent parts of the UK and Europe, and this should obviously remain in place. We may be an island race, but Britain has always been a country at the heart of Europe.

Consider one of the most evocative moments in modern British history. The summer of 1940: the Battle of Britain. In many ways it was, as Churchill said, our 'finest hour': Britain standing alone against a European foe, when the rest of the Continent had collapsed. Only twenty-odd miles of sea stood between Kent and the all-conquering Wehrmacht, and only the Royal Air Force prevented that same army from crossing the Channel and inflicting on Britain the same damage suffered by France and the Low Countries. But the story is not quite so simple. Who fought the Battle of Britain? British pilots in the majority, but also Poles, Czechs, Norwegians and others, men fleeing from occupied nations, who found a common bond with the British. One hundred and forty-five Polish pilots fought in the Battle of Britain, barely 1 per cent of the total, but they accounted for 7.5 per cent of all German aircraft destroyed. We must never detract from the sacrifice made by the British during the Battle of Britain, but we might also recognize the role played by other Europeans. Much earlier, an estimated two-thirds of the Duke of Wellington's winning army at the Battle of Waterloo was composed of Germans and Netherlanders.

Of course, co-operation with mainland Europe is mercifully not restricted to warfare. In numerous areas, across the centuries, the cultural, economic and political life of Britain has been shaped by developments on the Continent. Many of our political and legal institutions were introduced by the Norman conquerors. The Queen is the Supreme Governor of the Church of England partly as a consequence of the Reformation, a movement that began in Germany, and we should not forget that, in spite of being an enduring symbol of Britain, the royal family is one of the most cosmopolitan in Europe, linked to the ruling houses of Russia, the Netherlands, Denmark and Greece. It was only in 1917 that George V changed his family's name from Sachsen-Coburg und Gotha to the more pronounceable and very English Windsor. Before the fifties, when Britain opened its doors to citizens of its former dominions, the vast majority of its immigrants were from Europe. Huguenots from France (who had a sizeable community in Soho), weavers from the Low Countries and Jews from Central and Eastern Europe all brought words to the language and enriched our culture. It might even be argued that we entered the race for empire quite late, spurred on by the huge advances made by Spain and Portugal in the fifteenth and sixteenth centuries. The father of liberal thought, John Stuart Mill, did not create his theories in isolation – a continuous line stretches from him right back to the German philosopher Kant and further, to the French Revolution and its declaration of the rights of man.

Politically, culturally and in every sense, Britain is a federation of associated regions, and at the same time is tied inextricably to Europe. The first steps towards devolution have been made, but a long journey still lies ahead before the regions of England have autonomy on an equal footing with Wales, Scotland and Northern Ireland. If the process is not speeded up, England risks isolation from Europe, and Westminster governments risk increasing isolation from their voters.

Power to the People

Recent decades have seen a worrying reduction in the number of people who turn out to vote in elections, as well as in the membership of political parties. The anti-devolutionist camp argues that giving power to the regions will only increase voter apathy, but the contrary is more likely to be the case. People are uninterested in politics precisely because they cannot see how their opinion counts. If their region was given direct control over public spending and public policy, then they would see the immediate effects of turning out to vote, of joining parties and of campaigning to make a difference. I return again to my notion that the Britain of 2000 is not a complete democracy. In a sense, we live in a democracy because everyone has the *right* to vote, but in another sense, we will not really be living in a democracy until everyone is made to feel that their votes and their actions count. Giving power to the English regions is an important way of achieving this. It is the principle of subsidiarity, which formed a key part of the Maastricht Treaty: that decisions should always be taken at the most appropriate level of government. Nothing should be done in the capital that could be done better by the parish council.

In the early nineties, the issue of local government reform loomed large within my own constituency. This now has one of the largest single local authorities in Europe. Understandably, at the time there was a strong body of opinion in favour of establishing two authorities rather than a single, monolithic structure. Allan Stewart, who was then the Minister responsible for local government in Scotland, received an unprecedented amount of lobbying, by phone, fax, mail and personal address, and thought it very telling that, whether people were for the two-council option or against, they divided into two clear camps. Those involved in government phrased their arguments solely in terms of structure, spending arrangements and funding, while the 'real' people phrased theirs in terms of the amenities and resources of different communities. 'If we were split off from X, we wouldn't be able to use the library, swimming pool, buses, etc.' For Alan and myself, it provided a very clear example of the way people, as opposed to politicians, see issues and identify with concerns.

This is one reason why I support the concept of elected mayors. Currently, party opinion is divided over the issue but, following on from London, the die is surely cast. There are strong arguments in favour of pursuing such a policy.

First, as Liberal Democrats, we should be enthused by the evidence that voters relate as much, if not more so, to individuals as they do to institutionalized political parties. We should let our politics be free-ranging, rather than over-formalized. This is particularly relevant at the city and municipal level, where the issues at stake tend to be far more practical than ideological. An elected mayor has to carry the can: the voters have a figure with whom they can identify, for better or for worse. Just talk to a typical New Yorker or Parisian about issues relevant to their city: within minutes you will be well aware of their opinion of their city's administration in general and of the mayor in particular. That voter feels positively engaged in the political process, and exhibits a sense of ownership where the activities of the elected civic head are concerned. I believe that what works in New York, Paris and will soon be seen to work in London, makes sense for many of our great British cities.

Other, related, considerations are highly persuasive in favour of elected mayors. Greater political regionalism within England will be given added impetus by the emergence of high-profile, credible political personalities at a city level, as elected mayors will help to sharpen the focus of regional identity. Liberal Democrats should favour such new political structures which set up alternative sources of attention and power to the present Westminster-centric model.

Again, history teaches what the crystal ball cannot. I am endlessly impressed, on visits to cities such as Birmingham, Manchester, Liverpool and Newcastle, by the splendour of their Victorian municipal trappings. Walk around their city halls and breathe in deep the vision and determination of the regional grandees who championed the Empire and contributed so much to a sense of civic pride and dignity. When Michael Dobbs' entertaining novel *House of Cards* was filmed for television, Manchester City Hall was used as a double for the interiors of Westminster. The grandiose settings reflect the importance with which the city fathers viewed themselves and their legislature, and how they were viewed by others. It is that sense of civic commitment that we need desperately to invigorate today.

A much-missed personal mentor, the late Mark Bonham Carter, argued with characteristic perceptiveness at a party conference several years ago that the denuding of civic Britain under the Conservatives was tantamount to philistinism. The picture has scarcely improved under Labour. Local government and regional politics are still viewed from the Westminster vantage point, and Whitehall, too often, is the opponent, aggressor and obstacle. Britain is crying out for a profound change in its political culture, and the Liberal Democrats must be at the vanguard.

Power to the Polling Booth

Voter disengagement cannot be reversed solely through the devolution of greater power to the regions and by empowering local government. It would be foolish to believe otherwise, particularly as there is such widespread disaffection with the political process. If we are to make people feel that their vote matters, whether at the local, regional or national level, there has to be as much of a revolution in the way we actually vote. For that reason, electoral reform must be a part of any programme of devolution. The current first-past-the-post system is unwieldy and undemocratic. It means that only one MP is elected per constituency, so all the voters who did not vote for him or her are left unsatisfied. In 1997, 14.7 million voters cast 'wasted' votes – that is, 42.8 per cent of those who voted. A high proportion of those voters are the same people every time – for instance, Conservative voters in County Durham, or Labour voters in Surrey. It is not difficult to see why the turn-out figures for British elections are so low.

First past the post results in a lack of choice for voters. Candidates are selected by a small number of party members, and voters can only choose between parties. If the candidate selected for your party has views with which you disagree, you are left with no alternative choice within that party. It also leads to unequal representation. In 1997, the average number of votes per MP elected was 32,376 for Labour candidates, but 113,826 for Liberal Democrats. Labour won 43.3 per cent of the total vote, but this equated to 65.2 per cent of the seats in Parliament. They thus had the power to form a government, even though eleven out of every twenty British voters actually voted against them. It does not take a genius to see that such a system does not truly give power to the voters.

There is an added, in-built danger. To govern is to choose, but to govern upon too limited an electoral basis is to invite the wrong choices. The most graphic example of this danger has to be the Poll Tax. The genesis of the Poll Tax came about with a revaluation of Scottish domestic rates in the early eighties. This created uproar in the genteel ranks of the Scottish Tories, as it increased the tax burden on the wealthy, culminating in the announcement by George Younger (then Scottish Secretary of State) that there would be a fundamental review of domestic rates and that – in words that were to assume fateful dimensions – 'the status quo is not an option'.

The rest, as they say, is history. Tweed-clad Scottish Tories were more than satisfied with the resultant Poll Tax, although very few others were. Public policy had been based on the desires of a very limited section of the electorate, and pandered to the instincts and prejudices of rank-and-file activists instead of meeting the needs of the population as a whole. We have to draw lessons from this. The more narrowly defined the appeal, the more pernicious the policy output. This could be seen again in 2000, in the Tory pitch over asylum seekers in the run-up to the local elections. It was focused to satisfy a target audience, and at the same time furthered prejudice and intolerance.

This rigid electoral system – and its destructive consequences – is a major cause of public disaffection with the political process. How can people feel that their vote makes a difference, or that their interests are being faithfully represented, when the voting system is so clearly flawed and fraudulent?

A major step forward would be the instigation of a system of fair votes. One of the best is the Single Transferable Vote system (STV), which is already used in the Republic of Ireland, the Australian Senate and in electing the Northern Ireland Assembly. STV is a truly democratic voting system because it focuses power solely in the hands of the voters. Each constituency elects between three and five MPs, depending upon its size. Voters rank the candidates, putting a one by their favourite, a two by their second choice, and so on. If the voter's first choice candidate does not need their vote – either because he or she has enough votes to be elected without it, or because they have too few votes for it to make a difference, then the 'power' of the vote is transferred to the second choice candidate.

Under this system, no vote is wasted – all those cast go towards electing someone. It also allows for increased choice, beyond the traditional party boundaries. People can put a Labour candidate at number 1, a Conservative at number 2, and so on. Figures indicate that people already engage in this supermarket style of voting: they will vote Labour in General Elections, Liberal Democrat in local elections, Green for the European Parliament, for example. So people are already accustomed to viewing their vote in terms of 'the best person for the job', rather than an expression of loyalty to a single party. STV simply extends that practice to the way we create our own Parliament.

People argue that this system would disrupt the link between MPs and their constituencies. In actual fact, STV would increase the accountability of MPs to their constituents, since they share power with between two and four others and thus cannot rely on having a safe seat. Where people are able to cast votes on the basis of individual merit, MPs will have to work hard to maintain the loyalty of their constituents, and as a result will take pains to represent their interests in Parliament.

It is also argued – somewhat patronizingly – that the ballot papers would be too complicated for people to understand, but the first Northern Ireland assembly election in 1973 used the STV system, and there was a 70 per cent turn out, apparently not discouraged by the 'complexity' of the ballot paper.

With such a system in place, faith can return to the ballot box. At the same time, the process of devolution will give people the power to effect change over their immediate localities. The result will be a dynamic and democratic society, as closely in touch with its own government as it is with its neighbours in Europe.

Conclusion

The recent changes that we have seen in Britain, with new devolved political structures, particularly those involving more proportional voting systems, have resulted in increased choice for voters. Politics is an expanding buyers' market – more choices to make and more votes to cast. With several tiers of representation, voters now have the experience of casting more than one vote. Human nature being what it is, and with the public displaying a healthy disregard for the advice issued by the various parties, there is clear evidence that many people use their votes in different ways.

Thus, in the Scottish Parliamentary election, there were obviously many voters who cast their first constituency ballot for Labour, but who then went on to cast their second (regional list) ballot for another party. It looks as if the same phenomenon featured in the elections for London Mayor. More thoughtful voting is more sophisticated voting, and social changes coupled to political reforms means that fewer and fewer people are now voting on purely tribal lines. Such an approach should be encouraged.

In making this case, it is worth a moment's pause to look in the mirror. Would I, as the party leader, unswervingly vote Liberal Democrat? In a national context the answer would obviously be yes. Yet, when I look at the many good people who can be found among the ranks of the other political parties, I have to question this instinctive response.

If, in days gone by, I had been forced to cast my vote for an SNP candidate, then that person would have been the late Donald Stewart, MP for the Western Isles from 1970–87. Donald was a stalwart defender and promoter of his native Isles, as well as one of life's genuine gentlemen. We disagreed on just about everything, from the return of capital punishment, through Britain's destiny in Europe, to the matter of nationalism itself. But he was, correctly and with complete personal integrity, a valued and respected community representative.

I am prone to soft spots, and Donald evoked many. Anyone who can advise me, as Donald did, over a dram, after a debate on the Channel Tunnel (in which we had, needless to say, advanced diametrically opposing viewpoints) that it would all turn out to be a 'great waterlogged Concorde, lying at the bottom of the sea', has to be worth a vote. Similarly impressive was his comment to Scottish Tory landowning MPs that, where he came from, poaching was not so much a criminal activity, more a 'moral obligation'.

If forced to vote Labour, my cross would hover between the names of Tam Dalyell and Austin Mitchell. I would support the former on the basis of sheer professional respect, and the latter on similar grounds, with the additional impetus of a strong personal friendship. Without individuals of this calibre, Parliament would be a much poorer place.

Could I vote Conservative? Admittedly, that would be a high hurdle to jump, but on grounds of pro-European principle alone, I would cast my vote with Sir Edward Heath. I hope that I am not untypical (even if it is a little unusual for a party leader) in giving voice to the above thoughts. One of the most encouraging results from the Scottish Parliament was the triumph of Dennis Canavan as an independent candidate in Falkirk West. Such successes demonstrate the readiness of voters to disregard self-interested political directives from the top, and make up their own minds. As Roy Jenkins argued in his seminal Dimbleby lecture of 1979, the voters can tell 'a hawk from a handsaw'. So it must remain.

Increased voter flexibility is especially encouraging for a less class-based party such as my own. Traditionally, as our support is rather evenly spread across geography, gender, generations and social strata alike, we have tended to suffer as a result of having insufficient concentrations of voters. Hence the potency of the 'wasted vote' jibe. Now, however, the contours of British politics are shifting, revealing new faultlines. The new landscape offers our party, always so good at coming second, the serious prospect of coming first in many more contests.

Chapter Six

FREEDOM WITHOUT BORDERS:
BRITAIN, EUROPE AND THE
CHALLENGE OF GLOBALIZATION

'My country is the world, and my religion is to do good.'
THOMAS PAINE, *The Rights of Man*, Part II, 1792

At London's Tower Hill stands a monument to members of the Merchant Navy and fishing fleets killed during the Second World War. For the families and friends of those named on the memorial it is, of course, unique, yet in one sense, it is unremarkable. Every town and village throughout the United Kingdom has such a memorial listing those killed in the two world wars. Many British towns and villages also include the dead of other wars and conflicts, from the Boer War to the streets of Belfast.

The Tower Hill monument is very important for me personally. One of the 24,000 men named is Charles MacEachen, a Merchant Navy steward. I never met him. He was killed in 1943, aged just twenty-one, sixteen years before I was born, but he was always a presence in my family as I grew up because he was my mother's brother, and I was named after him. His death greatly affected my mother – to this day she recalls the expression on my grandmother's face when the fateful telegram arrived. Charles was, by all accounts, a vivacious, fun-loving prankster, and my mother has often told me how sad it is that I have missed out on having him as an uncle.

There is scarcely a family in Britain which has not experienced losing a relative in war. Even so, in today's era of peace, it is difficult to imagine the extent to which wars dominated life for much of the last century. Anybody who grew up during the Cold War, as I did, will remember the very real fear of nuclear annihilation with only four minutes' warning, which threatened the Scottish Highlands as much as Britain's large cities. The thought of all those public information films listing what to do in the event of a nuclear attack still fills me with foreboding. As does the rather off-hand advice by successive governments to shove the settee up against the door as protection against nuclear fallout.

Despite the threat of nuclear holocaust, my generation is the first in my family not to face the prospect of going off to war. Previous generations did so because of problems well beyond our own shores. My grandfather served as a sergeant in the Lovat Scouts, and ended up fighting in the Dardanelles, directly because of a shot fired at an archduke in Sarajevo. My parents' generation went to war because an Austrian jailed in Bavaria wrote a book about his ambitions for conquest in eastern Europe, and then gained the power to pursue his wild schemes. Throughout the last century, British people went to fight in Flanders and beyond because, in Neville Chamberlain's infamous words of September 1938, 'of a quarrel in a faraway country, between people of whom we know nothing'.

What is Globalization?

What Chamberlain never understood, and what people such as Winston Churchill knew, was that faraway countries do matter. We may know nothing of their people, yet those people still have the power to affect our lives profoundly. It has been so throughout the twentieth century, and it is even more so today. We even have a name for that trend – globalization – a word used to describe a series of processes that affect the life of the nation: its economy, culture and security.

In essence, globalization means the death of distance (a very benign bereavement). With the development of technology, especially that of the microchip, many traded goods became higher value, lighter and less commodity- and energy-intensive to produce. As a result, it does not cost so much to transport goods from the producer to the person buying them, more goods are traded and markets thus come closer together. In addition, more services can be traded, as cheap air travel allows for the frequent movement of skilled individuals. Architecture, civil engineering, education, medicine, entertainment and tourism are now increasingly shared services. The number of Australians and New Zealanders practising as nurses, dentists and vets in Britain is a classic example of this trend. (The Liberal Democrats have themselves benefited enormously from the expertise of migrating Kiwis like Neil Stockley, formerly Director of Policy, and Des Wilson, who ran the 1992 election campaign.) Due to the communications revolution, financial markets are also increasingly linked: an event on one side of the world has an immediate impact far beyond its national boundaries or even those of its neighbours. Most of these developments increase choice and opportunity for the British people.

Liberals, social democrats and now the Liberal Democrats, have been welcoming this trend for decades. We have looked forward to a day when nations would co-operate rather than retreat behind their own borders, behaving without regard for others. W. E. Gladstone was one of the nineteenth century's foremost advocates of international law. Out of that cause emerged the movements which argued for a League of Nations, a United Nations and a World Trade Organization.

Liberals recognized the implications of globalization long before most. They had another word for it: 'interdependence'. The Liberal Party's founding statement declared that international policy should be based upon 'a recognition of the interdependence of all the world's peoples'. That was written long before globalization became a buzzword. Walter Layton, the great Liberal intellectual and newspaperman, was one of the first people to develop the idea. As editor of the *Economist* in the 1920s, he wrote much about the growing interdependence of the world's economy, culture and politics. Layton was just part of the intellectual ferment which affected progressive thought throughout the twenties and thirties. As a result of this change in ideas, the end of the war saw a growing consensus in favour not only of bodies such as the UN, but also of global economic bodies and rules.

What is Wrong with the UN?

The UN is a global body created to maintain peace – one of the greatest missions of humanity, but it has not lived up to the ideals of its founders. Put simply, it doesn't work. One major problem is the instability of an institution which depends upon a resentful USA for 25 per cent of its revenues, which the Republican Congress resists paying. There is also the wider problem that the false idol of national sovereignty allows individual nations to veto UN action: powerful nations on the UN Security Council can prevent UN action by exercising their right of veto. That means that there can be agreement throughout the Security Council, with a massive majority, but the UN can take no action because just one country dissents. Often, that means China or Russia dissenting to protect an ally, as we saw in the way Russia behaved in the early stages of war in the former Yugoslavia.

There is only one good reason for this right of veto. It would clearly be wrong if a country profoundly disagreed with a course of action, yet still found its forces committed to a UN operation. British soldiers should never be forced to fight if the British Parliament disagrees with a particular military excursion. That, however, can be prevented by saying that while any country has a veto over the use of its forces, it cannot prevent a UN operation from taking place. The UN should become a body able to take majority decisions, one in which tyrants cannot act secure in the knowledge that one of their dubious allies will support them in the Security Council and prevent any necessary action. Nations who agree with the UN's decision could then commit their forces to the operation; those who do not, could absent themselves. That way we could have a United Nations which fulfils the dream of its founders.

Once reformed, the UN would be able to take on roles that it has so far been unable to fulfil. In particular, it must become capable of intervening in the affairs of countries which are seriously violating the human rights of their people. That was the role carried out by NATO in Kosovo, but it is a task that should be carried out by the UN on a global scale. Then we can tackle savagery not only in Europe, where countries are willing to challenge it, but in other parts of the world too. As NATO ensured justice in Kosovo, the UN might have done so in Rwanda, in the face of the West's reluctance to use troops where its direct interests are seemingly not threatened.

At present, the UN is simply not equipped to promote global security. Britain must argue for urgent reform so that this goal can be achieved, not least because British interests are directly affected by what happens in other countries, as a consequence of globalization. A butterfly flapping its wings in China may not cause dole queues here, but wars, civil unrest and natural disasters elsewhere do have a negative effect on British business and thus on the life of our nation. A recent trip to India taught me that, after the USA, Britain is the largest single investor in Indian businesses. Our large and successful British Asian community also provides an important link between the two economies. Turning a blind eye to the tense relations between India and Pakistan cannot be an option: supporting the UN is as much a matter of safeguarding national interests as one of international ethics.

We must change the legislation on the right of veto, so that the UN can do its job without members exploiting the right for their own political ends. As Paddy Ashdown has pointed out, Britain and France are uniquely well placed to spearhead these reforms, as they are the two permanent European members of the security council, with similar defence interests. The efficiency of the UN would also be greatly improved by the establishment of a military staff college to train UN forces in the duties of peace keeping. Britain has considerable expertise in this subject, and for that reason, the college should be based here.

At present, none of this is possible because of the UN's desperate financial condition. Members pay a direct grant to the UN, but there is no provision for taking action against a recalcitrant payer, as when the USA refused to pay its share for several years. Paddy Ashdown has suggested funding it differently – through a Tobin levy on all foreign exchange transfers. The Tobin levy, so named because it was suggested in 1978 by James Tobin, economist and Nobel Prize winner, would involve a small levy, of around 0.01 per cent, being implemented by major countries on all foreign-exchange transactions. Aside from providing financial resources, such a tax would throw some sand in the wheels of currency speculation. Such speculation thrives when markets are highly unstable, as they were in South-East Asia in 1997. This instability leads to investors panicking and pulling out of countries entirely. Some US$1.5 trillion are traded every day and only 5 per cent of this is anything to do with country-to-country trade. Ninety-five per cent of this figure is speculation – money effectively being bet on whether interest rates or currency values will change. A tax would diminish the degree of profit that speculators could expect and, by decreasing the amount of speculation, promote economic stability.

The Canadian Parliament and the Finnish government have already endorsed the Tobin levy. It is now time for Britain to do the same. Although the national governments levying the tax could keep the money they raise, there is a profound logic to the idea of using it to fund the UN: an international activity which is often a problem is taxed, and the revenue given to an international problem-solving body. The UN's current annual budget stands at US$2.536 billion. A Tobin tax on currency speculation could raise US$150 million more than this, and with such a cash injection, we would have a chance to create a body with real political and practical clout.

Why Britain Needs the EU

It is not only the UN that offers opportunities for international co-operation. British people are finding increasingly that they have the most shared interests with their European neighbours. Indeed, Britain is a European country, whose history has been inextricably tied up with that of its Continental neighbours. It is impossible to understand, for example, the historical relationship between Scotland and England without bringing in France, Norway, Spain and the Netherlands, and today, British people, in particular the business community, accept that by working with their neighbours, they all benefit. But politicians on both the Left and the Right are still not being honest. Britain is insufficiently engaged within Europe, thanks to a mixture of vague conditional promises on one side, and xenophobia on the other.

If Britain does not take a lead soon and become enthusiastic about involvement in the rest of Europe, we will inevitably repeat the mistakes of the past. There were real opportunities for Britain to take a lead in Europe in the late forties and fifties. Winston Churchill was one of the first to highlight the potential benefits of unity in Europe, when he spoke at a Congress of Federalist groups in The Hague in 1948 on the need for 'progressively effacing frontiers and barriers' in Europe. Soon after this, he became one of the first British politicians to back the idea of a European assembly, but Labour, in power at the time, rejected the idea. The Conservative Party, governing from 1951 to 1964, was little better. Instead of recognizing that moves such as the Schuman Plan of 1950 (which involved Franco-German control of their respective coal and steel industries) were major steps forward in reducing conflict on the Continent, Britain stood by and wanted no part. The biggest mistake made was to miss the boat on the Treaty of Rome, signed in 1957, which heralded the formation of the Common Market – the predecessor of the European Union. We refused to join the other six member states seeking greater harmonization of European economies because we maintained the groundless belief that full involvement in Europe would damage Anglo-American relations. I am always struck by the comment made by the former US Ambassador to Britain, Raymond Seitz: 'If Britain's voice is less influential in Paris or Bonn, it is likely to be less influential in Washington.'

Having seen the Common Market work, we then had to search round for another European game to play, and helped to launch the ill-fated European Free Trade Association, with Sweden, Norway,

Denmark, Austria and Switzerland. It had few teeth, and could do nothing to challenge the fact that British trade with the Common Market was growing steadily. It became inevitable that Britain would seek to join – a move which resulted in rejection in 1963. It took another two applications for Britain to join ten years later. A clear pattern emerged, which we are in danger of repeating in the decision on whether or not we join the euro. When any move forwards looks likely to happen in the rest of Europe, we tend to say that it won't happen. When it happens, we say it won't work. When it works, we say we don't need to be part of it. Then, finally, we realize that we have to be part of it, and enter on terms that are far worse than if we had joined earlier – with the result that right up until the nineties the image of Britain in Europe was one of an apparently reluctant Harold Wilson always seeking re-negotiations, or a handbag-swinging Margaret Thatcher demanding our money back. We lost out in 1957, lost out subsequently, and we must not repeat such mistakes again.

The whole of Britain's post-war political history has been dominated by the question of our relationship with Europe. With the curious exceptions of Eden, Home and Callaghan, the career of every post-war British Prime Minister has been dominated by the European question, and to a large extent history judges their worth as leaders on how well they have handled that single issue. The verdict is not favourable. They began by saying that European Union would never happen. Then as ever, they refused to believe it would work and, when it did, they still refused to take part. When they finally joined, they were surprised to find that it was not working in their favour. It is sad to reflect on the fact that for at least the last twenty years there has been scant attempt by those politicians in power to persuade British voters that European co-operation is in the country's national interest.

Such procrastination and resentment must not be allowed to dominate the European debate in the twenty-first century. Europe is a positive development because, in the age of globalization, nations can only regain control of their destinies if they share sovereignty and work together. The idea of Britain achieving anything in 'splendid isolation' is profoundly outdated.

It is also riven with errors because, as the average secondary school student will be able to tell you, the history of Britain is one of a continual influx and outpouring of different peoples. Danes, Celts, Jutes, Saxons, Romans, Jews, Huguenots, Indians and Africans have, over the centuries, all contributed to the life of our country. To refer to Britain as a community with a tightly bound socio-cultural identity which is separate and distinct from that of its neighbours, is to conjure up an image of a Britain that does not and has never existed.

My Scottish background makes it comparatively easy for me to see myself as a European. Scotland not only has a long tradition of close relations with the Continent (sometimes, in the case of the Auld Alliance with France, to England's chagrin!), but Scots are comfortable with the concept of layered nationality.

The same is true in Continental Europe. In the border towns between Holland and Belgium, people speak very similar languages and have the same religions – they are used to crossing the border to go to work, or just to do the shopping. But woe betide you if you should accuse a Flemish-speaker of being a French-speaker, or vice versa. The sense of national identity in both these countries is very strong, and it is not diminished by close relations with their neighbours. To borrow a phrase from a certain lady: 'Are the Germans any less German for being in the Community, or the French any less French? Of course they are not.' (Margaret Thatcher, 1975)

People in Holland and Belgium still remember the last war as a time of great hardship and loss, and that strengthens their resolve to co-operate. We would do well to remember the reasons that the EU was founded. Why has my generation not gone to war with Germany, as the two previous generations had to? It is because of the European Union. At the end of the Second World War, people in all major European nations realized that when the economic interests of countries are tied together, the prospect of war fades away.

We cannot risk jeopardizing European stability. Events in the Balkans have shown how rapidly things can change, and how rapidly old wounds can reopen. We must take the pro-European case to the country whenever we can, in order to prove some of the basic arguments, and debate with the Eurosceptics to highlight the weaknesses in their case. A key example is the case for British membership of the European single currency – the euro. We have much to gain from membership of the euro, and British politicians must give the people the debate they deserve.

In June 1999 I participated in a debate in central London, with that well-known Eurosceptic, John Redwood, on the motion 'This house believes that Britain should join the euro and abolish the pound.' There were some signs of hope: a contributor from the floor put the view that Britain's distinctive history and character, and the strength of its traditions, meant that it has nothing to fear from involvement in the EU. We are strong enough to resist being swamped, and strong enough to make a real difference. Far from meaning that it is not necessary for us to be part of the EU, our uniqueness makes it all the more possible to benefit from it.

Another contribution from the floor gave me a clear sign of the mountain that those of us in the pro-European camp have to climb. A speaker rose and proclaimed that he had been born in Swansea in October 1939, while German bombers tried to obliterate the city. He went on to say that we had won the war, and secured our freedoms, and that we had no right to deny historic British liberties to future generations by joining the euro. Had I been unkind, I might have commented that there were no German bombers over Britain in October 1939 – it was the period of the phoney war. But I was more struck by how well this summed up the anti-European case.

The anti-European case is not at all sophisticated. The sceptics try to argue that they are not anti-European, only anti-euro. In fact, the two amount to much the same thing because, by and large, the anti-euro case is imbued with paranoid fears over domination from the Continent, and a belief that, by joining the euro, we would be ending hundreds of years of proud independence. For reasons not entirely clear, membership of a common European currency is equated with becoming a satellite state of a larger and alien power, a weak, obscure and seldom-heard province of Belgium. These rather mystical appeals to xenophobia are far from new. Much the same was said by the doom-and-gloom prophets when our currency went decimal. They trotted out a similar argument against the Channel Tunnel, and they could also be found proclaiming the end of civilization when the House of Commons became televised. Their attitude is not that distant from that of those who opposed universal suffrage on the grounds that Westminster would be overrun by 'hordes of women'. What sort of a nation would we be living in if we had listened to them?

At the heart of their case is a profound fear – and this is where pro-Europeans can take heart. The antis will exploit fear to the utmost when we eventually have a referendum on joining the euro. They will themselves constitute a fairly fearsome bunch. Picture it. Margaret Thatcher, Tony Benn, Norman Tebbit and William Hague, perhaps even Ian Paisley, together at a press launch, ranting about the dangers posed by getting too close to our foreign neighbours.

A BBC poll at the end of January 2000 suggested that 69 per cent of the British public were against joining the European currency. This result is scarcely surprising, and nor was Ken Clarke's observation that it was the result of 'alarmist and exaggerated Eurosceptic campaigning'. He is correct, but I remain confident that the nation will eventually support those who want Britain to play a part in Europe. We must, however, persuade the people of one fact: *it is patriotic to be pro-European, because full membership of Europe can only be good for Britain.* Joining the euro will help Britain, because, in purely domestic terms, it will enable our businesses to access the EU single market, of over 370 million people, on entirely level terms with Continental businesses. The euro will be a major player in the global financial markets and it will become invaluable in securing the economic stability for which British businesses are crying out.

The British people will support the pro-euro case because it has logic on its side. This becomes apparent as soon as the key arguments of the anti-euro lobby are held up to scrutiny. We are often told that joining Europe has few real benefits because our economy is more world-oriented than those of the rest of Europe, but this simply is not true – four of the existing eleven members of the Eurozone export a higher proportion of their GDP outside that Eurozone than we do.

The anti-euro case has shown itself to be flimsy in the extreme. In February of this year, William Hague published his '5 reasons to keep the pound' pamphlet. Giving it a title like that was a risk, particularly when not one of the points listed is at all reasonable.

Mr Hague says that Europe is mired in recessions, and that we should steer clear of this bunch of losers. A unified interest rate would, he argues, bind us irrevocably to Europe's cycle of booms and busts. This is an utter falsehood: Europe is growing faster than Britain. Figures from the House of Commons Library,[1] suggest that economic growth in the UK is likely to be below the EU average in 1998 and 1999, having been above average in each year from 1993 to 1997. For example, UK growth in 1998 was 2.2 per cent, compared to a similar figure in Germany, 3.4 per cent in France and 2.7 per cent for the EU as a whole. We have also suffered recessions of greater severity and duration than our European counterparts. Interest rates have been consistently much higher in Britain than those in the Eurozone (by some 2.75 per cent as I write), and the reason for this is solely the ineptitude of previous UK governments at controlling inflation. It is also a fallacy to present the 'one size fits all' interest rate as some nightmare scenario. In Britain we already have huge regional diversity, particularly between North and South – and one interest rate for all regions. This has not led us to suffer economic collapse. There are also huge regional disparities within the countries in the Eurozone – for instance, the difference between Northern and Southern Italy. Unified interest rates have led only to greater stability in these countries.

Mr Hague also tells us that the euro has fallen dramatically against the dollar. This is true, but if strength or weakness against other currencies were a valid yardstick, then we should have ditched the pound years ago: in 1966, a pound bought eleven German marks. Now, it buys about three – not the greatest of success stories.

Mr Hague maintains that a single currency will lead to a single European superstate, with Britain somehow being bossed around by a collection of foreigners. This is scare-mongering of the worst kind.

Britain and Ireland shared one currency from 1921–79 and nobody could argue that this forced Ireland to become a satellite state of the UK.

In any case, Britain is not powerless in Europe. We have the right to veto any changes to its structure. The key decision-making body in Europe is the Council of Ministers, which is made up of the elected heads of government of each EU member state. We cannot be forced into anything that we do not want, or which might be detrimental to Britain.

Related to this, Mr Hague argues that the single currency will result in our taxes being set by people beyond our shores, but, as stated above, we have the right to veto any moves towards tax harmonization. The issue of tax harmonization has nothing to do with the single currency; it comes under the single market legislation, and it was a certain Margaret Thatcher who signed up to this on Britain's behalf.

Mr Hague also tells us that we are doing perfectly well without the single currency, so why upset the apple cart? This shows a markedly narrow outlook. Ruling out the single currency will cost jobs and damage businesses, and a volatile pound will make foreign investors wary of investing their money in Britain. We may be doing well at present, but, without harmony with Europe, any success will be short-lived.

We are also told that it would cost billions of pounds for all British businesses to adapt their systems to the euro, and that only a small proportion would benefit from the reduced costs of trade with Europe. This is more misplaced and misleading propaganda. The CBI estimates that moving to monetary union will cut business transaction costs by 0.4 per cent of GDP every year, and that the costs of changing over to the euro would be a one-off expense of no more than 0.5 per cent of GDP. Even if we do stay out of the euro, many British businesses will have to make the transition themselves, in order to trade with companies in the Eurozone. They will suffer far more if they do not have the backing of the government. The majority of British agricultural trade is with the Eurozone, so farming – that most hard-hit of occupations – would receive a much-needed boost from moving to a single currency.

We can see that not one of William Hague's '5 reasons' withstands scrutiny, and that they are linked by one factor: xenophobia, the belief that 'Europe' and whatever it stands for, is 'bad'. It is not quite so easy to see, through the fog of negativity and suspicion, what the Eurosceptics actually want. Where would a Hague government (heaven forbid) lead us? It might push for a free trade area with no strings attached, but the last attempt to do that, the European Free Trade Association, failed and broke up. Or perhaps Mr Hague wants to get out of Europe? His vision is far from clear, and there is a great danger that the Eurosceptics would only lead the UK into isolation.

When the exchange rate is right for British entry, membership of the euro will clearly be in Britain's business interests. Fifty-five per cent of our exports go to the EU, compared with only 12 per cent to the USA. We should surely welcome anything we can do to open up European markets further to British business. Those benefits would proceed apace, as soon as we joined the euro. A referendum will show just how much the British people support the idea. Politicians must recognize that Britain will not be manoeuvred into the euro by stealth, and, as much as membership of the European currency is desirable, I am adamant that many serious arguments have yet to be fought and many thorny issues resolved, in the glare of public scrutiny. As my colleague Vince Cable, MP for Twickenham and former chief economist for Shell, has suggested, the government needs to have an independent commission, consisting of people from business, academic, financial and political backgrounds, to advise on a suitable entry level.

How do we decide when to join? The Governor of the Bank of England, Eddie George, has said that there is 'never a right moment for UK entry'. Wim Duisenberg, the President of the European Central Bank, has even argued that we are decades away from joining. Others argue that sterling is overvalued, and that we must wait for it to fall before we join. It may be true that there will never be a time when the situation is 100 per cent favourable, but we should not be disheartened, because the time was ripe for British membership when the euro was launched, and there is no reason to believe that it will take decades to reach a similar situation. In any case, conditions rarely are 100 per cent favourable in business. Business people assess risks on a daily basis: progress in business is about weighing up pros and cons and then making the leap. Clearly, the risks of delaying and remaining outside Europe need to be assessed just as carefully as the potential risks of joining.

To support its policy of inaction, the present government says it cares more about the British economy than Europe, but the two issues cannot be viewed separately. Gordon Brown listed '5 tests' of the wisdom of joining the euro, which relate, for example, to the convergence of economic cycles and whether the City is prepared for entry. One of the tests is whether monetary union will encourage long-term investment in British businesses. While we cannot be sure whether it will, we can be certain that being outside the European Union will discourage investment. Respected figures within the business community have been saying so for years. Jacques Nasser, the President and Chief Executive of the Ford Motor Company, has stated: 'When we sit down and think about a major investment, our assumption is that the UK will be within the Eurozone at least during the lifetime of that investment.' A safe assumption, unless the Eurosceptics have their way. Dr Richard Sykes at ICI was even more forthright: 'If the UK remained outside the euro on a sustained long term basis, that would be disadvantageous to investment in this country.' Bernd Euler at Siemens was also gloomy about Britain's prospects if the anti-euro lobby were to prove victorious: 'If the UK decides to stay out forever, this will put UK-based companies, including Siemens UK, in a very difficult position.'

And just in the first month of 2000, the heads of two major Japanese companies warned that billions of pounds of investment are at risk because of the overvalued pound and the absence of any strong British commitment to joining the European currency. Toyota had been planning a new £200 million plant in Derbyshire, but the chairman of the company has gone on record to say that this is in jeopardy if we continue our isolationist economic policies. How much more evidence does the Chancellor need? If we hang back from joining the euro, foreign investors will start to hang back from Britain.

There can be no excuse for ruling out euro membership indefinitely or for two Parliaments, unless perhaps the real agenda is to disengage altogether, and that is not a serious option. Only by being constructively engaged in Europe can Britain have a real influence on the shape of the EU. No serious politician advocates withdrawal from Europe, yet if we are unwilling members, we will end up dealing with the consequences of decisions that affect us, but upon which we have had insufficient influence. This is precisely the state of affairs that the Eurosceptics dread and are paradoxically seeking to bring about.

This is the heart of my pro-euro message: it would be a patriotic move for Britain, because it would promote our interests, and it would allow us to exert a real influence in Europe. Those who agree must hit back hard at the arguments pushed by William Hague, John Redwood and others, highlighting the paucity of their own alternative – for it is no alternative at all.

Politicians will fail the people if they continue to discuss Europe solely in the context of the single currency. There are many other equally important issues where European co-operation is vital and where the EU has benefits for all. Europe can spread power to the people. It offers the chance for regions to become the most important level of government after the EU, with far fewer decisions taken in national parliaments. The EU regional framework can help to promote and strengthen diversity and empower people through devolved decision-making structures. This is of particular interest to the English regions, some of which are already making great strides in campaigning for regional assemblies. Finally, Europe can be a strong voice for human rights, social justice and democracy throughout the world, with, if necessary, the economic and military power that it takes to protect the weak and oppressed.

If we are to get that right, then Europe needs to reform itself, and we need to re-examine what we mean by a federal Europe, for federalism has to be one of the most misunderstood terms in politics today. Opponents of Europe use it to scaremonger and imply that it means a centralized and overtly bureaucratic superstate.

Nothing could be further from the truth, and, to prove that, one only has to look at federal countries throughout the world, such as America and Canada. They are far less centralized than most European countries, certainly less centralized than the UK, even taking into account the establishment of representative bodies in Edinburgh, Belfast and Cardiff since 1997. In both countries, the recent trend has been towards a more decentralized approach to politics: federalism allows that.

Federal actually means that different powers lie at different levels of government, which are connected to a central or federal government, which in turn exercises only the powers that the lowest levels of government have agreed to. This is how the USA came into being – by the agreement of the thirteen colonies that threw off British rule to become states. Admittedly, Britons view the USA as a single nation, and the President as the most powerful person in that nation. That is understandable because the President deals with matters that affect all the American states, and these larger issues are often the ones of most interest to us across the Atlantic, but in a federal system, the President and Congress are by no means all-powerful. There are significant powers reserved for state governments, and we should learn from that example.

The American model works well because people understand which powers are the responsibility of which level of government, and the distribution of those powers is clearly defined in the American constitution. This cannot happen in Europe at the moment because Europe has no written constitution. This glaring omission must be addressed: the duties and the sphere of influence of the European parliament need to be clearly defined, alongside the duties and the sphere of influence of national governments. With this constitution enshrined in law, Europe would have the power to act decisively with the agreement of all, and, just as important, Europe would be kept out of the areas in which it has no business.

Other reforms are necessary if Europe is to be truly representative of its people. The European Parliament needs to be given greater powers of scrutiny over the European Commission. The former is elected by the people of Europe, while the latter consists of ex-politicians appointed by their own national governments. It cannot be right that the elected body, the Parliament, does not have more control of the unelected Commission. The Common Agricultural Policy must be reformed so that resources are targeted to supporting economic, social and environmental goals in rural communities, rather than paying subsidies for over-production. That means supporting farming that is in keeping with the local environment and traditional family farms, rather than funding industrial farming, which produces butter mountains and wine lakes. The Common Fisheries Policy needs to be scrapped and replaced with a system that allows for regional management of fish stocks, ensuring that centralized rules do not cause problems for those remote from EU decision-making, such as the fishermen in my own constituency.

With the European Union reformed, Europe would only act in areas where it could be effective. The environment is a case in point. Problems such as pollution, resource depletion, global warming and threats to biodiversity do not respect national borders, and the UK's environmental policy must be backed up by the environmental policies of Ireland, France, Holland, Denmark, etc. Action on a global scale has to be the ultimate goal, but while we are striving for worldwide solutions, co-operation between neighbours is the only way forward. A key starting point would be to create a core bloc of countries who together have the power and influence to make a difference. Europe is such a bloc – or at least, it has the potential to be.

There are already a number of international agreements and treaties in place which cover topics such as toxic waste, endangered species, global warming and the spread of the deserts, but a great many environmental issues remain unlegislated. We need more comprehensive controls on forestry and fisheries, for example, and immediate talks on GM products. Only by co-operation with our neighbours in Europe can we have the clout to come down hard on environmental offenders – those who fill our air, rivers and seas with toxic waste, those who trade in endangered species, and those who illegally hunt, fish and fell trees.

With the collapse of Communism, a great many of our industrialized neighbours to the East are in financial crisis, and as a result, concern for the environment is low on the list of priorities, in spite of the high level of toxic emissions from their factories, cars and power stations. To put it bluntly, environmental awareness and standards are as low in the former Eastern bloc as they are in developing nations, and it is not hard to see how emissions of sulphur dioxide from factories in, say, the Czech Republic, affect air quality in Germany. Neighbouring EU states have to teach by example, but also offer development assistance, and provide the institutions and the expertise necessary to implement effective environmental policies in these countries.

Mention the environment to the average person and they will respond with 'global warming'. No environmental topic seems to have captured the public imagination quite so powerfully, and rightly so, for it is a very real threat. In 1997, the Kyoto Protocol set up the mechanism whereby companies who reduce their emissions of greenhouse gases can earn credits. Unfortunately, fifty-five countries – whose output of greenhouse gases amounts to 55 per cent of the total – have to ratify it before it can come into force. This in turn means that the USA, a major contributor to the emissions of greenhouse gases, does not have to join in, as long as most of the rest of the industrialized world does not, and the US Congress is currently hostile to joining. The faster the protocol becomes established, the better the prospects for the planet. The UK should take the lead and encourage other countries to ratify, so that the USA has no choice. If the EU was acting as a single bloc on this issue, then the USA would be under much greater diplomatic pressure to have ratified already.

As a nation with strong economic and cultural ties to the rest of Europe, it is similarly pointless to speak of a British defence policy. The defence of our nation can only proceed through full co-operation and consultation with our neighbours. We need to urge the EU to develop a common defence policy. At present Europe's voice on defence is weak or non-existent. This is due, in part, to an inefficient use of our defence resources: Europe spends two-thirds of the amount spent by the USA on defence, but has only one tenth of America's 'power projection capability' – its capacity to make a difference.

There is a body of thought which suggests that defence is a minor issue for Europeans, because all nations within the boundaries of the EU have achieved political stability, and also because defence technology has reached such a level of sophistication that modern warfare really means the computerized obliteration of military targets. We all saw the footage on television, during the bombing of Baghdad, of 'intelligent' missiles seeking out army bases.

That footage contributed to a dangerous complacency. Quite apart from the chaos in the Balkans, there are many potential threats to, within and from the nations on the fringes of Europe – for example in North Africa, the Middle East and the Caucasus. Russia is a hugely unstable landmass bordering on Europe, and possesses enormous firepower. We saw that over the Christmas of 1999–2000 with the bombardment of Grozny.

Despite greater efficiency in military technology, the effects of 'collateral damage' cannot be overlooked, as witnessed in Kosovo. In any modern conflict, 90 per cent of all casualties are likely to be civilians, and after any such conflict come the inevitable camp-followers of poverty, disease, homelessness and displacement, which in turn will affect any neighbouring states not previously involved in the war.

It is absurd for anybody to think that our status as an island renders us somehow immune to developments in the rest of the world. Remember the violence in St Leonard's, Hastings, as Kurdish and Kosovan immigrants clashed, or in Dover, where tensions between local inhabitants and refugees from Eastern Europe boiled over. Minor episodes perhaps, and certainly exaggerated in the press, but nevertheless telling symbols of our connectedness to the European political scene.

Europe is burying its head in the sand partly because, for more than half a century, the USA has kept a reassuring presence here. During the Kosovo crisis, the USA provided some 75 per cent of the NATO aircraft and 80 per cent of the NATO munitions utilized. The USA remains the dominant force in maintaining world peace, but this global dependence on a single state is potentially dangerous. Apart from anything else, Europe cannot count on future American governments always being prepared to commit troops and resources to problem regions close to our own back door. We should never underestimate the isolationist tendencies which occasionally feature on Capitol Hill.

Safety in numbers is obviously the way forward for Britain and its neighbours. The amount of money being spent on defence is dropping continually – in some cases, as in Germany, it has dropped by 50 per cent since 1989. It is logical for European countries to band together to share skills and equipment, training and procurement. The EU provides the structure for such integration and for the development of a common defence policy, but it has a separate defence organization at present – the Western European Union. This should be formally merged with the EU, to provide a more cohesive structure for EU defence and foreign policy.

The Eurosceptic scaremongers prophesy that, as soon as we join the common currency, our troops will be sent off to fight a war in which Britain has no interest and over which Westminster has no say. This is a blatant fallacy. There is no question of Westminster not having the final say on the use of British forces. In the first place, what conflict could conceivably involve our European neighbours that did not also directly affect us? In any case, British and Dutch marines have been operating together for the last twenty-five years, and Europe's defence industry is itself moving towards greater consolidation. Britain should be at the forefront of this development: ethically, because we have a duty to promote peace and stability across the world, and practically, because British people are directly affected by instabilities elsewhere.

At the same time as committing our energies to a Europe-wide defence scheme, we must work to ensure that the defence industry as a whole does not pose a potential threat to global security. Without the international arms trade, there would be no armed conflicts, so control of the arms trade has to be tackled on an international basis, with the co-operation and support of the EU. Britain should be far more proactive where abuses of the arms trade are concerned. In particular, we should look for ways to ensure that our defence manufacturers are vigilant about whom they sell their products to and whether they are being used for aggressive military action against neighbours, or for internal repression. As the arms trade is international, little can be achieved without action at an EU level. Member states should sign an agreement not to sell arms, or even military technology, for any purpose other than self-defence.

Britain has a major responsibility to bring such measures about. According to the Ministry of Defence, 50 per cent of the UK's defence industry output goes abroad, and New Labour has done little to ensure that these exports are not contributing to regional instability or abuses of human rights. In January 2000 alone, we saw three dangerous examples of British involvement in a largely unregulated arms trade: Indonesia, Pakistan and Zimbabwe, all within the space of three weeks. The current legislation is in desperate need of a revisitation. The Scott Inquiry into the sale of arms to Iraq took place four years ago – but what has changed since? At present, the British taxpayer has to underwrite export credit guarantees to the tune of £239m per year. These insure our exporters, including the arms industry, against foreign customers defaulting on payments, but when there is no control over where arms are going, or what they are used for, then there is a very real danger that the British public is unwittingly funding and arming oppressive regimes.

It is not as if the industry is some Leviathan beyond our control. We can insist that purchasers of arms and technology apply for a licence, and refuse to grant it if they do not consent to monitoring after they have made the purchase. We can make government directly responsible for the granting of such licences, and the EU responsible for the monitoring. We can insist that arms brokers operating within the EU adhere to a code of practice, and that, if any arms contract poses a risk to stability, or will cause abuses of human rights, no member state of the EU will agree to produce the goods. In short, the means exist to control the arms trade, so as to promote instead of endanger world peace. Britain has a duty to take the lead.

If Europe is to have serious clout in terms of defence or the environment, then it needs to enlarge. By including central and eastern Europe within its boundaries, the EU can become both more effective and more stable. That will help us all: if enlargement spreads security, prosperity and democracy across central and eastern Europe then our own security and prosperity will be increased, but enlargement can only take place after sweeping reforms to the EU budget, so that it is more transparent and more accountable, and administrative costs are reduced. Otherwise we risk creating an entity which is too cumbersome and unwieldy to act with efficiency.

The Global Marketplace

If we need to think differently about Europe then that is equally valid for the rest of our international policy. Today, international policy means far more than it has done traditionally. To many people, trade is now of much greater importance. That was brought sharply into focus by the Seattle round of the World Trade Organization talks, when the public disturbances that occurred at its fringes captivated the world's media and caused the collapse of the talks.

The opening of new markets in former Communist countries, the development of a single market in Europe and the growth of e-commerce all mean that our businesses trade in places that were once impossible to reach. Potentially even more explosive is the information that the Internet provides: the possibility for all and sundry to put forward their views and interests in a way undreamed of by most people even ten years ago. The world is now a much bigger place than ever before – and smaller at the same time. Bigger because there are so many more opportunities available, and smaller because these opportunities are far easier to reach.

All of this has implications for governments and their international policies. British governments used to have a foreign policy, which tended not to change from one government to the next. Disraeli's maxim that Britain did not have permanent friends, just permanent interests, reigned supreme. It was dealt with by the Foreign Office, headed by a Foreign Secretary, and tended to relate to treaties between nations on issues of war and peace.

In the wake of globalization, everything has changed. We are now more likely to talk of international policy than foreign policy, and thankfully, this relates far more often to economics and trade than it does to war. The priorities of British embassies more than reflect this changed culture. There is now realistic talk of expanding the rules that promote good behaviour by nations on a global scale so that, more than ever before, individuals have globally recognized rights. Consider the case of South Korea, a nation which has raised its living standards from those comparable to the Sudan in the sixties, to those on a par with Greece and Portugal on the eve of the millennium. With these economic advances, there has been a gradual but discernible movement towards a greater respect for civil rights, minorities and democracy.

This is welcome. I saw how valuable discourse between nations can be when, in the early eighties, I spent a year in the USA as a Fulbright Scholar at Indiana University. This experience was an important influence on my view of the world. My contemporaries at the university were from a range of backgrounds and hailed from all parts of the Union, but I remember that almost all of them had lived in more than one state. Most had moved, with their parents, at least two or three times; many had experienced the huge contrasts between the East and West coasts. The diversity of their experiences, compared to my own, impressed me. There seemed to be an assumption among Americans that continual movement, in search of new horizons and opportunities, was the norm. Perhaps it was a surviving vestige of the pioneer spirit. It is an attitude – a flexibility and an optimism – that has struck me whenever I have returned, and everyone should have the opportunity to learn from other countries as I had the chance to do.

That means not putting up barriers to co-operation. In 1945, J. M. Keynes argued that the protectionism and particularism of the inter-war years should never return. He understood that when nations retreated behind their own borders, there were only counter-productive consequences. The World Trade Organization was to emerge from Keynes' vision, via a tortuous route. We now live in a world in which trade has become increasingly free from the restraints of individual governments, and in which living standards have improved globally. There is no question now of any return to the damaging 'beggar-my-neighbour' protectionism of the thirties which did so much to contribute to the Great Depression in America and Europe. Since 1951, world trade has expanded seventeenfold, and world per capita income has doubled.

Yet there are severe problems with the system. Above all, in an overzealous pursuit of trade liberalization, other objectives, such as sustainability, the needs of developing countries, and fairness, are being lost. That is not the way it was meant to be. The WTO agreement said that there must be 'positive efforts' to ensure that developing countries get their fair share, but this has not been happening.

The dispute over the EU banana regime is a case in point. Small Caribbean states such as Dominica depend on banana exports to the EU. They account for about 70 per cent of all export earnings in Dominica, and much of its employment, but production is mainly on small family farms, on steep land, so they cannot compete with the massive outputs of the huge, flat plantations of Latin America. With the EU now trying to fall into line with the WTO ruling, which would give the already dominant multinational companies like Chiquita, Del Monte and Dole even greater access to EU markets, Caribbean banana growers are under severe threat. Unless they have more time to adapt to the competition, they will go under. The WTO should be capable of dealing with a problem like this, but instead it has made it worse.

The cause of developing countries should be a major concern for the future within the WTO. Further trade liberalization would help to promote economic growth in these countries, thus spreading the benefits of international trade more evenly. The EU Commission proposed that all industrialized countries commit themselves to tariff-free purchase of products from the least developed countries by 2003. It is a proposal which has yet to become reality, despite the obvious benefits for the developing world. Sustainable development must be included in the basic rules of the WTO, so that it becomes a fundamental objective of the international trading system. There are other issues to place on the agenda too: the environment, protection of public health, labour standards and animal welfare.

As a modern organization, the WTO has to become more democratically accountable. The rioting in Seattle should be condemned unequivocally but, as politicians, we have to be aware of its causes. People resort to violence when they can see no other way of making a difference. Violence is also a traditional response to the unknown, and that is exactly what the WTO has become to the public – a shadowy, powerful body that answers to no-one.

At a European level, this problem could be addressed if the EU Commission honoured its promises of greater transparency in the conduct of WTO negotiations. This would enable the European Parliament to scrutinize the WTO far more effectively, and citizens would be able to see and understand its movements with greater clarity. National parliaments and the European Parliament should also be given more access to important WTO documentation. At present, the WTO has a well-deserved reputation as the premier body for settling trade disputes between nations, but its dispute panels often refer to various less transparent, more elusive bodies of experts. For example, the Codex Alimentarius Commission – which sets food standards – and the International Council for Standardization – for technical standards – are dominated by people trained by, and working for, large multinational companies. As a result, wider public concerns may not always be fairly represented.

A case in point is the dispute over the milk hormone, bovine somatotrophin (BST), and reports that BST had made test animals ill. Nevertheless, the Codex Alimentarius Commission gave its approval to the hormone.

Before 1996, the Codex did not possess much power – it merely dispensed advice to nations who were too poor to fund their own food safety administrations – but, in that year, the World Trade Organization converted the Codex into a super agency, armed with the authority to issue 'rebuttable presumptions'. If the Codex issues a rebuttable presumption of harmlessness for a product like BST, no nation can prevent it from being imported. If they dare try, they face a hail of sanctions.

The WTO is using this kind of power to move towards a state of affairs where worldwide mutual recognition agreements (MRAs) are commonplace. These agreements essentially mean that any product or process approved in one nation is approved in all. This can include GM crops, milk hormones, medical devices, procedures and products. It is not hard to see how this kind of agreement favours huge multi-national companies, who want to be able to reach the maximum number of customers unhindered by 'excessive' regulations. Indeed, the establishment of MRAs is a key feature of the Trans-Atlantic Business Dialogue. This is a working party of 100 of the West's most powerful CEOs, created to advise governments on US–EU relations. In October 1999, the Trans-Atlantic Business Dialogue launched its Implementation Plan, which targets thirty-three key environmental, consumer and worker protection laws in various countries. It wants them all scrapped, on the basis of being detrimental to trade. Some of the World Trade Organization's activities are conducted less in the public interest, and more in favour of big business.

So far, among the national laws that WTO panels have ruled against and consequently weakened, are the US Clean Air Act, the US Endangered Species Act and Japan's food pesticide standards. It has also ruled against the EU's ban on imports of potentially health-threatening hormone-treated beef. When the EU attempted to defy the WTO by giving preferential access to the bananas produced by those small farmers in the Caribbean, it was hit with sanctions of $190 million. Crucially, in every single one of these cases, the WTO panels sided with the corporate parties involved. In the case of the Clean Air and Endangered Species Act, these were Venezuelan and Brazilian oil companies respectively. In the case of the Japanese legislation, they were the major Asian shrimp exporters, and US-owned fruit and beef consortiums benefited from the WTO rulings on bananas and imported beef.

Trade and the environment are inextricably linked but, as we can see, the WTO is doing insufficient to promote environmentally responsible practices in and between nations. On top of the bully-boy tactics represented by 'rebuttable presumptions', the 'burden of proof' rule currently requires countries to prove that goods are unsafe or damaging to the environment or public health, before they can try to ban their import. Instead, surely exporters should be forced to provide greater evidence of safety? It is often not possible to prove that something is entirely safe, but one could seek to ensure that a product has undergone a stringent testing programme, similar to that carried out on medicines. Since pollution does not recognize borders, and since most pollution stems from production processes rather than products themselves, neighbouring countries should be allowed to discriminate against goods produced in an environmentally unfriendly way. Countries should be allowed the same discretion over any products or processes where there are public health concerns, such as BST.

The WTO needs to return to its pre-1996 position and refocus with alacrity on the needs of developing countries. There are some obvious ways in which this could be done. There should be an annual environmental assessment of the WTO's operations, carried out by the United Nations Environment Programme. Rules that make it difficult to enforce agreements limiting pollution could be modified, and there could be much closer co-operation between the WTO and the International Labour Organization, to tackle problems such as forced labour. Underpinning all of this, there must be much greater transparency in the WTO's decision-making.

If the WTO can be made more open, and more responsive to the needs of developing countries, than we will have travelled some way towards tackling the great challenge of international policy for this generation of politicians and the next: global poverty. Liberal Democrats are deeply concerned about the inequalities that divide Britain. These deny millions of people the opportunities that they deserve, but poverty in Britain is usually only relative. The poorest people in the world, those who lack the most basic requirements for existence – food, clothing and shelter – live well beyond our shores.

Our Debt to the Developing World

Global inequalities have increased steadily for the past two centuries. This has resulted in huge differences between continents. Of the world's 200 richest people in 1998, it is very telling that only eighteen came from sub-Saharan Africa and Latin America. Moreover, the assets of the top 200 were greater than the combined income of 41 per cent of the world's people.

Like most Britons, I was shocked by the television images of the devastation caused to Mozambique by floods in late February and early March 2000, and I applauded our decision to commit immediate aid to the country. Mozambique was one of Africa's success stories, but as the figures below demonstrate, it is still one of the world's most vulnerable nations. By contrast, we were among those with the greatest capacity to help, as the following figures from 1997 demonstrate:

UK GDP per capita: $20,730
Mozambique: $740

UK life expectancy: 77.2
Mozambique: 45.2

UK infant mortality per 1000: 6
Mozambique: 130

UK daily calorie intake: 3,237
Mozambique: 1,799

UK adult literacy: 99.0 per cent
Mozambique: 40.5 per cent

My first direct exposure to the plight of people in other nations came when I was sixteen. My sister had moved to Canada some years previously, and I was fortunate enough to travel to the far north of British Columbia for a visit. I was introduced to the problems of the Native American reservations: unemployment, poverty and alcoholism. We were introduced to the oldest woman in the community, and my sister asked her whether she thought life on the reservation was much different from the way her ancestors had lived. I remember the old woman's answer vividly: 'When the white men came, they had the Bibles and the Indian had the land. Now it's the other way around.'

For some time after, I was very interested in the history of North America's indigenous peoples, and was ashamed of the way colonialism had decimated populations and destroyed cultures. Eventually, I came to see that many political flashpoints around the globe – Palestine, for example – were also the legacy of the colonial past, of a time when the big players carved up the cake among themselves. As a citizen of one of the main culprits, I could not see how we could turn our back on situations that our forebears had created. I still cannot. Nowadays, I do not see the issue in terms of blame and guilt. Plenty of the world's problems were not created by Britain or any other colonial power, but we have a duty to care and to do something *because we can.*

It was an especial privilege to have been in South Africa during the 1995 Rugby World Cup. Setting aside the ignominy of being introduced to President Mandela as the violinist Nigel Kennedy, the optimism and enthusiasm across the whole country was irresistibly infectious. After the opening game in Cape Town, I left the stadium to see even the poorest citizens – the street cleaners and refuse collectors, without exception black – celebrating wildly and waving the national flag. This was a truly galvanic moment for the country, but it was far from an isolated peak of emotion. I later travelled further throughout the country, seeing rural areas of unbelievable poverty, but the energy, the enthusiasm and the sense, above all else, of belonging to a nation that has a future, was widespread, not least because South Africa is such a youthful country, high in natural resources. At this moment the extent of the vast untapped potential of the developing world became vividly clear to me personally.

One of the most positive aspects of globalization is that more and more people feel similarly. They are outraged about the poverty of people in faraway countries, and they recognize that these people deserve the same opportunities to fulfil their potential as themselves.

We increasingly feel that we have a responsibility to the poor, wherever they may be, and we want to act on their behalf and in their support. The arguments advanced in the Brandt Report of over two decades ago remain valid and persuasive today. I recall, as a student, being influenced greatly by Dr David Owen, a month after the 1979 general election, when he argued against one of the first foreign policy decisions of the incoming Conservative government, which was to cut overseas aid by 15 per cent. That approach was short-sighted then, and the developed world's attitude remains inadequate now. We should rediscover the central thrust of the Brandt Report – namely that we have both a moral *and* self-interested need to be far more bold with the ambitions of our aid efforts. The morality behind ending world poverty and hunger is absolute, but we need also to recognize the longer-term necessity of locking-in emergent economies to the developed world, from the point of view of our economic growth in the future.

Few people nowadays subscribe to the idea that people in the developing world are scroungers, happy to survive on handouts from the West. It has become increasingly apparent that what they need is opportunity, but this cannot happen while countries in the Third World have to spend more money paying interest on loans from the West than on education and public health.

The debt burden of the world's poorest countries amounts to 93 per cent of their income. Every citizen of Zambia now owes the country's creditors $790 – more than twice the average income. It is clear that such debts are unserviceable: they will never be paid off, and the interest is only being met because the debtors are diverting resources from crucial areas. They are thus locked into a cycle where indebtedness leads to further poverty, which in turn prolongs the debt.

It is reasonable to ask why any responsible Western government ever allowed the situation to arise. The problem is that the process of international lending and borrowing is rarely conducted in the public eye. Loans are agreed in secret, negotiated between local elites in the Third World countries and powerful creditors like the World Bank and government export credit agencies. Of the debts owed to Britain by the world's poorest countries 96 per cent are owed to the Department of Trade and Industry's Export Credit Guarantee unit – the money was lent as an inducement to buy British exports.

Former Chancellor Nigel Lawson made sympathetic moves over the subject of Third World Debt, urging the USA to lower its interest rates and weaken the dollar. Export credit guarantees were actually brought in as part of Lawson's debt relief programme, to encourage British companies to trade with those Third World countries who agreed to a rescheduling of their debts, but Lawson insisted that the case of each country be looked at individually. In doing so, he denied the possibility of finding a global solution to what was, and always will be, a global problem.

Since then, public awareness of the situation has increased, largely as a result of organizations like Jubilee 2000, which calls for a one-off cancellation of all unpayable debts. In June 1999, the G8 summit agreed to cancel $100 billion of the debt. This was followed by bold moves by both President Clinton and Chancellor Gordon Brown, both of whom agreed to 100 per cent cancellation of the debts owed to their nations by the world's poorest countries. Gordon Brown has taken the process further by calling for a taskforce to speed up debt relief.

I salute Gordon Brown's efforts, but I do not believe he has gone far enough. He agreed to waive the debts owed to Britain by twenty-six countries, but Jubilee 2000 has identified a total of fifty-two countries whose debts are unpayable. In addition, only around half of the total sum is owed as debt to individual countries. The rest – around $177 billion – is multilateral debt, owed to the World Bank and the International Monetary Fund. It will take consolidated action by *all* the G8 leaders to persuade these bodies to cancel the multilateral debts.

The criteria for those deemed worthy of help are restrictive and outdated. To qualify for debt relief currently, nations consistently have to meet a number of rigorous economic criteria over a number of years. Of the fifty-two countries that Jubilee 2000 has identified as being in desperate need of debt relief, only forty-one meet the current criteria. This means that some extremely poor nations, such as Nepal, have no hope of ever qualifying for debt relief.

The G8's provision of $100 billion in debt relief was widely applauded, but these nations have only written off those debts which were *unpayable*. While this is a good start, it still leaves many of the world's poorest nations facing crippling repayments on those loans which the G8 deems payable. In some countries, such as Mali, this actually means that repayments have increased. Formerly, all of Mali's debts – both the payable and unpayable loans – were gathered together under a single umbrella, and that country made single, scheduled payments which amounted to a fraction of the total owed. With the removal of the unpayable debt, the payment umbrella has been removed and thus nations like Mali are obliged to start repaying their other debts in full.

It is not enough for Britain simply to cancel the debts of twenty-six countries. We need to exert pressure on our allies to bring about a cancellation of all multilateral debt. Germany's new government has recently climbed down from former Chancellor Kohl's intractable position, and declared that Jubilee 2000's demands are justified, but as yet there has been no action in that direction. Japan has written off a small amount of the debt owed by Bolivia – a symbolic move for a government previously opposed to debt relief, but still a drop in the ocean. The same is true for France, which has cancelled debts from Central American countries, in the wake of recent environmental disasters, but has made no moves towards a more universal position. Unilateral action by Gordon Brown and Clinton only addresses part of the problem, in some cases exacerbates it and does nothing at all for those nations who do not qualify for membership of the poorest twenty-six.

The solution is not simply to throw money at poorer countries. Political corruption sometimes means that money sent for aid ends up being used for military purposes, or simply funnelled into offshore havens. We need to set up structures whereby foreign aid and its uses can be monitored: the best aid often comes in the form of skilled doctors and teachers, and textbooks and medical equipment.

Nowhere is the exchange of skills with the developing world more relevant than in the fight against HIV and AIDS. The UN estimates that in 1998, 1.7 million young people contracted HIV in Africa. In the four worst affected countries, up to a quarter of all people aged 15–49 were HIV positive. The reasons for this epidemic are plain to see. Death from AIDS is, at the bottom level, due to poverty of information: lack of basic health education and access to condoms. Many European countries and major cities have managed the crisis without a major epidemic. We need to send our skilled professionals to Africa to pass on their knowledge. The practice of twinning European cities and hospitals with African counterparts would help to establish channels of communication. Given that the NHS is currently suffering from a shortage of trained staff, it would make sense for our hospitals to open their doors to more personnel from the African countries, so that there was a two-way transit of skills and expertise.

There is little mystery surrounding the problems which affect developing countries. Currently, population growth in such countries hugely outstrips income growth. The control of population is inextricably linked to the predicament of women in the developing world. Women in these countries are subject to shocking inequalities in terms of their life chances and opportunities. The UN estimates that an African woman is around 500 times more likely to die during pregnancy than her Scandinavian counterpart. Women's access to education in developing countries is highly impaired: an estimated 60 per cent more women than men in the developing world are illiterate. So aid has to address gender inequalities. Family planning and access to maternity care should be a spending priority.

Britain cannot afford to take a back seat when it comes to the problems of world poverty. There tends to be an attitude in this country that overseas development policies are safest in the hands of Brussels decision-makers, and unfortunately this attitude has coloured the way British governments approach the issue. In fact, the EU is not nearly as active as it should be. The EU provided $0.7 worth of aid per capita to countries with the lowest income, compared with

$1.4 to those of middle income, and $4.5 to others. While I thoroughly endorse membership of the EU as the only way to get things done on a global scale, we have to campaign for a redirection of EU aid money, so that it goes where it's most needed.

The World Bank and International Monetary Fund also need to change. They promised to deliver permanent debt relief, so that countries could stop spending their money on exorbitant repayments and redirect the money to areas like education and health, but two countries who received debt relief in 1998, Uganda and Bolivia, have already returned to unsustainable levels of debt. In what sense have they been helped? Any initiatives must offer a *permanent* exit from debt, provided the countries concerned commit themselves to a programme of eradicating poverty and to the protection of human rights. If the richest nations truly mean what they say about eradicating world poverty, then they cannot consider easing up on debt relief.

Conclusion

In conclusion, Britons have a duty to care about what happens in the rest of the world, if only because we are all directly affected by it. Examples of the way life in Britain is changed by events beyond its shores arise continually – and there is no doubt that the trend is on the increase. Last year, in my own constituency, we had an early lesson ourselves. During the campaign for elections to the Scottish Parliament, we had two Croatian politicians and a Bulgarian working with us, as part of a scheme organized by the Westminster Foundation. It was an enriching exercise for all. They learnt from us, and we learnt from their experiences of the momentous events that their countries had undergone in recent years. Coming from countries where democracy is only in its infancy, they had a freshness and an enthusiasm for the political process that was both impressive and infectious. They also prompted us to question some of the things we do during elections. The Croatians wondered why, for instance, did we not spend much time talking to people who said they intended to vote for other parties? Why weren't we spending more of our time seeking to change people's minds?

Co-operation like this – the exchange of ideas and expertise with Croatians and Bulgarians – was unimagined little more than ten years ago. It is a welcome change from the dark days of the Cold War. And those who argue that, as an island, Britain must safeguard its independence, are not so much stuck in the past as deeply deluded. Far from losing our national identity – that much uttered but seldom-defined phrase – we cannot expect our social, economic and cultural life to flourish at all if we isolate ourselves from Europe and the world at large. Our future is as a key player, pressing for vital reforms within the UN, the EU and the World Trade Organization. The alternative is to have no future.

CONCLUSION:
A SENSE OF IDEALISM

Since I entered Parliament in 1983, these are among the things I have got wrong:

1. My most regrettable vote in Parliament is one I never cast. The Child Support Bill went through Parliament essentially unopposed, and I did not vote on it because all the parties supported it as a non-contentious issue. I now realize that it was a disaster, resulting in the creation of the hugely unpopular Child Support Agency, whose practices have proved so unsympathetic to the needs and circumstances of parents.

2. When in 1992 the Liberal Democrats passed a policy in favour of holding a Royal Commission on Drugs, I was one of those who argued that the party should try to minimize national attention on this policy. I now recognize that – particularly in the light of medical findings on the therapeutic uses of cannabis – this debate needs to be held publicly, and I have made that case openly.

3. In the mid-eighties, I did not believe that the environment would become such a major campaigning issue for the Alliance. I now believe that the environment is a matter of national emergency. I also admit that, had we been more proactive in promoting environmental issues, we would not have suffered such heavy losses in votes to the Green Party in the 1989 Euro-elections.[1]

4. I did not protest vociferously enough when British police suppressed demonstrations against the visit of the Chinese president

Jiang Zemin, in late 1999. When our own police force is suppressing dissent on behalf of an authoritarian government, everyone who cares about liberty and democracy should be besieging our own government with protests. I regret greatly that I did not exercise my right to raise the issue in Prime Minister's Questions, and thus force the government to justify itself.

Readers may wonder why I am reciting this list. At this stage, I will only say this. I am listing some of my failings as an MP in the hope that my colleagues will follow suit, in the hope that, by admitting our mistakes, politicians can restore public faith in politics, and save democracy from an early death.

I genuinely believe that true democracy – one in which every citizen participates – is a sickly child in the Britain of today, and that it needs urgent care and attention to restore it. If we do nothing, and choose to leave the business of government solely to Westminster, and voting to the handful of citizens who still feel that it matters, then I fear for the future of politics.

Changing the Face of Politics

I have spoken a great deal about the profound influence of the Watergate scandal upon my embryonic political thinking. I freely admit that I rushed home from school to catch the updates because the scandal and salacious details intrigued me, but I also gained, at a very young age, a sense that the world was not what it seemed. We were brought up to respect people in authority and to consider their word as good as law. I was extremely fortunate and perhaps unusual in never having been let down by parents, teachers, and other elders, but I was far from naïve. President Nixon most certainly let me down, and I grew up with the firm conviction that power could be a dangerous thing. As I became increasingly involved in politics, this translated into a concern for public integrity.

That's why I find it hard to keep a sense of humour about parliamentary sleaze. Westminster is still dominated by the 'gentlemen's club' ethos that can treat wrongdoing as a harmless foible. But when MPs resort to underhand methods, they not only let down the people who voted for them, they let down the whole notion of democracy.

No wonder Parliament is less respected than it once was. In British political tradition the Executive (that is, the Prime Minister and Cabinet) should be accountable to Parliament, yet this is increasingly a theory rather than the reality. Prime Minister's Question Time is a stagey and confrontational bearpit, and rarely can a government backbencher with aspirations seriously challenge his or her own leaders and hope to get on. Our political culture is such that suggestions from other parties are rarely taken on board by government, and, to be fair, those initiatives are too often only made for the sake of party-political point scoring. Perhaps most worrying is that ministers often choose to make their key announcements outside Parliament, holding MPs and the role of MPs in contempt.

People see Parliament as irrelevant, and do not choose to get involved in political parties. I am afraid that parties will attract fewer and fewer members, less and less fresh blood, and fewer and fewer new ideas. Young people in particular are far more attracted by single-issue groups, which don't involve any of the seemingly messy compromises which party politics does, and are understandably 'purer' and more attractive. When our parties are no longer able to draw on new talent from a cross-section of the community, politics will truly be in freefall.

Adopting a different approach, an honest approach, should be part of changing the business of politics itself. We need to change the way in which we go about our politics, to restore a sense of faith and trust in the political process. A crucial element in this, I believe, is to uphold the principles of integrity and honesty in office. If an MP is to be truly honest, it follows that this honesty should extend to admitting his or her mistakes. That's why I began this chapter with my own confession. Non-politicians frequently have to admit to errors, and if politicians were to follow suit, then the public might have more confidence in them. I am simply trying to start the ball rolling. My list is, of course, confined to the mistakes that I am aware of and is not exhaustive – I am certain the public and my colleagues could add to it, but at least I have made a start.

The consequences of refusing to admit one's mistakes are dire. The Prime Minister offers a case in point. It is very interesting to look at how the public perceives Tony Blair today. When he became Prime Minister, one of his unique selling points was trust. He could hold out his hands to the British people – if you watch his early TV performances, that's exactly the gesture he adopted – and say 'trust me', and by and large they believed him. But now, after three years of spin and the slick repackaging of old spending plans, the gloss has worn off. People are cynical about the Prime Minister, and opposition politicians know this. We know that we can stand up in the House of Commons and criticize the government on the NHS, and that whatever the PM does to defend his record, the nation will not believe him. They are losing their faith, as various leaked Downing Street memoranda have recognized.

I take no pleasure in that. When Labour first launched its famous 'five pledges', my own view was that they were likely to be delivered, and that this would be a new dawn for British politics. I have been proved wrong, because Labour has become obsessed with dressing up the facts and figures, so much so that people do not know whom to trust. At the next election, I am sure that Labour will tell people that they have delivered all five pledges – even if it hasn't. How refreshing it would be to hear a Labour politician say that they had delivered on two or three or four, but that they had to put forward new ideas on how to meet the remaining targets. Would not such an admission give people more faith in the political process than the continual dogmatic assertion that the government was, is and always will be in the right?

Having said that, admissions of failure from politicians can only ever be a starting point. If we are to restore trust, then we also need to look at the overall framework of politics. That means more focus on long-term solutions to problems, rather than short-term fixes. There were two graphic examples of this in the first months of 2000. First we had the floods in Mozambique. There was a massive public debate about how many helicopters were being sent there, but there should have been just as much attention paid to the long-term problems such as climate change and underdevelopment, that led to the problem in the first place. When the waters subsided, Mozambique slipped off the news agenda, but something similar will happen again if there isn't more attention paid to long-term issues. The same can be said of the problems faced by the workers at Rover's Longbridge. All the attention has been on short-term fixes. We certainly do need to act to save British jobs, but we will do that far better by creating favourable conditions for British business in the long term, especially by tackling the exchange rate problem.

At the same time, people will never trust politicians while they continuously seek to hide what they do. Genuine freedom of information legislation would give people much greater confidence in the decisions taken on their behalf, because they would be able to find out what ministers were up to. At the moment, if a British government minister has a meeting with a politician from the USA or the Irish Republic, it is far easier to find out about the business of the meeting using Irish or American sources than British ones. How can that be healthy for the quality of our democracy?

Our present electoral system disenfranchises a large proportion of voters and practically compels them to lose interest in politics. The mother of one of my members of staff has voted for the Alliance or the Liberal Democrats in every election since 1983. That's four general elections, elections for around sixteen local councillors, and four European elections. In each of those elections, the party she voted for has gained between twelve and 31 per cent of the vote in her constituency, but her vote made no difference until 1999, when it helped to elect Andrew Duff as the Liberal Democrat MEP for the Eastern Region of England. Finally, under a fairer voting system, her voice was heard. In that time, how many other people had lost faith, feeling that politics offered them nothing, that there was no point in voting, because it doesn't change anything? Without fair votes for all elections, we cannot pretend to live in a democracy.

To make people's votes really count we must also recognize that politics isn't solely about what happens in Westminster. Much has been done to decentralize power in the UK, with the establishment of representative bodies in Cardiff, Belfast and Edinburgh, but it is an unfinished revolution, and it must continue. The Welsh Assembly should have far greater control of Welsh affairs, on my visits to Northern Ireland, I'm often told that the Assembly needs a wider economic role, and the regions of England need a clear voice. Then, people would be able to see the effect of their vote working upon their immediate environment.

Reconnecting Politics and the People

One of the major advantages of changing the way we go about politics is that politicians will have to reach out to a much broader cross-section of the people if they ever hope to govern. At the moment, they don't have to do that, and I can see elections being fought over a series of increasingly narrow issues, based on a sense that only by appealing to Middle England will people get elected. We saw this in the 1997 election, in the way both Labour and the Tories courted those who had the greatest interest in paying less tax. We see it now, as William Hague trawls the country with the jingoistic cry of 'save the pound', rather than embarrass his supporters by talking about saving futures in our inner cities.

There is a danger that British politics will become more Americanized. Now, I am a great fan of many things American, but that enthusiasm does not extend to the way in which politics is run by big donors, who have a massive influence on the selection of candidates for the top jobs, and I am not impressed by the pitiful levels of turnout that are a defining feature of US politics. The idea that less than 50 per cent of Americans can be bothered to vote in a presidential election should frighten anyone who cares about the health of Western democracy. It is a dire warning of what will happen in Britain if current trends continue.

Apart from being misguided, an approach based on appealing to a small section of the electorate assumes that politics is only about one thing: winning elections. Although it is true that politicians need to win elections to implement our policies, they can become over-obsessed with the race, forgetting the prize at the end. There are many other duties incumbent upon politicians, such as their obligation to contribute to informed public debate. A well-developed public discourse, based on facts and principles, not hysteria, is a mark of any healthy society. I am afraid that the standard of debates on the subject of Europe suggests that we are far from healthy: the 'Up Yours, Delors' mentality is alive and well and living on the floor of the House, and could be seen vividly in the debates on homosexuality in early 2000.

Politicians must engage with the whole community, not just the eloquent and readily informed parts of it. Unless they do so they will exacerbate a very unhealthy development in our society. We are already a renowned nation of ironists, and rightly proud of it. The danger is that with further disenchantment from politics, we will become a nation of cynics, losing any sense that collective action can make a difference, and any sense of the 'get up and go', and innovative spirit which, let's face it, has made a tiny island a key player in world history, economics and culture. People will start to find instead that they can get by quite nicely, thank you, providing for their own, and not worrying about their fellow citizens. All the 'me and now' values that disfigured eighties Britain will return to haunt us.

Opportunities for All

The dwindling opportunities that many of today's Britons face must be a major concern. I firmly believe that the start of the twenty-first century is a wonderful time to be alive. Not for my generation the turmoil of my parents' or grandparents' generations: the disease, the grinding poverty and the unstable economies. In Britain 2000, we no longer face the threat of invasion by a foreign country, or the risk of spilling the blood of our bravest and best in Flanders Fields. In spite of that, the opportunities that our society has to offer, the so-called peace dividend, are far from available to all. We have an education system that, despite the best efforts of its devoted staff, fails too many children. We have a health service that rations or delays treatment so that people die because of sheer inequalities. Perhaps understandably, those who can afford it, opt out. They send their children to a private school. They opt for a private hospital. I am ashamed to live in that kind of society.

I have tried, throughout this book, to show why I believe the things I do. I hope it will now be apparent that my background, growing up on a croft in the Highlands, and my subsequent experiences in Glasgow, America and Westminster have, above all else, committed me to one principle. I want everyone to be free. To experience that, they must have equal opportunities, equal life chances. And that's why I am a Liberal Democrat.

We entered the twentieth century with a rigid class system, in which opportunities for advancement were denied to millions of people. Many of those divisions still exist at the start of the twenty-first century, and unless we recognize them, we will be failing vast swathes of the population who have no option but to rely on crumbling public services. The result will be the death of democracy – for we cannot think that the roughly 14 million British people living on or below the poverty line have any sort of freedom.

Inequalities will be worsened if we become a society divided along the lines of the information-rich and the information-poor. The Internet, satellite and digital TV, and the often overlooked massive increase in radio stations, have all expanded the amount of information available to people on an immeasurable scale, but they all come with a price attached. Ensuring access for all is a priority.

Playing Our Part in the World

Despite the amount of information flowing in from all parts of the globe, Britain may still turn in on itself. The world is a dangerous place: if wars take place far from our shores, they can still affect us.

Even co-operation with other countries can seem risky, and some fear it will somehow dilute the heady brew of the British character.

That attitude could lead to two dangerous developments. The first is that we miss out on the benefits of international co-operation, and a reformed, democratic Europe. Shared sovereignty could bring us control over factors beyond our borders, like the economy and the environment. Politicians must face up to the fact that the nation state is dying, even if nationalism is not, and that we need to take global institutions more seriously than ever before.

The second danger is that we will fail to fulfil the great potential that we have for dealing with global problems. Ever since I saw the first pictures of the Biafran famine victims, I have believed that richer nations have a duty to help their poorer neighbours. The moving scenes during the Live Aid concert in 1985 proved how many ordinary Britons felt exactly the same. When we have it within our power to save lives in Africa or Asia, through sharing expertise or providing aid, then we should do so with vigour. If we become an introspective, protectionist island, and allow millions to starve and live in poverty, we will, in effect, be committing an historic and international crime.

Idealism and the Voter of 2020

We have to recognize some of the fundamental shifts that have taken place in politics in recent years which will inevitably make the ideologies of the past irrelevant. It will not be possible to categorize the voter of 2020 as a socialist, or a conservative. Instead, the voter of 2020 will be a variety of things: internationalist, green, committed to properly funded public services, technologically aware and liberal. That could make the voter of 2020 a natural Liberal Democrat supporter – but only if he or she hasn't lost faith in politics altogether.

That's where idealism steps in. I entered politics because, like many of my peers and colleagues, I had strong ideals. Over my seventeen years in politics, my idealism has not abated, but I have witnessed it withering away nationwide, to the point where, at least among the young, to have ideals is akin to being blinkered and old-fashioned. Before we can go to work on the nation and its problems, we have to repair the mechanism for change. Politicians have to restore a sense of idealism to politics.

To do this, we have to know what our ideals are, and stamp them in large letters across the political arena. That means talking about basic principles and big issues. An acquaintance of mine is a novelist and screenwriter, and he once told me that, before starting to write anything, he made sure he could say what his story was about in one sentence. Once he knew what that one sentence was, he could begin. If he had trouble coming up with that one sentence, it was a sure-fire indication that his story was not worth telling. This is equally true of politics – to engage people, we need to talk about core values. If we don't know what those values are, or we can't communicate them to the citizens, then we should not be politicians.

My key principle is a firm belief in liberty. As a youngster, learning about the shootings of Martin Luther King and Bobby Kennedy within two months of each other had a profound influence on me. I was appalled, but their deaths made me determined not to live in a society where the bullet dominated over free speech. I came to believe that everybody should have as much freedom as possible, without infringing the freedom of others, to make the most of their natural potential.

For a believer in liberty, involvement in politics is essential, because liberty is threatened by a variety of factors which have to be confronted at government level: inequality, instability, resistance to international co-operation and environmental hazards, to name a few. I believe that, used in the right way, doing the right things, government can enhance and strengthen liberty. This sounds fairly abstract, but unless politicians find ways of articulating their principles, then the quality of our country's political conversation will be low. If we never talk about the basic beliefs, then it's no wonder that voters, and even political commentators, ask 'What's it all about? Why do you bother?' How many people in the street could say they honestly knew what Tony Blair's or William Hague's key principles were?

If politicians remind themselves why they are in politics, and communicate that to the public they represent, then voters will have a much clearer understanding of what the parties stand for. They will be able to appreciate the fundamental issues behind disputes over levels of NHS funding or the national curriculum. It might become apparent that, when politicians disagree, they are doing so over real issues of principle, rather than sheer opportunism. That was my own experience over the issue of asylum seekers during the Romsey by-election campaign. Once the public has a sense that we are indeed people with genuine beliefs, then their faith will be strengthened.

Linked to my fundamental commitment to liberty is my belief that the pursuit of social justice should be the major task of government. When I entered Parliament in 1983, one of the cutting-edge ideas of the time was libertarianism. In its mid-eighties form, it was the passion of the more wild-eyed Young Conservatives. Their creed ran roughly as follows: government enslaves people by taking their taxes from them, and spending the revenue in ways over which they have little control, essentially preventing them from doing many things that they might want to do. Therefore, all those who follow the true faith of liberty should 'roll back the frontiers of the state' to make people more free. They did not accept the idea that, by redistributing wealth and tackling inequalities in society, government can actually promote freedom.

I take a different view. I do not accept that creative government action means less freedom. It seems to me preposterous to assert that people are more free when government does less. If government did nothing to provide decent health and education services, then many people in Britain would be manifestly less free, because they would not be able to provide these services for themselves. The same applies to public transport, welfare benefits, and social services. If government withdrew from these areas, then the best services would only be available to the lucky few. Government has a clear obligation to meet market fail-ures, and provide the best public services for all our people, so that every-one has the maximum life chances. For me, social justice, protected and enhanced by government, equals more freedom. To promote liberty, government needs to do less, do more and do different.

Decentralizing power in Britain and changing politics are areas where we must 'do different'. Social justice falls firmly into the 'do more' part of the equation, as does environmental policy, but that doesn't mean government becomes a 'Green Giant', infringing people's right to choose. It means encouraging the growth of a green culture in Britain, in which it is clear that the environment matters to daily life, and stacking the system, so that people are encouraged to use public transport wherever they can. It means ensuring that, in the economic sector, markets work so that they deliver positive environmental gain, not the pain of pollution. Come election time, governments should face judgement on the extent to which they have improved our environment.

Protecting the environment is part of a modern approach to politics. Another aspect of that modern approach is the way government approaches technology and innovation. Although I have said that I want government to do more in the field of social justice, it is my strong belief that in the field of regulating business, government should do a lot less. By and large, when progress and innovation in technology takes place, it does so regardless of government policy. So long as government has provided a solid educational base and funding for blue-sky research and development (and I am committed to both), innovation takes place as a result of the creative spark of individuals or small groups of people. Often, they need the risks of an open market to provide stimuli, but they do not need endless regulation by government, which is exactly what the DTI provides. A good example is the 112 pages of regulations that come with the minimum wage (see chapter three). Any government that cares about innovation has to strip bureaucracy and jargon to the minimum.

Politics in Britain must have a future, and it will, once we change the way it works, so that it is more inclusive, more idealistic, and more relevant. It must not attempt to contain forces – like the global economy or the pace of technological innovation – which are beyond the remit of modern nation-state governments acting alone, but must instead unleash, nurture and support the creativity that bubbles away in Britain, particularly at the local level. Government has to recognize its role in helping individuals achieve their dreams, whether by helping communities defend themselves against identikit shopping malls and corporate domination, or helping disadvantaged youngsters to boost their self-esteem. Once politics adapts to this new role and becomes comfortable with it, the voters will start to develop a far clearer idea of why those strange beasts like myself who engage in politics, bother at all. It will lead to a mature and constructive political conversation in Britain, and it will provide a future of freedom for all. It's that which motivates my political life. And I am determined to do everything I can to ensure that our democracy does have such a future. It can and it must.

NOTES

Preface

1 Gordon Brown, speech, *Hansard*, 17 March 1998, col. 1110.
2 Gordon Brown, speech TUC Conference, HM Treasury website, 9 September 2000.
3 8 May to 14 August 2000, and again 12–27 October 2000.
4 The Prime Minister said 'On Wales: I made a wrong judgement. Some battles you have to walk away from.' *Observer*, 9 April 2000.

Introduction
WHY AREN'T THE VOTERS VOTING?

1 The business of shouting 'Hear, hear' in agreement is a classic example of parliamentary anachronism. In daily life, we congratulate one another by clapping – why should Parliament be different? It has happened on two occasions in my time in Parliament. The most recent was when Betty Boothroyd announced that she was standing down as Speaker of the House of Commons. The first was when John Major walked across the floor of the House to congratulate Eric Heffer after a speech on the Gulf War. Eric was desperately ill at the time with cancer, and died soon after. Tony Benn remarked to me then that he had never witnessed such an occasion in his long years as an MP.
2 In 1974, 67 per cent of people felt that MPs were out of touch with the people who elected them. In 1990, after the televising of Parliament, that figure was still 65 per cent. 'Audience Reactions to Parliamentary Television', Bovill, McGregor and Wober in *Televising Democracies*, Routledge, 1992.
3 *The Times*,.19 April 2000.
4 *Non-Voting: Causes and Methods of Control*, Charles Edward Merriam and Harold Foote Gosnell, University of Chicago Press, 1924.

Chapter One
FREEDOM FROM POVERTY: THE FORGOTTEN NATION

1 'Call for Labour "family reunion"', *Independent*, 4 March 2000.
2 East Surrey experienced a 68.8 per cent drop in unemployment figures, while Banbury experienced a 68.4 per cent drop. In contrast, Pendle only saw a 14.9 per cent improvement, and Burnley 15.2 per cent. House of Commons Library.
3 Nick Davies, *Dark Heart: The Shocking Truth About Hidden Britain*, Chatto and Windus, 1997.
4 Ivan Turok and Nicola Edge, *The Jobs Gap in Britain's Cities: Employment Loss and Labour Market Consequences*, Joseph Rowntree Foundation, 1999.
5 This attitude is only possible because of the current first-past-the-post electoral system, under which Labour is guaranteed tenure over a number of safe seats and the votes of those who oppose it do not count. Under a system of proportional representation, (as used in the elections for the Scottish Parliament and Northern Ireland and Welsh Assemblies), voters have more than one choice of candidate. As a result, there are no safe seats, and no party can afford to ignore whole sections of the populace.
6 D. Piachaud, 'The Prospects for Poverty', *New Economy* 5, 1998.
7 Nick Davies, op. cit.
8 Peter Kilfoyle's accusation was that Labour is ignoring its traditional heartlands. Again, this trend is reinforced by the current electoral system.
9 Jonathan Freedland, *Bring Home the Revolution; How Britain can live the American Dream*, Fourth Estate, 1998.

Chapter Two
FREEDOM TO BREATHE: THE GREEN FUTURE

1 Friends of the Earth Press Release, 30 May 1999 (1998 figures).
2 *Guardian*, 6 June 1997.

Chapter Three
FREEDOM FROM GOVERNMENT: PEOPLE AND THE STATE

1 So-called because the Conservative Chancellor 'Rab' Butler replaced Labour's Hugh Gaitskell in 1951, but the policies didn't appear to change.
2 Ramsay Muir, *The Faith of A Liberal*, Lovat Dickson, 1933.
3 As did Lloyd George. Hobhouse's formula, that freedom means nothing without a background of social rights, was the basis for the National Insurance Act, the foundation of the modern Welfare State.
4 I believe there is a pronounced element of psychological imbalance in the New

Labour spirit. Excessive arrogance walks hand-in-hand with genuine self-doubt, social sentience can be found alongside harsh repression. If New Labour make mistakes in defining their new natural audience, this is because they are no more adept at defining themselves. All of this foretells a short, sharp and essentially negative general election campaign when the time comes. The early indications are not encouraging. The likely effect will be to drive down voter participation still further. Labour looks hell-bent on securing a second-term victory without due regard for the long-term costs.

5 *Guardian*, 5 April 2000.
6 Nick Davies, *Guardian*, 7 March 2000.
7 It should be noted that the HIDB was, in the first instance, a Liberal concept – promoted in the early sixties by such leading lights as Jo Grimond and Russell Johnston.
8 Ian Sanderson, Fiona Walton and Mike Campbell, *Back To Work: Local Action on Unemployment*, Joseph Rowntree Foundation, 1999.
9 Richard Berthoud, Maria Iacovou, *Guardian*, 11 February 2000.
10 Trefor Lloyd, *Young Men, the Job Market and Gendered Work*, Joseph Rowntree Foundation, 1999.
11 ACHCEW Commission on the NHS, *New Life for Health*, Vintage, 2000.

Chapter Four
FREEDOM TO INNOVATE: SCIENCE AND DEMOCRACY

1 Some readers might be interested to learn that this quote was included in Kennedy's speech by his speech-writer Edgar Cahn – the man who invented time-dollars (see chapter one).
2 *Economist*, 15–21 January 2000.
3 NOP Survey, 1999.
4 NOP Survey, 1998.
5 House of Commons Library.
6 Data Monitor.
7 Quoted in foreword to *e-commerce@itsbest.co.uk*.

Chapter Five
FREEDOM TO GOVERN: THE GREAT DEVOLUTION DEBATE

1 *Identity and Politics, A Discussion with Michael Ignatieff and Sean Neeson*, Centre for Reform Paper No. 2, 1998.
2 Nicholas Bromley, Richard Grayson, Jay Liotta, Margaret Sharp and Ryan White, *Funding Federalism: A Report on Systems of Government Finance*, London, 1998.
3 Ibid.

4   Simon Partridge, *The British Union State*, Catalyst, 1999.
5   Ibid.

Chapter Six
FREEDOM WITHOUT BORDERS: BRITAIN, EUROPE AND THE
CHALLENGE OF GLOBALIZATION

1   House of Commons Research Paper 00/56: Economic Indicators.

Conclusion
A SENSE OF IDEALISM

1   In that election we ended up with no MEPs. The figure rose to two in 1994
    and ten in 1999.

INDEX